COMPUTER JURISPRUDENCE

LEGAL RESPONSES TO THE INFORMATION REVOLUTION

MICHAEL D. ROSTOKER • ROBERT H. RINES

Franklin Pierce Law Center
Academy of Applied Science

OCEANA PUBLICATIONS, INC.
New York • London • Rome

Library of Congress Cataloging-in-Publication Data

Rostoker, Michael D.
 Computer jurisprudence.

 Includes bibliographical references.
 I. Rines, Robert H.   II. Title.
KF390.5.C6R67   1985   343.73'0999   85-15290
ISBN 0-379-20790-7   347.303999

Manufactured in the United States of America

TABLE OF CONTENTS

CHAPTER 4   COMPUTER CONTRACTS

Tape Supplement: *Legal Approaches to Computer Contracting*
Tape Supplement: *User-Vendor Computer Litigation*

CHAPTER 5   COMPUTERS AND PRIVACY

CHAPTER 6   COMPUTER CRIME

Tape Supplement: *Evidentiary Considerations of Computers*

CHAPTER 7   ELECTRONIC FUNDS TRANSFER

PREFACE

As modern society moves through the early stages of the information age, the legal and technological communities are grappling with problems for which existing rules of law may not apply. Most of these problems center on issues of privacy and proprietorship. How, for example, can individuals control the kinds of data gathered on them and how that data will be used? To what lengths can an employer legally go to protect the transfer of new technological developments to a competitor, given the mobility of personnel within the computer technology field? Can such questions be adequately resolved through the application of existing legal concepts? Or is there a need to design a new system of approaches?

In considering these issues, those familiar with the history of law in Western societies, especially its development in Great Britain and the United States, will no doubt experience some *deja vu*. The legal profession has stood on this threshold before.

During the agrarian age and early years of the industrial revolution, individual rights to be free of unwanted intrusion were indirectly protected under the penumbra of rights granted in property law. However, with technological advancements in optics one individual could intrude upon another in the form of viewing that person without crossing any boundaries of land and thus not violating the narrow trespass theory of *quare clausum fregit*. Several decades later advances in photography removed the need for relatively long durations of posing with its inherent consent. A photographer could obtain and use for commercial gain a non-permitted image of another without violating provisions against criminal theft or property trespass (*de bonis asportatus*). The rules and protection of the law as it had evolved during the agrarian age were insufficient to cope with these technological challenges. As the bar and bench wrestled with fitting the new problems into the pigeon holes of the old laws, legislators attempted to promulgate prophylactic measures that dealt with individual incidents. The solution, in hindsight, was both simple and somewhat obvious. Eventually the legal community devised the new tort of invasion of privacy.

The legal and technological communities may again be facing dilemmas for which the current system of laws may be incomplete or inadequate. The purpose of this book is to probe that possibility by providing a thorough understanding of the impact computers are having on the laws in our society.

This book is the major component of a three-part course of study and reference. The other two parts are a tape series presented by leading practitioners in the computer law field who discuss typical and special experiences in select problem areas, and a primer in video tape part that supplements the book's introduction to computer technology and terminology.

The intended users of this book are a diverse population ranging from those with general legal expertise but no previous understanding of computers, to computer-knowledgeable non-lawyers, to those having neither substantial computer nor legal backgrounds, including business persons and students. For the person with a legal background, the book has a familiar format, presenting historical, conceptual and practical aspects of such legal areas as contracts, proprietary rights and privacy. Extensive analyses and citations are presented in language understandable to readers from disciplines other than law. While not using a how-to or case book approach, the book will indicate directions for problem solving which are also extensively supplemented in the tape series. In addition to legal issues arising in the United States, the book examines international considerations, specifically with the Far East and Europe.

For non-lawyers, including academics, government, business and technological professionals, this book provides an introduction to the legal considerations surrounding the adoption and use of computer technology in our society. Readers unfamiliar with computer terminology and function should use the primer video tape supplement since the summary primer presented in the book is intended for review and not as a self-sufficient educational tool. Additionally, the practical problem approaches in the tape series supplement should prove valuable.

This book represents an integrated approach to a complex body of technology and law which has been under study for several years at the Franklin Pierce Law Center in Concord, New Hampshire, U.S.A. Some of the basic materials were initially compiled by a team of selected graduate students and professional experts in the diverse fields of law involved, aided by the guidance of leading national and international practitioners of computer technology and law. These initial contributions were subsequently shaped into the unified and directed study resulting in this book.

Michael D. Rostoker, Esq.
Robert H. Rines, Esq.
Concord, New Hampshire, 1985

ACKNOWLEDGEMENTS

Appreciation is extended to the numerous persons who have made this book a reality. Although a complete list of participants would be somewhat unwieldy, special appreciation is extended to the following persons:

To Gail Kelley, for exceptional editorial advice, commiseration and support beyond the call of duty.

For independent research and writing which helped in the genesis of this book, the following faculty and graduates of the Franklin Pierce Law Center are gratefully acknowledged:

Chapter 2 - Prof. Homer Blair, Jennifer Tegfeldt;
Chapter 3 - Jennifer Tegfeldt;
Chapter 4 - Arlene Halliday, Jennifer Tegfeldt;
Chapter 5 - Arlene Halliday, John Murphy, Joseph Nicastro;
Chapter 6 - Carla Ottaviano;
Chapter 7 - R. Timothy Phoenix.

For assistance and support in the preparation of materials, evaluation of ideas and gratuitous suggestions: Elizabeth Black, Sheila Cassavaugh, Prof. Thomas Field, Marlyn Flanders, Jeff Haymes, Prof. Marcus Hurn, Prof. Bill Joyner, Steven Krantz, Sara Laumann, Steven Matzuk, Nancy Metz, Paul Neubauer, Irene Page, Jeffrey Ralph, Richard Schmidt, Nancy Richards-Stower, Prof. Robert Shaw, Robert Speirs, Dean Robert Viles, Richard Wilder, Nancy Wood and Chou Fu Ying.

CHAPTER 1 - COMPUTER TECHNOLOGY

A PRIMER ON COMPUTERS

I. INTRODUCTION

The computer has permeated the very fabric of the modern world. Rapid changes abound in the manner of conducting our lifestyles, from contacting associates and purchasing goods to earning a livelihood. These changes, in great part, have occurred due to the acceptance and rapid advancements of computer technology.

During the early stages of computer development, these devices existed as great electronic behemoths secured in sterile and austere surroundings, with a dedicated, specially trained 'priesthood' supporting and directing the new technological marvel. However, the computer has recently become smaller, less expensive and more 'user-friendly' with regard to moderately trained individuals, further permeating the fabric of everyday routine in modern society.

Along with the advancements that computers have provided follows the need to understand the terminology and structure of computers. Ignorance of the capabilities and use of computers, in the near future, will be a handicap as severe as present-day modern language illiteracy. Computer-literacy, therefore, becomes a paramount concern prior to undertaking the study of the various societal and legal responses to the computer in the information revolution.

II. THE COMPUTER SYSTEM

In its simplest form, a computer is a device that can perform computations without human intervention. Such computations can take one of three forms: arithmetic operations, logical operations or input/output operations. Arithmetic operations include the standard mathematical operations of addition, subtraction, multiplication and division along with more complex procedures such as square root, factoring and powers of numbers. Logical operations require the computer to determine states of quality, such as whether one quantity is less or greater than or equal to a second quantity. Input/output operations include the receiving of information by the computer machine and the causing of an action by a machine, such as printing particular numbers on a page or rotating a mechanical robot arm. However, the computer can only perform one of these operations, as directed, at one time, but at such an accelerated rate of operative speed, that the computer appears to be performing many functions simultaneously.

Computer systems are generally subdivided into three general classifications: Mainframe, mini and micro. These divisions are traditionally related to thresholds in size, price, speed of processing and the 'bit' size of the internal electronic processor. The 'bit' is a logical binary digit or on/off switch, and bit size represents the number of bits or size of a logical word that the computer can recognize at one time. The bits are grouped into 'bytes' which represent characters to a computer, with one byte commonly consisting of eight bits, as will be described in more detail later in the chapter. A mainframe computer is represented by large and fast electronic hardware, a 32 bit processor and a pricetag from one-half to $3 million. Mini-computers have relatively small and fast hardware, about the size of a large filecabinet with a 16 bit processor and approximately a $20 thousand to $200 thousand overall price. Micro-computers have the smallest and slowest of electronic hardware, nominally an 8 bit processer, and are fairly inexpensive, generally betweeen $100 and $15 thousand. Such bench marks are not absolute, especially within the last few years, as 16 bit micros and 32 bit minis abound while the operational speed of some micros now comfortably exceeds the best speed of last decade's mainframes.

Far greater specificity can be obtained, however, in the description of the components that comprise a computer system. In general, there are four such basic components: input/output (I/O) devices, a central processing unit (CPU), mass storage devices and software. Of these, the first three are visible, material electronic or electro-mechanical devices called hardware. The last, software, describes the evanescent sets of logical instructions and data used by the computer system electronics in performing directed operations. An even greater degree of understanding can be obtained by schematic representation of the functional modules of the computer system, each module being composed from a set of the four basic components.

A general schematic representation of a computer system would thusly contain the connected basic modules discussed below:

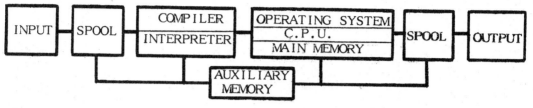

Input

The first of computer system modules is the input device. Such devices share in commonality the ability to convert real-world data and events into electrical impulses. Example input devices include card-reading devices, which sense the location of coded holes punched into paper cards or tapes; keyboards, which recognize the striking of desig- nated characters on a typewriter-like pad; disk and tape readers, which sense the existence of magnetic zones on a metallic oxide coated surface; optical and audio scanners, which sense discrete quantities of differentiated electro- magnetic radiation; and many other devices.

Spool

The spooling device is a hardware and software device used to minimize the differences between input/output and com- puter processing speeds. Since the computer CPU is capable of performing its routine operations very rapidly, generally 1000 to 1 million per second, normal input means are sub- stantially slower than the computer's access needs. For example, the fastest of typists may input from 5 to 10 characters per second. This is at best two orders of magnitude below the operational speed or access/recognition speed of a standard computer CPU. The spooling device, therefore, as a programmed mass storage device, collects data obtained from one or more input devices and holds the data until the computer CPU is ready to receive the data. The spooler then transfers the data to the CPU at its approximate operating speed. A second spooler can be used to act as a buffer between the operational speed of the CPU and various output devices.

Compiler/Interpreter

The compilers and interpreters of a computer system are the software translating routines that convert a high level language (source) program into computer-understandable (object) instructions. The primary difference between a compiler and an interpreter is in the manner of such translation. A compiler translates an entire source code program at one time, producing a very efficient translated machine readable object code. An interpreter translates each line of source code separately into object code. The compiler therefore produces a faster code while the interpreter software is much less expensive and allows for immediate sectional translations.

Central Processing Unit

The computer CPU is the primary 'working' portion of the computer system. The CPU is hardware, capable of performing arithmetic, logical and input/output functions. Characterized as being of a certain number of 'bits', or binary logical on/off switches, generally 8, 15 or 32, the CPU provides a 'window' for the computer to recognize codes of symbolic characters. The CPU hardware is primarily involved with the retention and sensing of the various bit registers. Capable of holding a particular charged state for a finite duration, these electronic switches symbolize the binary code for all symbols and characters recognized by the computer.

The first computer used a series of electrically powered vacuum tubes as the bit registers. Power passing through the tube was sensed and translated as a binary 'on' bit, no power being defined as an 'off' bit. Massive power requirements and resultant undersirable heat output, coupled with frequent tube failure, heralded the introduction of the transistorized computer CPU.

The transistor, three wires imbedded in a drop of semi-conductive material, normally housed in a container less than pea-sized, provided a low-power, long-life successor to the thumb-sized vacuum tube. As with the tube, power passing through the transistor signified an 'on' condition, with no power signifying an 'off' condition.

Substantial evolution of the transistor circuit has resulted in construction of the modern silicon wafer semi-conductor, or chip CPU. Also referred to as integrated circuits, or 'IC s', these semiconductor chips, which vaguely resemble mechanical caterpillars, are essentially transistor circuits that have been micro-miniaturized and photo-etched onto a wafer of silicon and embedd in protective plastic.

Operating System

The operating system is the software that monitors and governs the activities of the computer system and ensures system reliability. Thus, the control, processing and file management components of the operating system are the background software that provides a basic environment under which the user-defined application programs operate.

The control programs are generally divided into three sections: job management, resource management and job control routines. A 'job' is the primary compiled object code version of a user-defined application program with its connected data, subroutines and functions. Connecting the various portions of the extended program or job, scheduling the use of the computer system's resources for the job and providing system recovery and error detection for a failed job are the primary responsibility of the control programs of the operating system. Specifically, the job management routines determine the order of processing precedence and duration of allowed CPU processing time for each job input to the computer; the resource management routines designate what computer system resources are accessible to a particular job; and the job control routines schedule which jobs are passed or switched into and out-of designated system memory locations.

The operating system processing programs include both a run-time error monitor and a series of service programs. The run-time error monitor recognizes job and operating errors while the job is in operation, or 'running'. The service programs perform the remaining operating system processing functions and are predominantly represented by a linkage editor, which connects application programs with needed subroutines and functions; a librarian, which allows access to the system control and definition library; and the system utilities which control the imbedded functions, such as random number generation.

The file management programs represent the final component of the computer's operating system. File management is directly related to the structure and order of computer-internal data. To control internal collections of inter-related data used for application programs, the file management programs often include a data base management system (DBMS). In compliment to the DBMS internal control, the operating system text editor is used to control the input and output of data, especially the interactive display and editing of pre-compiled program software.

Many examples of operating systems exist in common usage since the advent and overwhelming acceptance of the personal computer (PC). Notably, the TRS-DOS (pronounced 'tris-dos') is the Tandy Radio Shack-Disk Operating System. Other examples include the International Business Machine's IBM-PC DOS, the VMS, or virtual memory system, and the UNIX operating system developed at Bell Laboratories.

Memory

Memory is the term used to refer to the computer system hardware capable of storing large volumes of data with rapid update and retrieval capability. As the basis of the computer system mass storage device component, memory is divided into either main or auxiliary categories.

Main memory, commonly referred to as the RAM (random access memory) of a system, is that quantity of memory immediately accessible, or 'on-line', to the central processing unit. The predominant concern in the choice of main memory involves the speed with which data can be switched into or out-of memory in transference with the CPU. More specifically, the speed of the memory should be as close to the operating speed of the CPU as possible.

As with the hardware of the central processing unit, the memory hardware is a collection of binary switches capable of an 'on' or 'off' state representing coded data. Early memory circuits consisted of vacuum tube arrays, with their inherent power and failure problems. Transistor circuits replaced the more cumbersome tube arrays, and were in turn predominantly replaced by core magnet memory.

Core memory provided an alternative to the volatile power circuit memories that lost all data when system power failed, by the expedient of stringing a series of magnetic ferrite doughnuts along the intersection of wires. Passing electric current through the wires enabled the shifting of the doughnuts' magetic poles, signifying the necessary on/off bit state. Since the magnetic poles, once shifted, retained their orientation, power loss did not cause data loss in the memory. Core memory, still in use for certain specialized applications, was so popular that for an entire generation of computer professionals the term 'core' was synonymous with main memory.

Modern main memory is predominantly composed of silicon wafer semiconductor chips, of the same nature if not form, as the CPU chip. Recent techniques in circuit micro-miniaturization or very large scale integration (VLSI) have permitted as many as a million circuit elements to be condensed onto a single one-quarter by one-quarter inch silicon wafer chip. Such capacity permits even the least powerful, micro-computer driven personal computers to be equipped with main memory capacities measured in thousands (kilo) of computer

words/characters, referred to as bytes (b), or kilobytes (kb)
of RAM.

The auxiliary, or 'off-line', memory is the mass data
storage that is not directly accessible to the CPU. The
primary consideration in the choice of auxiliary memory is the
volume of storage available rather than the speed of
update/retrieval.

The most common devices used for auxiliary memory are
magnetic tapes and disks. Magnetic tapes, either reel-to-reel
or cassette, and disks, accept and hold the imposition of
magnetic dot patterns when necessary. Also available are
laser disks, which change and read the reflective surface
pattern of a plate-like disk, and magnetic bubble chips which
are commonly synthetic garnet chips with an internal matrix of
polarized magnetic bubbles. All storage is performed, as with
main memory and CPU, by a series of bits representing
individual characters. To access these data bits from the
auxiliary memory, they must be transferred into main memory,
much as a human reads a book into memory, to be directly
accessible by the CPU.

Output

Output devices are the hardware that are capable of
converting computer-generated electric impulses into real
world data and events. In general, a human computer user is
most concerned with obtaining a desired output from the
system.

The output may be in the form of graphs, symbols or
text, produced by printers, plotters, graphics devices or

on a cathode ray tube (CRT) screen. Alternatively, the output may be in the form of the movement of a robot arm, the sound from a speaker or any other electrically generated event.

III. COMPUTER OPERATION

Most computers today are general purpose; that is, they can be directed or programmed to perform a number of varied tasks. Communication to the computer as to the desired task and method of procedure for solving the task, is facilitated by a computer language.

Computer languages are generally divided into three categories: low, high or very high level. Low level languages, such as assembler and machine languages, are very close or identical to the actual internal object code understood by the computer system. High level languages, such as BASIC, COBOL, Fortran, APL, PL/1 and others, use English-like statements and equations to produce a translatable source code program for the computer. Very high level languages, such as the data base management system (DBMS) languages '1022' and 'SPEED' or operating system interactive command languages, allow a substantial number of preselected routines to be run in response to a single command.

Once a program, or ordered set of instructions to the computer, has been decided upon, the computer operator must determine the parameters of how the system will execute the program. Execution can be accomplished in either batch mode or as a transaction-oriented program. Batch processing is the preparation of the program with an entire set of presorted data needed for calculation, then delivered in a single 'batch' to the computer. Transaction-oriented programming, in the alternative, provides processing as each individual operation or calculation in the program is required. The latter method is also called query/response programming.

Two other considerations as to the mode of processing involve whether the procedures are to be accomplished in 'real time,' and whether the programmer is 'on line'. Real time refers to processing coincident with an on-going activity, which is producing information quickly enough to control the dynamic activity. On line refers to whether the programmer has a direct access to the CPU as data and instructions are input. This capability of not apparently waiting for the computer to finish other jobs to respond is also called random processing.

As to the actual instructing of the computer, as previously mentioned, the computer only recognizes a preselected number (byte) of electronic on/off switch registers (bits). The computer stores and recognizes data and instructions by predetermined codes of bits. Two of the most common of these developed codes for encoding computer characters are the Extended Binary Coded Decimal Interchange Code (EBCDIC) and the American Standard Code for Information Interchange (ASCII). The computer, in the CPU and memory devices, can recognize and change data and instructions as directed, as by 'flipping' the magnetic doughnuts in core, noting and passing power through electrical circuits in semiconductor chips or by the polarization of magnetic surfaces on a disk or tape. A sufficiently large quantity of storage bits in an ordered array, as in memory, provides the computer with the capability to store and process instructions and data as the CPU methodically reviews and responds to the contents of designated memory locations.

A useful glossary of terms used in the industry follows.

IV. GLOSSARY

Access Arms, Magnetic Disk The mechanism that positions read-write heads over tracks on magnetic disk storage devices.

Acoustic Coupler A special type of modem which allows a standard telephone headset to be attached to a terminal to allow the transmission of data.

Actuator The access arm on a disk storage unit that swings in and out over the proper location.

Address That portion of a computer instruction that references the location of the data to be processed.

Addressing, Data Communications A technique used in data communications networks to establish contact with a remote terminal.

Addressable Storage The method used to reference data in storage by assigning a unique number to each storage location.

ANSI American National Standards Institute.

Applications Packages Prewritten programs for common applications.

Arithmetic/Logic Unit (ALU) The electronic circuitry in the central processing unit that controls all arithmetic and logical operations.

Arithmetic Operations The performing of calculations on data by the internal electronic circuitry in the central processing unit.

ASCII Code American Standard Code for Information Interchange: a seven bit code widely used in data communications.

Assembler Language A symbolic programming language that uses symbols and abbreviations to represent the function to be performed.

Asynchronous Transmission in Data Communications The transmission of a single character at a time preceded by a start bit and followed by a stop bit.

Audit Trail Provides the ability to trace any processing back to the original source data.

Automatic Programming See Programming, Automatic.

Auxiliary Storage Devices Devices, generally magnetic tape and magnetic disk, on which data can be stored for use by computer programs; also known as secondary storage.

Backup File A copy of a current file used if the current file is destroyed.

Band Printer A type of high-speed printer that uses a rotating belt or band with embossed characters which are struck by a hammer.

Bar Codes Vertical marks or bars on prerecorded tags which can be sensed and read by a machine. The width and combination of vertical lines are used to represent data.

BASIC A programming language developed at Dartmouth University for use in academic computing, but now widely used on personal computers and small business systems.

Batch Processing The accumulation and processing of data as a group.

Binary Digit A single bit.

Binary Number System A number system with a base 2 that uses two symbols (0 and 1) to represent values.

Bit (Binary Digit) The smallest unit for storing data in main computer storage.

Blocking The storing of two or more logical records on magnetic tape or disk to form a physical record for the purposes of more efficiently storing and processing the records.

Bubble Memory A type of memory which is composed of small magnetic domains formed on a thin crystal film of synthetic garnet.

Bug An error in a program run, resulting in improper or lack of output.

Bursting The process of separating each page of continuous forms.

Byte A given number of bits considered as a unit to form a storage location.

Card Reader A device capable of reading the data stored in a punched card and transmitting it to main computer storage.

Cards, Punched See punched cards.

Cathode Ray Tube Terminal A device used as a computer terminal which contains a television-like screen for displaying data. Most CRT terminals also have typewriter-like keyboards.

Central Processing Unit Electronic components which cause processing on a computer to occur by interpreting instructions, performing calculations, moving data in main computer storage, and controlling the input/output operations. It consists of the arithmetic/logic unit and the control unit.

Chain Printer A type of high-speed printer which contains characters on a rotating chain.

Channel An electronic device associated with a computer system that controls the physical transfer of data between the input/output device and main computer storage.

Channels, Communication The lines or data links over which data is transmitted, including standard telephone lines, coaxial cables, microwave transmission, satellite, and fiber optics.

Check Digit A calculated digit appended to a numeric field to assure validity when referenced in the future.

Coaxial Cables High-quality communication lines normally laid underground or under the ocean.

COBOL Common Business Oriented Language: one of the most widely used business programming languages.

Coding The process of writing instructions for a computer.

COM (Computer Output Microfilm) A technique used to record output from a computer as very small images on roll or sheet film.

Common Carrier A company or organization which contracts with state or federal governments to carry the property of others.

Communications, Data See data communications.

Comparing, Logical Operations The ability of the computer to compare data and perform alternative actions based upon the results of the comparison.

Compiler A program that receives a series of computer statements written in a symbolic form and converts the statements to machine language instructions.

Computer A device which can perform computations, including arithmetic and logic operations, without intervention by a human being.

Computer Center The area in a company that is used to house the computer system and the people who program and operate the computer system.

Computer Crime See crime, computer.

Computer Operator An individual who operates the computer system.

Computer Program A series of instructions which directs the computer to perform a sequence of tasks that produce a desired output.

Computer Programmers People who design, write, test and implement the programs which process data on a computer system.

Computer System The actual computer hardware, and operating software, which consists of the processor unit, operating system software, compilers and inter-preters, operator console, input devices, output devices, and auxiliary storage devices.

Computer Users The people who utilize the output from a computer system in their daily activities.

Concentrator A device which accepts information from many terminals over slow-speed lines and transmits the data to the main computer over a high-speed line.

Console Terminal A device through which the computer operator communicates with the processor unit.

Control Break The change that occurs when a record is read in which the control field is different from the control field in the previous record.

Control Programs Programs that are a part of an operating system that provides for automatic control of computer resources.

Control Unit The part of the central processing unit that directs and coordinates the enitre computer system.

Control, System The method used to assure that only valid data is accepted and processed on a computer.

Conversion See parallel or direct.

Core Dump See dump, core.

Core Storage See storage, magnetic core.

CPU See central processing unit.

Crime, Computer The use of a computer system to steal, embezzle, or maliciously access or destroy data or files used with computer systems.

CRT Terminal See cathode ray tube terminal.

Cylinder The amount of data that can be read with a single positioning of an access arm on a magnetic disk.

Daisy Wheel Printer A printing device consisting of rotating spokes or arms which contain embossed characters.

Data A representation of facts, concepts, or instructions in a formalized manner suitable for communication, interpretation and processing by humans or machines.

Data, Storage and Retrieval The process of recording and extracting data from auxiliary storage devices using a computer.

Data Banks A collection of data which is stored on auxiliary storage devices.

Data Base A collection of interrelated data stored together with a minimum of redundancy to serve multiple applications.

Data Base, Hierarchial A data base in which there is a fixed relationship between the elements in the hierarchy.

Data Base, Network A data base in which each of the elements is linked to each other through pointers.

Data Base Administrator The person who is responsible for creating, updating, and controlling access to a data base.

Data Base Management System A series of programs which is used to establish a data base, update the data base, and query the data base.

Data Collection Those operations to obtain data in an uncontrolled environment from those doing the work being reported on.

Data Communications The transmission of data from one location to another using communications channels such as telephone lines, coaxial cables, microwaves, or other means.

Data Communications, Line Speed The speed at which data is transmitted over communications channels.

Data Definition Language A language that is a part of a data base system which allows for the definition of files and records, and their relationship.

Data Entry The process of preparing data in some machine-processable form for entering data directly into a computer system.

Data Management Programs Programs supplied as a part of a system's software that handle such operations as the blocking and deblocking of records, accessing files, etc.

Debug To examine computer system components to remove errors.

Decision Tables Graphical representations of logical decisions that must be made concerning conditions that can occur within a program.

Decollating The process of removing carbon and separating the multiple copies of a report.

Desk Top Computers Computer systems which are small enough to be placed on top of a desk for use.

Digitizer A data entry device which can scan images and transmit those images as digital impulses to a computer.

Direct Access Storage Device An auxiliary storage device on which data can be stored and retrieved in any order, sequentially or randomly.

Direct or Relative File Organization A file in which records are stored in a location based upon the key found in the record.

Disk, Floppy See floppy disk.

Disk Cartridge A type of removable disk storage commonly contained in a single disk for recording and retrieving data.

Disk Drive A device consisting of a spindle on which a disk pack can be mounted for electronically storing data.

Disk Pack A unit which consists of multiple metal platters connected to a common hub. Each platter is coated with a metal oxide on which data can be electronically stored.

Distributed Data Base The concept of distributing portions of a data base at remote sites where the data is most frequently referenced.

Distributed Data Processing The distribution of computing power and data using minicomputers at locations where processing is required.

Documentation, Program The detailed recording of the facts about a program through supporting materials and within the program itself.

Drum Printer A type of high-speed printer that features a cylindrical drum which rotates to position characters for printing.

Dump, Core A printout of the contents of main storage.

EBCDIC See extended binary coded decimal interchange code.

Education, Computers in In education, computers are now used for computer-assisted instruction as an area of specialized study, or as a tool to support classes in all disciplines.

Egoless programming Programming attitude based upon the concept that a program is not one's personal possession but open to all to view.

Electrographic printer A non-impact printer that uses specially coated paper on which the image is "burned" or formed by various means.

Electronic Fund Transfer A method of receiving and paying for goods and services by which funds are transferred from one account to another electronically under control of one or more computer systems.

Executing Instructions The process of analyzing machine language instructions on a computer and carrying out the functions to be performed.

Extended Binary Coded Decimal Interchange Code (EBCDIC) A widely used coding system for representing data in computer storage and on auxiliary storage devices.

Fiber Optics Technology based upon light-weight, smooth hair-like strands of transparent material used for transmission of data and sound at high rates of speed.

Fields A unit of data within a record.

File A collection of one or more records.

File Organization The methods used to organize records so that they are accessible by computers.

File Updating The processing of additions, deletions and changes against a master file.

Fixed Word Length Computers Computers using a representation of data in main storage in which all values are stored in a fixed number of bits regardless of the size of the number.

Floppy Disk An oxide-coated plastic disk about 8" in diameter enclosed in a protective covering that can be used for magnetically storing disks.

Floppy Disk Reader A device which can read data stored on a floppy disk.

Flowchart Symbols Standard symbols used to flowchart programming logic.

Flowcharting The process of graphically depicting the detailed steps in the solution of a problem.

FORTRAN A high-level language designed for scientists, mathematicians, and engineers.

Front-end Processor A sophisticated, programmable communication control unit consisting of a computer designed to handle communication functions to relieve the main computer of these tasks.

Full Duplex Line A data communications channel that allows data to be sent in both directions at the same time.

General Purpose Computers Computers which can perform any task by changing the application program in main computer storage.

GIGO Garbage in, garbage out.

Graphic Display Terminals CRT terminals capable of displaying not only letters of the alphabet and numbers, but graphs and drawings as well.

Half-Duplex Line A channel that allows data to be sent in both directions but not in both directions at the same time.

Hexadecimal Number System A number system with a base 16 that uses 16 individual symbols to represent values.

Hierarchical Data Base See data base, hierarchical.

Hierarchy Chart A chart used in structured design to show the relationship of modules within a program.

Hierarchy of Operations in High-level programming language, the sequence in which calculations are performed.

High-level programming language A programming language far removed from the internal characteristics of the machine.

Hollerith Code The coding system used to record data on punched cards.

Impact Printers Printing devices which print by some print mechanism striking paper, ribbon, and characters together.

Indexed File Organization A file organization method in which records are stored in ascending or descending sequence and are referenced by an index which permits sequential or random retrieval.

Input Data used for processing on a computer system.

Input Errors Errors that occur when data is converted to a machine-readable form or when data is entered into the computer for processing.

Input/Output Operations A basic data processing function that requires the reading of data and producing some output from the data read.

Input/Processing/Output The sequence of events that occurs when data is processed on a computer system.

Input Units Units that are part of a computer system which present data to the processor unit for processing.

Inquiry A request from a terminal operator to a computer system for information.

Instruction Register An area of storage in the central processing unit where machine-language instructions are stored and analyzed prior to execution.

Instructions, Computer, The unique numbers, letters of the alphabet, or special characters that, when interpreted by the computer circuity, cause a particular operation to be performed.

Intelligent Computer Terminal A terminal with the ability to process data using the electronic components within the terminal without the need to access the power of a large computer.

Interblock Gap A blank space typically 0.6 inches wide that separates records or groups of records on magnetic tape.

Interpreter A program that reads source statements and immediately causes the statements to be executed one at a time.

Interrupt An electronic signal which indicates to the central processing unit that the transfer of data between an input or output device and storage has been completed.

IPO Chart Input/processing/output chart used in structured designs to assist in designing the structure of a program.

Job Control Language (JCL) A language that serves as a link between the operating system and the application programs to define jobs being processed, programs to be executed, and provide for job-to-job transition.

Keypunch A device used to punch holes in cards for card reader input devices.

Key-to-Disk Shared Processor System A data entry system in which multiple key stations are used to enter source data into a minicomputer for storage on disk.

Key-to-Tape Data Recorder A data entry device used to manually record data onto magnetic tape.

Large Scale Integration (LSI) Method of constructing electronic circuits in which many thousands of circuits can be stored on a single chip of silicon.

Laser Printers Very high-speed printers, printing in excess of 20,000 lines per minute.

Leased Line A permanent communications channel used to connect a terminal with a computer system.

Libraries, System Areas on direct-access auxiliary storage that are used to store load modules, object programs or subroutine and source statements.

Light Pen A device which allows data to be entered or altered on the face of a CRT terminal.

Line Speed See data communications, line speed.

Linkage Editor Programs that are a part of the operating system that are used to transform object programs into load modules.

Logical Record Individual records stored on an auxiliary storage device.

Loop The repeating of a sequence of instructions.

Low-Level Programming Language Programming language, which is closely related to a particular machine.

Machine Language Instructions A series of numbers, letters, and other bit configurations which can be interpreted by the electronic circuity of a computer, causing operations to be executed.

Macro A statement specified in an assembler language that generates a number of machine language instructions.

Magnetic Core Storage See storage, magnetic core.

Magnetic Disk A form of auxiliary storage in which data is stored on a rotating disc.

Magnetic Ink Character Recognition (MICR) A method used in the banking industry for encoding checks and other documents using a magnetic ink that can be sensed.

Main Computer Storage See storage.

Magnetic Tape See tape.

Mainframes Large computers which are capable of processing large amounts of data at very fast speeds with access to billions of characters of data.

Maintenance, System An ongoing process after a system has been implemented to correct errors and make changes as required to meet changing needs.

Manufacturing, Computers in In manufacturing, computers are used in product design and control of the manufacturing process itself.

Mass Storage Devices Very large-scale auxiliary storage devices.

Matrix Printers A printer that forms characters by a series of small dots.

Memory See storage.

Memory, Programmable Read Only (PROM) A type of memory whose contents can be read but cannot be altered when used as a part of the computer system; it can be modified by the user before being assembled as part of the system.

Memory, Random Access (RAM) A type of storage in which data can be written into and read from the storage element.

Memory, Read Only (ROM) A type of memory from which data can be read and used but not altered.

Memory, Semiconductor A type of memory in which transistors etched on crystals of silicon are used as a storage device.

MICR See magnetic ink character recognition.

Microcomputer A computer system commonly consisting of a CRT, keyboard, and limited storage based upon a microprocessor and costing less than $10,000.00.

Microelectronics The science of creating very small electronic circuits on a thin wafer of germanium or silicon.

Microfilm See COM.

Microprocessor The electronic components of an entire central processor unit created on a very small single silicon chip.

Microsecond One millionth of a second.

Microwave Transmission The transmission of data through open space on a line of sight path by electromagnetic waves.

Millisecond One thousandth of a second.

Minicomputer A computer system which has smaller computer storage, slower processing speeds, and lower cost than large computer systems.

Modems A device which accepts a digital signal and converts it to an analog signal or accepts an analog signal and converts it to a digital signal.

MPU Microprocessor unit.

Multidrop Lines A communication network in which more than one terminal is on a single line connected to the computer.

Multiplexer An electronic device which divides a channel of a certain speed into a series of channels of a slower speed.

Multiprogramming The concurrent execution of two or more computer programs on one computer system.

Nanosecond One billionth of a second.

Network Data Base See data base, network.

Networks, Data Communications A system composed of one or more computers and terminals.

Nibble A half of an eight bit byte.

Nonimpact Printers Printers which use a specially coated or sensitized paper that responds to stimuli to cause an image to appear on the paper.

Object Program The machine language instructions resulting from a compilation of source statements.

OCR See optical character recognition.

Octal Number System A number system with a base 8 that uses eight symbols to represent values.

Office, Computers in the Computers are widely used in word processing activities for inquiry and updating files. Computer terminals are replacing the typewriter as an office tool in many companies.

Operand That portion of the computer instruction that commonly indicates the address of data to be processed.

Operation Code The portion of a computer instruction which indicates the operations to be performed.

Operating System A collection of programs that allows a computer system to supervise its own operations.

Operations Department The department that is responsible for carrying out the day-to-day processing on a computer once a system is operational.

Optical Character Recognition (OCR) The reading of data by scanning the location or shape of the data on a document.

Optical Scanning Devices Devices that read or otherwise sense data on forms for processing on a computer.

Order Entry System The system which defines the procedures used when processing an order.

Output Information that is produced as a result of processing input data.

Output, External Output used outside an organization.

Output, Internal Output used within an organization.

Output, Transaction-Oriented   See   Transaction-oriented output.

Output Units   Units which are part of a computer system that can display, print or otherwise make available to people the results of processing data.

Paging   The ability to display an entire screen full of data on CRT terminal under terminal control.

Parity Check   A checking method in which a bit is associated with each character stored so that all characters will contain an odd (or even) number of bits.

Pascal   A programming language designed to make it easy to write programs using structured techniques.

Personal Computer   A microcomputer designed to be operated by a single user.

Physical Record   A group of records placed together on an auxiliary storage device.

PL/1   A programming language developed by IBM for use as a general-purpose language in both business and scientific applications.

Plotter   A device capable of producing drawings as hard copy output from a computer.

Point-to-Point Line   A direct communication line between a terminal and a computer system.

Polling   A method used in data communications networks in which each terminal is interrogated in sequence to determine if there is data to be sent.

Print Statement   A programming statement used **to cause** data to be output by the computer.

Printed Reports   Reports which are printed by printers attached to the computer system.

Printers   Devices which are connected to the computer system and which can prepare printed reports under the control of a computer program.

Privacy Act of 1974   A law enacted in 1974 to protect rights of citizens from invasion of privacy.

Procedures   A series of logical steps by which all repetitive actions are initiated, performed, controlled, or completed.

Processing Programs Those programs that are a part of the operating system which perform commonly required functions; they include the language translator and the service programs.

Processor Unit The unit which stores the data and contains the electronic circuitry necessary to carry out the processing of the stored data; it consists of the central processing unit and main computer storage.

Program See computer program.

Program Design The process of developing the structure of a program and the detailed steps required for the solution of a problem.

Program Documentation See documentation, program.

Programmers See computer programmers.

Programming The process of writing instructions for a computer.

Programming, Automatic An early term used to describe writing a computer program in a notation other than machine language.

Programming Language, High-Level See high-level programming language.

Programming Language, Low-Level See low-level programming language.

Programming Languages The software supplied as a part of the computer system that provides a means of instructing the computer to perform operations.

Programming, Machine-Language The writing of instructions for a computer by means of numbers, letters of the alphabet and special characters that can be understood by the electronic circuitry.

Programming, Structured See structured programming.

Programming, Symbolic Programming using simple words or abbreviations to express the operations to be performed.

Programs, Unreliable Programs that do not always produce consistent results.

PROM See memory, programmable read only.

Pseudocode A method used to express the logic required in the solution of a problem using English-like phrases.

Punched Cards A piece of lightweight cardboard capable of storing data in the form of punched holes recorded in predefined locations.

Punched Card Reader See card reader.

Query Language A language provided as a part of data base management systems that provides for easy access to data in a data base.

RAM See memory, random access.

Random Access The ability to retrieve records in a file without reading any previous records.

Random Access Storage Devices See direct access storage devices.

Random File Updating The process of updating files in which each master record is individually retrieved without searching through each master record sequentially.

Records A collection of fields related to a specific unit of information.

Relative File Organization See direct file organization.

Remote Job Entry Entering jobs in a batch processing system at a location remote from the central computer site.

Reverse Video The ability to reverse standard display on CRT terminals to highlight characters, words, or lines.

Ring Network A network in which there is no central computer, but a series of computers which communicate with one another.

ROM See memory, read only.

RPG Report program generator; a programming language designed to provide an easy method of generating routine business reports.

Satellite, Communications Communications relay stations positioned thousands of miles above the earth, used in transmission of data from and to earth stations.

Scrolling The ability to move lines displayed on a CRT terminal screen either up or down.

Searching The process in which records are examined to locate a specific record in a file or table.

Second Generation Computers introduced in 1959 that were transistorized.

Secondary Storage See auxiliary storage.

Sector A series of individual storage areas on magnetic disk.

Selecting The process of extracting specific types of data from a group.

Sequence Control Structure A basic control structure used with structured programming.

Sequential Access Data retrieved from a file, one record after another, in a predetermined sequence.

Sequential File Updating The processing of additions, deletions, and changes against a sequential file.

Sequential Files Those files in which records are stored one after another, normally in ascending or descending sequence, based upon some control field.

Serial Printers Printers that output one character at a time.

Simplex Lines A channel which allows data to be transmitted in one direction only.

Software Programs written for computer systems.

Software, Application Computer programs written for computer systems to solve a particular type of business or mathematical problem.

Software, System Programs written to aid in the operation of a computer system.

Software Industry The group of companies that specializes in writing system or application software.

Sorting The process of arranging records in ascending or descending sequence.

Special Purpose Computers Computers which are developed to perform specific tasks.

Star Networks A network which contains a central computer and one or more terminals connected to the computer system.

Storage, Main Computer Electronic components which can electronically store letters of the alphabet, numbers and special characters.

Storage, Size of Main Number of bytes comprising main storage.

Storage, Magnetic Core A widely used form of internal computer storage for many years, which consisted of very small ring-shaped pieces of material which could be magnetized in one of two directions.

Storage, Manufacture of The process of converting raw material into electronic components used to store data in the processor unit.

Storage, Vacuum Tubes One of the first methods used to store data electronically in main storage.

Stored Program Concept The concept in which instructions are stored internally in the main storage unit of the computer.

Structured Design A method of designing programs in which a large program is decomposed into small modules, each of which performs a given function.

Structured Programming A method of programming in which three basic control structures are used to develop programs.

Subroutine A group of instructions which is used a number of times in a program and can be called as needed.

Supervisor A program that is part of the operating system that controls and schedules the resources of a computer system.

Switched Line A type of data communications line in which connection is established with a computer over a regular telephone network.

Symbolic Programming See programming, symbolic.

Synchronous Transmission Transmission of data based upon a timing mechanism in which data is transmitted at fixed intervals.

System A series of related procedures and devices designed to perform a specific task.

Systems Analysis The process of analyzing existing systems for the purpose of evaluating possible improvements in methods and procedures.

System Design That phase of a system project in which the new system is created.

System Development That phase of a system project concerned with scheduling, programming, and documenting a system.

System Flowchart A series of symbols designed to graphically illustrate the procedural steps in a system.

Tape Magnetic A 1/2" wide piece of Mylar on which data can be stored electronically. Typical lengths for tape are 600 feet, 1200 feet, and 2400 feet.

Tape Coding, Magnetic The coding structure used to represent data on magnetic tape.

Tape Density, Magnetic The number of characters per inch that can be recorded on magnetic tape; common densities include 800, 1600, or 6250 bytes per inch.

Tape Library An area in a data processing department where tape reels are stored when not being used on the computer system.

Tape Reels A plastic container on which magnetic tape is stored for processing on a computer system.

Terminals, CRT See cathode ray tube terminals.

Terminals, Data Communication A terminal used in a data communication system for the transmission and reception of data. These terminals may consist of CRT terminals, small computer systems, or other types of I/O devices.

Terminals, Dumb A terminal whose only processing capability is to accept keyed data and transmit that data to a computer.

Terminals, Hard Copy A computer terminal that can produce printed output.

Terminals, Intelligent See intelligent computer terminals.

Testing, Program The process of checking to assure that a program produces reliable and accurate results.

Track, Magnetic Disk The concentric recording positions on megnetic disk.

Transaction-Oriented Processing System That type of system in which data is entered into the computer at the time the transaction occurs.

Transaction-Oriented Output Output normally displayed on a CRT terminal in a transaction-oriented processing system.

Translator See compiler.

TRS-80 A microcomputer system made by Radio Shack.

Unbundling The separate pricing of hardware, software and related services.

Updating The process in which files are changed, with additions, deletions, and changes, to reflect the latest information.

Utilities, System Programs that are a part of an operating system that are used to perform frequently used applications such as file-to-file conversion and sort-merge operations.

Variable Word Length A method of storing data in which each digit, letter of the alphabet or special character is stored in a single storage location; the number of storage locations required will vary with the size of the field.

Very Large Scale Integration (VLSI) Method of constructing electronic circuits in which hundreds of thousands to millions of circuits can be stored on a single chip of silicon.

Virtual Storage A storage method in which portions of a program are stored on auxiliary storage until needed, giving the illusion of unlimited main storage.

Voice Input A device that allows vocal input to be accepted and interpreted in a form processable by a computer.

Voice Output An output device which converts data in main storage to vocal response understandable by humans.

Word Processing The storage, manipulation, and processing of data as needed in the preparation of letters and reports using terminals and related devices.

CHAPTER 2 - INTELLECTUAL PROPERTY PROTECTION OF COMPUTER TECHNOLOGY

I. INTRODUCTION

Intellectual property is a term which is growing more popular to mean patents, trademarks, copyrights, trade secrets and know how.[1] Industrial property usually does not include trademarks, but includes the other items of intellectual property.[2] Proprietary assets or proprietary rights are terms having the same meaning as intellectual property.

The various components of intellectual property may be used to protect various aspects of computer hardware and software. However, because technology usually develops faster than the law, there has been a substantial amount of confusion regarding how best to protect computers, and particularly computer software.[3]

This has been particularly true because lawyers, not familiar with technology, and non-lawyers, not expert in intellectual property law, have frequently become involved in different aspects of computer law.[4]

It is often not easy to determine the best way to protect software, because of the different strengths and weaknesses of copyrights, patents, trade secrets and trademarks. Although a reader will gain an understanding of the issues and potential solutions to intellectual property protection of computer software, as in any field, it is suggested that the reader investigate any particular situation with a skilled expert at an early stage in order to get the best results.

Much of the difficulty in effectively protecting software derives from its nature. The ability of software to assume various forms (as programs, documentation or data bases) complicates efforts to determine what can be protected.

In the late 1970's the British Computer Society, concerned with the uncertain state of British law regarding
proprietary protection for software, encouraged the government to recognize programs as a form of "industrial and
artistic property."[5] In weighing the heavy investments in
programming against the protection offered, the society found
the government's policy of granting patent protection for
combinations of programs and engineering hardware far from
adequate. Since computer programs could be readily conveyed
internationally, the Society recommended coordinating national
laws with the authorities of major technology exporters,
such as the United States. Today, the absense of any uniform
national intellectual property legal protection in the face
of an increasingly demanding worldwide software market and
the possibilities for unauthorized use of software, continues
to generate domestic and international concern.[6]

II. PATENTS

In the United States, patents and copyrights are based
on the United States Constitution.[7] Article I, Section 8,
sets forth the powers of Congress. Congress can collect
taxes, regulate interstate commerce, coin money, declare
war, provide for the Army and Navy, and provide for other
broad functions.

The eighth power is quite unusual in that it is the
only power which tells Congress how it must do a particular
thing. Section 8 states that Congress has the power "to
promote the Progress of Science and the useful Arts by
securing for limited times to authors and inventors the exclusive right to their respective writings and discoveries".

This does not say that Congress has to promote the progress of science and useful arts, but if it decides to do so, it must do so by the required securing for a limited time the exclusive rights to the authors' and inventors' respective writings and discoveries. Congress can institute an award system or give medals to authors and inventors, but it can be argued that it could not do this unless it had secured exclusive rights for a limited time to those authors and inventors. Only then could Congress do these additional things, if it chose to, under some other power.

In the United States, "[w]hoever invents or discovers any new and useful process, machine, manufacture, or composition of matter, or any new or useful improvement thereof, may obtain a patent therefor,..."[8] The present patent laws, from which this comes, were passed by Congress in 1952, but the first U.S. patent statute was enacted in 1790 and is one of the earlier patent statutes among the world countries.[9] However, it is believed that the city-state of Venice in Italy put into place what apparently is the world's first patent law on March 19, 1474.[10]

Because of the statutes passed by Congress under the power given pursuant to the Constitution, patent law is federal law. The various states of the United States do not have patent laws and the rights of the inventors are enforced exclusively in federal court.[11]

Patents are frequently referred to as "monopolies". However it should be clearly understood that a patent does not give the patent owner a right to do anything. On the contrary, it gives the owner a right to exclude others.[12] Thus, the patent law states that "[w]hoever without authority makes, uses or sells any patented invention,...infringes the patent."[13]   While one could think of a patent as a negative monopoly, a right to exclude someone from doing something, the term "monopoly" is nearly always used to refer to a positive monopoly, that is a person can do something no one else can do. Therefore, the term 'monopoly' to describe a patent grant is a misnomer in that an owner of a patent does not necessarily have the right to make, use or sell the invention covered by the patent.

Thus, the owner of a patent covering all telephones could not make a dial telephone, if the dial telephone was an improvement invention patented by a later inventor.   On the other hand, the inventor of the dial telephone could not make a dial telephone because that would be dominated by, and would infringe, the basic telephone patent.   Thus, each of the two patent owners would be required to obtain the approval of, or a license from, the other in order to make a dial telephone. A third party would need a license from both patent owners in order to make the same dial telephone.[14]

Therefore, when one is considering a new product, even one which may involve patentable subject matter, it is very important to make a patent infringement search at an early stage of development in order to see whether that product will infringe a patent owned by someone else. If patent protection is then desired, the inventor must consider the three threshold issues to patentability: utility, novelty and unobviousness.

A.   UTILITY

United States patent law states that only inventions of sufficient utility to society warrant patent protection. Therefore only inventions that fall within certain ranges of subject matter are considered proper for patent protection. Such patentable subject matter is defined as "...any new and useful process, machine, manufacture, or composition of matter, or any new and useful improvement thereof,..."[15] The statute also states that "[t]he term 'process' means process, art or method, and includes a new use of a known process, machine, manufacture, composition of matter, or material."[16] A process is an act, or series of acts, to produce a similar result. If the process includes more than one act, or step, the order of the steps may provide the novelty necessary for patentability. This is true even if all the steps are old. It is the particular combination of steps which may be new. Also, even if the particular combination of steps is old, patentability may lie in the materials used in the process[17] or the material being combined in the process.[18] Finally, a new use for an old process may be patentable if it is non-obvious[19] in accordance with the statute.[20] More extensive analysis is not needed at this juncture, but can be found in the well known patent law treatises. [21]

The next category of statutory patentable subject matter is a "machine".[22] A machine includes a number of parts which are arranged to produce a definite, predetermined and unitary result.[23] The way the parts of the machine are arranged, as well as the nature of the parts themselves, are what defines or distinguishes one machine from other machines.

Analogous to the discussion above relating to processes, the patentability of a machine may rest in the way in which the various parts are arranged even if all of the parts are old.[24]   Rather than using the term "machine," frequently other equivalent terms such as "engine" or, more commonly, "apparatus" are used.

The next category is a "manufacture," or more properly an "article of manufacture," which has been interpreted to mean that which is excluded from the other statutory classes of patentable subject matter.   A structure such as a building may be regarded as a manufacture.[25]   Another statutory category is a "composition of matter" which includes chemical compounds and physical mixtures.   A composition of matter may be patentable based upon the novelty of the ingredients, or the new combination of exclusively old ingredients. The remaining statutory category is an "improvement".   It is rare when a patent is not an improvement on another patent. Even the first patent issued by the U.S. government on July 31, 1790, in which Samuel Hopkins was the inventor, refers to the invention as "an improvement in making of pot-ash and pearl-ash."

Many in the U.S. regard Thomas Edison to be the inventor of the electric light.   Edison, however, would have been the first to admit that his invention was an improvement on others as there were many validly issued U.S. patents which purported to cover electric lights.   However, the other electric lights lasted only a few seconds and were not practical.   Edison invented the first practical light bulb which permitted electric light to be used on a commercial basis.   What Edison actually invented was electric light using a carbon filament.[26]   The first claim of that patent was "an electric lamp for giving light by incandescense, consisting of a filament of carbon of high resistance, later described, and secured to metallic wires, as set forth." While it can be argued that improvements are a separate category of invention, all inventions are essentially improvements over the existing prior art, whether they are compositions of matter, machines, processes or any of the other forms of statutorily allowed subject matter.

B.   NOVELTY AND UNOBVIOUSNESS

Even if an invention is within one of the statutory categories of patentable subject matter it will not be patentable unless it has sufficient novelty as set forth in the patent law.[27] For many years people have tried to provide a satisfactory definition of invention; such has not been successful. Thus the framers of the patent law, to avoid the nebulous question of what constituted an invention, mandated that "a person shall be entitled to a patent unless..." particular conditions exist. Patentability, therefore, is described in the statutes by terms of what is not patentable. An invention, within one of the categories of patentable subject matter, must still be novel. To be novel, an invention must not have been identically disclosed or described within one of the statutorally forbidden categories.

The first novelty bar to patentability is frequently called anticipation. An inventor shall not be entitled to a patent if "the invention was known or used by others in this country, or patented or described in a printed publication in this or a foreign country, before the invention thereof by the applicant for patent."[28] The law assumes that everyone, including inventors, know all of the prior art, or previously disclosed inventions. Even though the invention was original to the inventor and the inventor was, in fact, unaware of the competing prior art, knowledge of that prior art is presumed, and will therefore result in a bar to obtaining a valid patent grant.[29]

As mandated in the statute, there are a number of ways that an invention can be anticipated. If, prior to the invention by the inventor, the invention was known or used by others in the United States, the invention was patented in the U.S. or a foreign country, or if the invention was described in a printed publication in the U.S. or a foreign country, the invention will have been anticipated by the prior art and patent protection is barred.

The next category which prevents novelty in an invention, is sometimes referred to as the "one year" rule. An inventor is not entitled to a patent if, more than one year prior to the date of the application for patent in the U.S., the invention was patented in the U.S. or a foreign country; described in a printed publication in the U.S. or a foreign country; or in the public use or on sale in the United States.[30]

It is particularly important, and is not frequently emphasized by U.S. patent lawyers, that the one year bar is a feature of U.S. law and is not the case in foreign countries, except Canada and the Philippines. These other countries require an "absolute novelty" to exist such that any publication of an invention prior to filing an application for patent would be a bar to protection. Thus even though one would have a year after the publication of an invention in the U.S. in which to file for a patent application, this publication would prevent the obtaining of a patent in many foreign countries.

Domestic patent law also provides that if the inventor has abandoned the invention he will not be entitled to a patent.[31] The law does not state what determines abandonment. However, abandonment is primarily regarded as an issue of fact dependent upon the intent of the inventor.[32]

Prior foreign patenting of the invention may also be a bar to patentability.[33] An inventor is not entitled to a patent if the invention was first patented, or was the subject of an inventors certificate, by the applicant in a foreign country before the date of the patent application in the U.S. on an application for patent which is filed more than twelve months before the filing of the U.S. patent application. This has relation to the need to obtain a license to transfer valuable technology abroad, as discussed in more detail in Chapter 3. Of note is that the filing of a U.S. patent application automatically acts as an application for a foreign license permit from the U.S. government.

Another condition which prevents the patentability of an invention occurs if the invention was made by someone else who described the invention in a patent, which is filed in the U.S. before the invention of the applicant.[34] Also, of course, the inventor is not entitled to a patent if he did not make the invention himself.[35]

The final condition for patentability, under the novelty threshold, relates to what is known as "priority". The inventor is not entitled to a patent if the invention is made in this country by another who had not abandoned, suppressed, or concealed it and the invention was made by the other before the applicant's actual invention.[36] This provision is a basis for what is known in the U.S. as an "interference", a very complex legal contest within the U.S. Patent and Trademark Office to determine which of two inventors is entitled to a patent; the required proofs of the successful party to an interference being the first in priority, or the first to have conceived the invention, with an uninterrupted effort to reduce the invention to practice.

Even if an inventor has overcome all the above novelty requirements to a patent, and the invention is not identically disclosed or described as set forth above, there may still be no entitlement to a patent, if the difference between the applied-for invention and the prior art is such that "the subject matter as a whole would have been obvious at the time the invention was made to a person having ordinary skill in the art to which such said subject matter pertains."[37] This so-called "non-obviousness" is probably the basis for more arguments, discussions, and appeals within the U.S. Patent and Trademark Office, and for more litigation, than any other part of the patent law. In fact, entire books have been written on this one issue.[38] This threshold, however, arose as an attempt by Congress to provide an objective test of patentability to replace the unwieldy concepts of "invention" and "flash of genius". The U.S. Supreme Court has said that this clause in the statute was intended to be simply a better expression of the previous requirements of invention, when it was incorporated into the 1952 Patent Act.[39]

C.   COMPUTER SOFTWARE PATENTS

For many years considerable confusion has surrounded the granting of patent protection for computer software. Under an "apparatus" theory, protection may be afforded a program which, by controlling a computer, creates a new and unique machine.[40] If a program further controls a new and useful process it may be granted protection under the theory that such a program is a "process." Nonetheless, patentability may not be granted if the idea is a scientific truth or mathematical expression. This principle resulted in the courts' development of the mental steps doctrine in *Cochrane v. Deener*[41] and *O'Reilly v. Morse*[42] in which any idea that could be carried out by the human mind without mechanical intervention would be denied patentability. The patent would, thus, only be allowed where novelty and nonobviousness rested in at least one physical step of the process.[43]

In an attempt to clarify the resultant confusion, the Supreme Court in *Gottschalk v. Benson*[44] held that patents must necessarily be denied when a claim attempts to obtain a 'monopoly' over a mathematical algorithm. Claims for programs which combined apparatus and process elements were to be granted patentability under rulings of the Court of Customs and Patent Appeals (CCPA) and now its successor, the Court of Appeals for the Federal Circuit (CAFC).[45] To determine if the claim contained nonstatutory subject matter, the CCPA in *In re Freeman*[46] required an analysis of whether the algorithm was directly or indirectly recited in the claim and/or whether the claim, in its entirety, wholly preempted the algorithm. In a subsequent case, *Parker v. Flook*,[47] the court applied the *Gotschalk* and *Freeman* tests in holding that patent protection must be denied for a computer program where the only novel element in the invention was the addition of an algorithm.

In *Diamond v. Diehr* , the Supreme Court rejected the *Freeman* test in granting patentability to an invention which relied in major part on the constant monitoring of a process by a programmed computer.[48] The court reasoned that a patent grant could not be denied where a mathematical algorithm, incorporated in a computer program, was only a step in a larger process which, as a whole, performed patentable subject matter functions. In the subsequent case of *Diamond v. Bradley* , the court similarly held that software designed to access otherwise inaccessible hardware elements and microprogramming "firmware" designed to update a computer's register are appropriate subject matter for patents.[49]

Patents in the United States provide statutory protection for a software concept but not for the expression of that concept.[50] While patentability rests on the satisfaction of requirements for utility,[51] novelty,[52] and nonobviousness,[53] the statutory language does not clearly indicate whether software falls within the subject matter limitation of a "process, machine, manufacture or composition of matter, or any new and useful improvement thereof."[54] In requiring claims to be analyzed as a whole, rather than at the "point of novelty," the courts have explained that the statutory nature of a claim is not altered by the fact that in several steps of the process a mathematical equation and a programmed digital computer are used."[55] The involvement of a computer in a claim does not, therefore, by itself negate the presence of statutory subject matter.[56] Even in view of the favorable decision of *Diamond v. Diehr*, licensors seeking patent protection for computer software risk commercial loss until the conflicting theories applied by the Supreme Court, in *Freeman* and *Diehr*, the Patent and Trademark Office, and the Court of Appeals for the Federal Circuit are resolved.[57]

Patent protection, whether granted in the United States or in a foreign jurisdiction, is well suited to encourage proliferation of the technology by providing a broad scope of protection. Once a U.S. patent is obtained, the inventor has the exclusive right to exclude others from making using or selling the claimed invention. A U.S. patent grant, lasting up to 17 years, can be maintained through the payment of the regular maintenance fees to the U.S. Patent and Trademark Office. If the patent is infringed, the patentee may obtain injunctive relief to restrain further infringement, damages to the extent of profits accrued by the infringer, and the destruction of all infringing software. Properly handled, the holder of a patent in the United States may also realize the tax benefit of capital gains treatment of patented technology.[58]

For all the advantages offered by patent protection, a patent does not guarantee success in a proprietor's efforts to commercially exploit the software investment. If litigation arises, preliminary relief may be very difficult to obtain for claims based on a patent whose validity is in doubt. Also, many commercially useful programmable processes and machines may prove unpatentable because they cannot meet the requirements for novelty and non-obviousness. A licensor is burdened with the comparatively high cost of securing patent protection. In addition, there is an average waiting period in the United States of about three years between the filing and ultimate issue of a patent. Finally, in view of the rapid changes in software development, a licensor may hold a patent, valid for 17 years, on a program for a computer discarded years previously as obsolete. For these reasons, the selection of patent protection may only be appropriate for a software product when:

> 1) the value of the software to the licensor more than compensates for the expense of obtaining a patent;
>
> 2) the software has a definable inventive concept patentable under statutory requirements;
>
> 3) the market life of the product is sufficiently long to justify the expense of obtaining patent protection; and
>
> 4) the concept may be adequately expressed in features which can be patented.59

Another difficulty with obtaining patents on software is found in the requirement under the patent law of complete disclosure. The law provides that the specification or description of the invention shall "contain a written description of the invention, and of the manner and process in making and using it, in such full, clear, concise, and exact terms as to enable any person skilled in the art to which it pertains, or which it is most nearly connected, to make and use the same, and shall set forth the best mode contemplated by the inventor in carrying out his invention."[60] This is felt by some to be a substantial burden in that some software may require many pages to disclose adequately for U.S. patent disclosure purposes. There have been continuous arguments as to what is regarded as an adequate or sufficient disclosure under the statute, and software disclosure is merely another aspect of this problem.

While the issuance of a patent in the United States will protect the software domestically, it provides no protection in a foreign jurisdiction. Foreign patent laws, as noted before, require absolute novelty of the invention for the granting of a patent. Full disclosure, as required in a United States patent application, would preclude protection in a foreign jurisdiction if a licensor did not file for a patent in that country within the one year period provided for under the Paris Convention.[61] Patent protection for software, however, has been consistently denied by all countries on the European continent, except Sweden.[62] Yet, the issue of patentability of software has not been readily dismissed by jurisdictions which recognize that the patent coverage for software inventions permit the public access to new software that would otherwise be maintained in secrecy.[63]

Common concerns for the provision of adequate software protection prompted an international symposium sponsored by the World Intellectual Property Organizaton (WIPO) in November of 1979, to discuss a treaty for uniform legal protection of software. Based on the state of legal uncertainty in each jurisdiction, the symposium recommended the application of copyright protection when patents were unavailable.[64] Until individual nations recognize patentability as a means for protection for software, a licensor is limited to protecting software by patent only in the U.S.. In foreign jurisdictions, licensors may evaluate alternative forms of statutory protection, such as copyright, or rely on non-statutory trade secret protection.

III. COPYRIGHTS

As discussed previously with reference to patents, copyrights are based on the United States Constitution, which gives Congress the power to "promote the Progress of Science and the useful Arts, by securing for limited times to authors and inventors the exclusive right to their respective writings and discoveries."[65] Under this constitutional power the first U.S. copyright law was passed by Congress in 1790.[66] After two major revisions in 1831 and 1870, the Copyright Act of 1909 was passed.[67] After extended congressional discussion and pendency, the Copyright Act of 1976 was finally passed, entering into effect on January 1, 1978.[68]

Until this 1976 copyright law, as enacted, there existed a dual system of protection in the U.S. The first system was based on Federal statute and the second based on state law, which could be either common law or statutory law. However the Copyright Law of 1976 preempted all state common law copyrights and copyrights based on the statutes of the state.[69]

The two most important requirements for eligibility under the copyright law for protection are 'originality' and 'fixation.' As provided for in the statute, "copyright protection subsists...in original works of authorship fixed in any tangible medium of expression..."[70] There is no requirement for novelty as is the case in the patent law, but the originality which is necessary to qualify for copyrightability requires creation by the author without copying from someone else.[71] Thus there may be two or more identical works, each entitled to copyright protection, if these works are created independently and not copied from each other.

A simple illustration may be necessary. If a first author writes a book about the life of George Washington, this does not preclude another author from writing a second book about George Washington. If the second author uses independent research, even though many of the sources are the same, and expresses the idea involved in his own words and does not copy from the first author, the second author's book would not infringe the first author's copyright and each author could obtain a copyright. Of course there are many books in the library on the life of George Washington and each contains particular authors' methods of expressing their ideas and the facts involved. Additionally, if a photographer prepares equipment and takes a picture of the Empire State Building, a copyright on the picture would not preclude others from erecting equipment on the same spot, with the same lighting and producing their own, albeit near duplicate picture. The copyright would, however, prevent another from impermissibly copying the first photographer's picture.

Copyright law specifically provides that "[i]n no
case does copyright protection for an original work of
authorship extend to any idea... concept... or discovery."[72]
Thus a copyright only protects the copyright author from
one who truly copies the copyrighted work. If another
develops a similar, or even the same item, independently,
the second author is not regarded as a copyright infringer.
Of course whether the second person copies the work of
the first, or had access to the work of the first, is often
a major part of the discovery effort in a lawsuit for copyright infringement. Under the copyright law which went
into effect January 1, 1978, a copyright is created when
the work of the authorship is 'fixed' in a final form the
first time. Another way to state this is that all copyrightable works are protected under the federal laws from
the moment they are created. Federal registration and
notice of copyrights are still necessary elements, however,
for a successful litigation for infringement. Such notice
requires the word "copyright" or a "C" in a circle, the
date of creation and the copyright owner's name. An example
notice might be: "Copyright 1985 VANGUARD Corp., all rights
reserved." Finally, under present law, computer programs
are regarded as copyrightable subject matter even though
there is no specific statement in the statute that expressly
grants that computer programs are copyrightable.[73]

In one of the most recent opinions on the applicability of copyright protection to software, the United
States Court of Appeals, Third Circuit[74] held that even
though 17 U.S.C. §102(a)[75] does not expressly list computer

programs as works of authorship, the legislative history of
the Act suggests that programs should be copyrightable as
literary works. [76] The court cited the creation of the
Commission on the New Technological Uses (CONTU) as evidence
of congressional intent to define the application of copyright
to computer software. [77] Traditionally, the Copyright Office
granted registration to programs, as consistent with its
policy to resolve questions of copyright in favor of the
registrant. [78] In evaluating the legitimacy of such practice,
CONTU determined that some form of statutory protection was
necessary in order to encourage continuing creation of
computer programs. [79] In its final report to Congress, CONTU
recommended the repeal of Section 117, to indicate that any
computer use of copyrighted programs is a potential
infringement under the new section, codified with the same
number. A rightful possessor of a copy of a computer program
is authorized to make additional copies if, 1) the new copy is
an essential step in using the computer program or 2) the copy
is for archival purposes only. CONTU also recommended the
following definition for the term 'computer program' to be
added to Section 101 of the Copyright Act:

> A 'computer program' is a set of statements or
> instructions to be used directly or indirectly in a
> computer in order to bring about a certain result. [80]

The Court of Appeals observed that both recommendations
were adopted under the Copyright Act Amendment of 1980 [81]
despite vigorous debate that the statute would
unconstitutionally disturb the tangible embodiment versus
original means of expression dichotomy which distinguishes
patent and copyright protection. [82]

The potential for software to be written in symbolic computer language and electronically translated into computer elements has necessitated, through litigation in the United States, determination of the form of computer program which may be the appropriate subject of copyright protection. In *Data Cash Systems, Inc. v. JS & A Group, Inc.*, [83] the court held that the object code representation of a program in memory could not constitute a copy since "the ROM is the mechanical embodiment of the source program," not a "copy" of it. [84] The court also stipulated that copyright would protect the ROM only if appropriate copyright notice, in either human readable or machine readable form appears on the contents of the ROM or its package.

In contrast, in the case of *Tandy Corp. v. Personal Micro Computers, Inc.*, [85] a computer program in the tangible form of an object code ROM chip was considered an appropriate subject for copyright. The court reasoned that in instances where a visual display or pertinent part of the program was copied and impressed on a chip, infringement had clearly occurred. Thus, any ROM bearing this information could not be considered, under 35 U.S.C. §117, as properly obtained copyrighted material and would be subject to suit for infringement.

The abandonment of the requirement for visual perceptability for a copy has extended copyrightability to include protection of both source code and object code. [86] Under 17 U.S.C. §102(a), a copyright protects works in any tangible means of expression "from which they can be perceived, reproduced or otherwise communicated either directly or with the aid of a machine or device." The courts have held that the statutory requirement of fixation is satisfied through the embodiment of expression in ROMs. Copyrightability of programming, whether as an application program or a systems program, is not dependent on the function each serves within the computer machinery.[87] As stated in the CONTU report, and relied upon by the *Apple v. Franklin* court,

> Programs should no more be considered machine parts than videotape should be considered parts of projectors or phonorecords part of sound reproduction equipment.... That the words of a program are used ultimately in the implementation of a process should in no way affect their copyrightability. [88]

Copyright protection for a software product, as opposed to the exclusive right to an idea afforded under patent protection, offers a licensor an easily secured statutory safeguard for his software investment. Under the 1976 Copyright Act, software is copyrighted as soon as it is rendered in a final and tangible form.[89] In foreign jurisdictions, the time of adherence of copyright protection varies. In the United Kingdom, for example, copyright protection adheres regardless of whether the software product has been registered or published.[90] While copyright in the U.S. protects only the original expression of the software, the duration of this protection is the author's life plus 50 years, or 75 years for works written for hire.[91] The remedies available to the owner of a program whose copyright is infringed include injunctions, damages, and accountings of profit. Such an owner may also require the delivery and destruction of all infringing copies. Levy of similarly substantial penalties for unauthorized copies is characteristic of foreign copyright protection, particularly in the United Kingdom.[92]

Copyright protection of computer software is increasingly likely when the technology is licensed among major western developed countries.[93] These nations have recognized software as copyrightable when its expression exhibits the individual style and creative stamp of the author-programmer.[94] International conventions, such as the Universal Copyright Convention (UCC) and the World Intellectual Property Organization (WIPO), of which most developed countries are members, have identified the application of copyright protection as the most feasible safeguard for uniformly protecting software internationally. According to a 1977 WIPO proposal, drafted in concert with CONTU, such a uniform system would require no registration or deposit for securing copyright. Unlike the requirements of the 1976 Copyright Act of the United States, such practice is typical of foreign copyright systems.[95] The WIPO proposal further would limit the scope of protection under copyright to 20 years from use or 25 years from creation, in deference to the limited product lifetime of programming in industrial use.[96]

The proposal, however, fails to provide statutory damages and fees in the event of infringement. Because cost of litigation can exceed actual damages, such failure places a software licensor at a definite disadvantage. The WIPO proposal further neglects the issue of preemption. In attempting to conform to the WIPO standards for copyright and trade secret, a licensor may be forced to rely on only one system of protection for his software, to the detriment of any interests left unprotected by the chosen statutory scheme. Such a result clearly contravenes the purpose for creation of a statutory protection plan and dissemination of the software into public use. Until a proposal for uniform statutory treatment is adopted as an amendment to foreign national copyright laws, licensors will be subject to the individual application of copyright laws of foreign jurisdictions.[97]

IV.   TRADE SECRETS

Classification of software as trade secret or know-how offers an alternative to protection offered by federal patent and copyright statutes.[98] Most of the favored status of trade secret or know-how licensing derives from its frequent combination with the license of patent rights. Yet, without the definition of scope, as provided by patent claims, the determination of the extent of trade secret or know-how rights has depended on judicial construction.

Typically, know-how has been defined as the knowledge of the company of how to make, market, sell or distribute a product.[99] It consists of any formula, pattern, device or compilation of information used in a business to gain an advantage over competitors.[100] The Supreme Court, in the case of *Kewanee Oil Co. v. Bicron Corp.*, explained that the subject of a trade secret must be secret and unavailable to public knowledge or general knowledge in the trade or business.[101] Disclosure of the secret was held not to destroy its secrecy if it was revealed to another "in confidence, and under an implied obligation not to use or disclose it."[102] Thus, the holder of a trade secret is protected against disclosure or unauthorized use of the trade secret by those to whom the secret was entrusted under express or implied restriction of nondisclosure or nonuse. Trade secret protection is not afforded to information that does not possess sufficient or at least minimal novelty to justify its classification as a trade secret.[103]

In determining the existence of trade secret, the Restatement of Torts advised consideration of 1) the extent to which information is known by others, 2) the extent of measures taken to protect the secret, 3) the value of the information to the business and to its competitors, and 4) the difficulty with which the information may be acquired by others.[104] Although case law does not place a duty on the licensor to make such a determination, it is clearly in the licensor's best interest to identify what portion of his know-how constitutes valuable trade secret. By nature, trade secret law can extend protection for methodology underlying computer programming but does not protect against independent development or reverse engineering. Since licensing significantly magnifies the risk that information may be publicly disclosed, licensing agreements should be structured to clearly identify and protect sensitive information.

In order to protect trade secret interests, the following are important considerations:

1) confidentiality agreements signed by anyone to whom the secret will be disclosed;

2) security measures ensuring restricted access to trade secret information;

3) nondisclosure agreements and reasonable covenants not to compete signed by employees;

4) predisclosure interviews for all employees to whom the secrets are disclosed; and

5) debriefing interviews for all terminating employees with access to trade secret information.105

The most important thing about a trade secret is
that the item to be protected must be kept secret and only
disclosed to others who have agreed to keep it secret.
Obviously in some cases, portions of computer software
must be revealed to customers. If this is the case, to
keep it a trade secret, the producers must require that
the customer or anyone else having access to the trade
secret sign an appropriate nondisclosure agreement. Such
agreements note a covenant to keep the confidential material
secret and not to disclose it to anyone else unless they
have a 'need to know' and unless they also have signed
a similar nondisclosure agreement. Additionally, the secret
material should be kept locked in appropriate rooms or
file cabinets, with only those who have signed a nondisclosure agreement having access to it.

It is customary to explain to those who are asked
to sign the nondisclosure agreement that they should sign
the agreement not because of a lack of trust but that in
order to enforce the trade secret in court a demonstration
is necessary to prove that the information owner has actually
kept it a secret and has taken positive steps to do so.
Having everyone with access to the confidential information
sign a nondisclosure agreement is a common way to help
convince the court that the owner regards it as a legitimate
trade secret. Notification of value is also a good indication of
intent to keep confidential the information, so it is suggested

that owners mark copies of the trade secrets, including magnetic disks, disk jackets and boxes with a stamp or a sticker that reads: "Confidential - Trade Secret." An appropriate notice should also be placed at the first page or the start of the trade secret material. It is also recommended that this notice be placed at the end of the trade secret material and included in other parts of the trade secret material as well. A typical notice follows: "NOTICE: This material is the property of VANGUARD Corp. It is confidential and is a proprietary trade secret which is not to be disclosed to others without written permission from the owner." As an important caveat, just because appropriate agreements have been prepared by a lawyer, the trade secret may still be easily lost if the agreements are not used properly and a record is not kept of them. Constant attention is required. A trade secret should be regarded as analogous to government classified material and the same techniques should be used to protect it as are used to protect such classified material.

In applying trade secret protection to computer software, the courts have debated preemption when the software is also protected under copyright.[106] However, where the trade secret claim and copyright claim were not equivalent, the courts have held that state statutes protecting software by trade secret would not be preempted by federal copyright law.[107] A close reading of the Copyright statute, Section 301, indicates that the nature of copyright and trade secret protection does not represent preemption conflicts as long as the applicant does not seek to enforce the same or equivalent right under both state and federal law. By statute, copyright extends only to the expression of an idea.[108]

In contrast, proprietary concepts are readily protected as trade secrets. Where the respective requirements of each are met, one may rely on both trade secret and copyright protection as comprehensive safeguards of an idea and its expression without risking loss of a software investment by preemption.

Congress expressed some concern in connection with the computer software protection act of 1980 with the simultaneous application of copyright and trade secret laws to computer programs. As discussed by Clarence E. Eriksen and J. Timothy Headley,[109]:

> The final CONTU Report to Congress and the legislative history of the Computer Software Protection Act of 1980 recognized the simultaneous application of copyright and trade secret laws to computer programs. The CONTU Report provided:
>
>> The availability of copyright for computer programs does not, of course, affect the availability of trade secret protection. Under the act of 1976 only those state rights that are equivalent to the exclusive rights granted therein (generally, common law copyright) are preempted. Any decline in use of trade secrecy might be based not upon preemption but on the rapid increase in the number of widely distributed programs in which trade secret protection could not be successfully asserted.[110]
>
> Similarly, the 1980 House Report stated:
>
>> During the course of Committee consideration, the question was raised as to whether the bill would restrict remedies for protection of computer software under state law, especially unfair competition and trade secret laws. The Committee consulted the Copyright Office for its opinion as to whether Section 301 of the 1976 Copyright Act in any way preempted those and other forms of state law protection for computer software. On the basis of this advice and on the advice of its own counsel, the Committee concluded that state

remedies for protection of computer software are not limited by this bill. 111

Some are concerned that a deposit of a copy of the printout of a computer program with the Copyright Office is a publication that would destroy the secrecy of a trade secret. In answer to this question the Copyright Office states that deposit of copyright material is not an actual disclosure of a trade secret. 112

In an international market, one may attempt to rely on industrial secret laws to implement trade secret protection. 113 While such laws exist in most developed countries, enforcing the law is difficult due to differences between civil law and common law jurisdictions. 114 In civil law jurisdictions, for example, protective orders essential to the maintenance of the secret may be more difficult to obtain than in the United States. Minimal allowable discovery complicates the burden of proof for theft of trade secrets if the infringing products have an altered appearance. By electing arbitration proceedings, a licensor may obtain discovery as well as preservation of the trade secret through secured proceedings. Since many countries treat arbitration awards as contractual matters, enforcement is easier with this approach than with court judgments. Where local court sovereignty would be at issue, one analysis suggests that if an arbitration clause allows the award to be enforceable in any competent court governed by the 1958 United Nations Convention, awards may be enforced directly in the nonvenue country's court without docketing the award first in the local court. 115

While foreign jurisdictions permit recovery of damages based on a contract when trade secrets have been misappropriated, one's commercial advantage in the trade secret is lost upon its public disclosure. Therefore, regardless of foreign or domestic jurisdiction, the efficacy of trade secret protection for software, and continued commercial value of the trade secret, will depend on the nature of any agreements involved and any emphasis on preserving the security of the trade secret.

V.   TRADEMARKS

In contrast to patents and copyrights, the U.S. Constitution does not include specific language giving Congress power to regulate trademarks. Many felt that Congress's power under the patent and copyright clause of the Constitution gave Congress the power to regulate trademarks and in 1870 Congress passed the first federal law which provided for trademark registration.[116] However in the Trademark Cases,[117] the U.S. Supreme Court held the 1870 Act unconstitutional stating that the only power Congress had to regulate trademarks had to originate from the commerce clause.[118]

The first effective federal trademark registration law was passed in 1905.[119] The present federal trademark law is known as the Lanham Act and is sometimes referred to as the Federal Trademark Act of 1946.[120] However, federal jurisdiction over trademarks extends only to marks used in interstate and foreign commerce. The United States also has what is known as 'common-law' trademarks.[121] Trademarks can also be registered with many state governments.

Trademark use, not registration, actually creates an entitlement to trademark rights. Thus trademarks cannot be registered under federal law or state law until the trademark has actually been used in either interstate or foreign (federal registration) commerce or within the state involved (state registration).[122]

The Lanham Act defines a trademark as "any word, name, symbol, or device or any combination thereof adopted and used by a manufacturer or merchant to identify his goods and distinguish them from those manufactured or sold by others."[123] It is important to note that a 'trademark' is not the same as a 'trade name'. A trade name is usually a company name or commerical name used to identify a par- ticular business, while a trademark can be considered as a brand name of a product.

The same trademark can be used on different goods. This signifies to the public that the goods come from the same source and the quality is controlled by that source whether or not the public knows the name of that source.[124] By putting the same trademark on different products, the trademark owner implies that the various goods are of a comparable quality. Thus a trademark carries with it the owner's good will and reputation and, as such, is a very important and valuable merchandising tool.

A trademark may be a word,[125] a group of words,[126] a group of letters,[127] a distinctive configuration,[128] a package design,[129] a pictorial representation,[130] or even a distinctive design or configuration on a shoe sole.[131] The important aspect of this protection, is that for U.S. trademark protection, and before a registration can be obtained, there must be actual use in interstate commerce.[132]

One particularly interesting feature of U.S. trademark law is that the Lanham Act provides that, except as expressly excluded in four paragraphs of one section of the statute, nothing in the Act shall prevent the registration of the mark used by the applicant "which has become distinctive of the applicant's goods in commerce."[133] The four exclusionary paragraphs of the statute provide that no trademark by which the goods of the applicant may be distinguished from others shall be refused registration on the principal register unless it:

a.   is immoral, deceptive, or scandalous or disparages or falsely suggests a connection with persons, institutions, etc.;

b.   is a flag or coat of arms or other insignia of the U.S., state, municipality or foreign nation;

c.   is a name, portrait, or signature of a particular living individual without written consent; or

d.   resembles a mark which is registered in the U.S. Patent and Trademark Office or a mark previously used in the U.S. by another and not abandoned, as to be likely, when applied to the goods of the applicant, to cause confusion or cause mistakes or deceive.[134]

It is therefore due to this non-exclusion that the forms mentioned previously, including pictorial representation, groups of words, etc. may be registered, because the law does not prevent them from being registered as long as they have become distinctive of the applicant's goods in commerce.

It should be clearly understood that the owner of a trademark on a product can not prevent another from selling the same product, but the non-owner cannot call it by the same trademark or brand name.[135] Thus a trademark is not a 'monopoly' on a product as some have accused.[136] Edward S. Rogers has rebutted the monopoly argument as follows: "There is no element of monopoly involved at all... A trademark precludes the idea of monopoly. It is a means of distinguishing one product from another."[137] Chief Judge Markey, now of the Court of Appeals for the Federal Circuit, in commenting on the defendant's arguments that to protect the Levi Strauss pocket tab trademark would be to continue a monopoly, stated that the "perjorative use of 'monopoly' implies that Strauss's trademark right is harmful and anti-competitive. On the contrary, the pocket tab trademark gives the public a reliable indication of source and thus facilitates responsible marketplace competition."[138]

A U.S. district court has stated that "...a trademark does not in any way represent a monopoly...on a particular product"...While patent laws were enacted to encourage invention and development of new products, trademark laws were intended solely to protect the consuming public from deception and confusion, [which often result] from imitation of the distinguishing trademarks of established products."[139]

As an example, 'Apple' is an important trademark of Apple Computer, Inc.. 'Apple' can be used with other combinations of words and symbols, such as 'Apple II' for computers which are improvements over the original Apple computer.

Obviously then, a trademark is not limited to one particular product. A company such as General Electric will use the trademark "General Electric" or "GE" on a wide variety of products. When this trademark is placed on a new product it has significant market value because many customers are familiar with GE products and would tend to buy another product with that mark on it because they regard the quality of products made by GE as satisfactory for their purposes. Thus the primary importance of a trademark is for use in marketing a product. Certainly 'VisiCalc', 'Easy Writer', 'Word Star' and 'Magic Pencil' are important and valuable marks and are certainly of significant importance in marketing the products which bear these trademarks.

It is important to remember that a trademark is always used as an adjective, not a noun. Thus there must also be a generic word associated with the trademark. You don't buy an 'Apple', you buy an Apple Computer. If the trademark is used as a noun it may ultimately be used generically as a name of a type of product. If this happens for any significant period of time the trademark will be lost to the owner and anyone can use it. This has happened to a number of well known words such as aspirin, escalator, linoleum, cellophane, etc.

In addition to using the trademark as an adjective, it should be used distinctively with either an initial capital letter or all capital letters, possibly within quotation marks and with some indication that it is a trademark. One method of doing this is to use a small "TM" as a superscript after the word at least the first time it is used in a particular advertisement or document with an appropriate statement, somewhere in the advertisement or document, that the word is a trademark of the owner of that particular mark. The "R" in a circle can be used only after the trademark is registered on the principal or supplemental register in the U.S. Patent and Trademark Office and should not be used before this time as there are certain penalties and disadvantages involved.

For software protection, it is appropriate to pick a name for a computer program which is only to be used for a year or two, use the TM superscript identification, and note the ownership of the trademark, as common-law trademark rights are only obtained by actual use in the U.S., as noted earlier. The trademark need not be registered to obtain these rights. However, if the mark will be used for more than two or three years it is worthwhile to register the trademark, which will cost something more than a copyright and less than a patent. Registering a trademark should be done by a trademark lawyer. Keep in mind that nearly all lawyers have no experience or knowledge about trademarks and one should find a trademark lawyer to handle trademark applications.

Many patent lawyers are skilled trademark lawyers but many are not. There are many people who are skilled trademark lawyers but not patent lawyers. The reason for using a trademark lawyer for obtaining a trademark is the necessity that each detail is accomplished properly. A skilled trademark lawyer can also instruct the client in its use and, most importantly, make a trademark search to see if others have registered the mark or are using it in commerce. This is particularly important to undertake before initiating the spending of significant amounts of money in an advertising campaign on the mark. If the mark being used is owned by someone else, the trademark owner can prevent other use. This can be very expensive, especially after money and time have been spent getting the mark known in commerce by the non-owner.

VI. MASK PROTECTION

On November 8, 1984, the Semiconductor Chip Protection Act was signed into law.[140] The law was designed to protect the specific computer related innovation involved in "maskworks fixed in a semiconductor chip product."[141] Such products have the multiple patterned layers of conducting, insulating and semiconductive 'doping' deposits used to create a specific electronic circuit chip.

The 'maskwork' which is protected, is in effect the "series of related images" which are fixed in final form "in a semiconductor chip product when its embodiment is sufficiently permanent or stable to permit the mask work to be perceived or reproduced."[142] More generally, these masks provide the patterns needed to photolithograph and etch the computer circuit onto a silicon chip.

The act provides a form of registration based protection not unlike the copyright. Such similarity extends to the annexation of the Act to the end of the existing copyright statute. Forms for registration are also available from the Copyright Office and notice is similar, requiring the placing of an "M" in a circle, "M" or "Maskwork" with a date and an identified owner on the goods.[143]

However, unlike a copyright, mask work protection is limited to the time of registration, and is only eligible for protection if:

(1) on the date the work is registered or first
     commercially exploited anywhere in the world,
     the owner is a national or domiciliary of this
     country, a national, domiciliary, or sovereign
     authority of a foreign nation that has signed
     a treaty with the United States pertaining to
     the protection of "mask works" or is a "state-
     less person";

(2) the work is first exploited commercially in
     this country; or

(3) the work is contained within the scope of a
     Presidential proclamation pertaining to the
     "mask works" of foreign nationals, as detailed
     in the law. 144

Some review of the application is provided, and
protection will be denied if the mask work is not original or
"consists of designs that are staple, commonplace or familiar
in the semiconductor industry or variations of such designs,
combined in a way that, considered as a whole, is not
original." 145 The duration afforded for protection is ten
years and protection begins at the date of registration or
prior commercial exploitation anywhere in the world.

The owner of the mask work, again in similarity to a
copyright, has exclusive rights regarding the reproduction of
the work and the importation or distribution of any
semiconductor chip embodying the mask work. 146 There are,
however, certain limitations on the mask work owner's
exclusive rights. Unauthorized users of the work will not be
liable if the use was for evaluation techniques or teaching
purposes, 147 or if a purchaser, without notice, obtains
pirate chips. 148

Unlike the other forms of intellectual property
protection discussed, foreign nationals are limited in exer-

cising protective rights to mask works. Foreign applicants must either petition the Secretary of Commerce or obtain a Presidential proclamation granting protection.[149] Such domestic prejudice is similar to many foreign forms of intellectual property protection as discussed below.

VII.   INTERNATIONAL PROTECTION

While the legal system in the United States appears to be proceeding along a course of trying to fit the problems of software and other data information protection and utilization into existing legal structures, designed with public policy, economics and incentives considered centuries ago and on the basis of then-understood concepts of invention and artistic and literary works, and creating new 'band-aid' types of special protection, there is strong evidence that these ideas are lacking in the needs of today's society.

Until very recently, they appeared to veer in a direction that might also have resulted in them not being honored by significant industrial countries of the world, including more specifically, Japan. At this writing, however, Japan appears to have settled for emphasis upon some form of copyright protection in line with the urgings of the United States and western countries.[150] Brazil, however, still appears to favor a separate program protection law.[151]

Among the salient conclusions that the Japanese reached before buckling under to the copyright concensus are that the economic activities involved in software, programs and related subject matter are different in nature and objective from the cultural works underlying the concept of copyright law.[152] It was observed that software programs

and the like can only realize value when put to use, and
that the concept of use has allegedly no place in the philosophy of copyright law. The potential hampering of the
development and promotion of software under the limitations
of the very nebulous concept of adaptation rights of copyright law was another area of concern. The Japanese conclusion was that the concept of moral rights to works under
the copyright law is both unnecessary and inappropriate
for goods such as programs used in economic activities.
And there was the further conclusion that the kind of con-
ciliation, arbitration and dispute resolution required for
an effective system was entirely outside the scope of the
legal concepts of the copyright law. [153]

The current concepts of patent law in the exclusion
of developments based on logical rules, the humanities
and social sciences, were deemed totally unsuited for the
protection of programs. The requirement of complete publication of details was considered as possibly negating
the significance of appropriate protection. Further, despite
the tremendous amounts of effort and time involved in development of a program, there are very few that can satisfy
the patent law concept of inventiveness. Limited life
cycles of some programs also appear to negate the value
of current patent concepts.

With regard to contract law protection, it was noted
that only the parties to the contract are bound. In addition, sales of multi-purpose programs including software
products to unspecified users is an increasing way of doing
business and is not protected by individual contracts. [154]

The Japanese, therefore, proposed a new program rights law in the nature of a registration system, having some formalities of examination, with information to the public on what is purported to be protected as defined by the originator. This system would enable use and copying through arbitration in return for proper value, with measures devised to prevent unreasonable infringement on the rights of the originator. A system of program examiners with appropriate legal and technical backgrounds was to be established to aid in the settlement of disputes.

The above, of course, must be taken in the context of a current (and undoubtedly temporary) relatively "have-not" society in software development compared to the United States, United Kingdom and other western countries; but the analysis of inadequacies in current legal concepts is still worthy of attention.

In debating these and related issues with key software developers and users, representatives from industry (large and small), university, government and the legal and economics professions, study groups from the Franklin Pierce Law Center Patent Trademark & Copyright Research Foundation and Germeshausen Center for Innovation and Entrepreneurship Law have reached the conclusion that at least three techniques may be a future trend that all nations can find acceptable for the protection of software.[155] This is apart from those rare circumstances where patents may be appropriate or circumstances where trade secret or confidentiality agreements may have some usefulness (as distinguished from wide areas where counterfeiting or piracy can easily destroy any trade secret rights). These are in order of effectiveness and potential utility:

1. Technological protection by destruction, blind and non-reproducing techniques, and by changing keys or access codes--always with the utmost security on such codes.

2. Some form of copyright-like protection, but not just treated as subject to general copyright law. Rather, it is proposed to provide some kind of descriptors of what is alleged to be "new"; very rapid securing of rights; a sensible protection time; and competent and very prompt dispute resolution (which seems to rule out the current court system). Late twentieth century public policy considerations regarding the appropriateness of compulsory licensing should be determined (with the precedent of the phonograph record compulsory licensing of the U.S. Copyright Law)[156] and weighed against the economic and other incentives to create the work.

3. A licensing scheme similar to that of the American Society of Composers, Authors and Publishers providing for the pooling, licensing and accounting for software, program and related information that may be appropriate for such treatment.

These rapid developments in planning come at a time when nations, particularly in the far east, that have never extended copyright protection and in some instances have never had a patent system, are recognizing the need for and benefits of such intellectual property protection. Taiwan, long a seat of counterfeiting, is considering copyrights.[157] Korea has recently proposed a copyright law, albeit preferential for residents of Korea and works originally published in Korea, but currently lacking protection for computer software.[158] The Peoples Republic of China, having as of April 1, 1985 adopted a new patent law, later described, is now turning to considerations of copyright.[159] This patent law recognizes the computer's input into patentable invention. The Federal Court of Australia in *Apple Computer Inc. v. Computer Edge Ptg. Lid.* has recently ruled that computer programs manifested in source code are "information capable of conveying an intelligible meaning" and are protectable as literary material, with object code versions being protected as translations thereof.[160] Malaysia is also introducing its own patent law,[161] with copyright protection presently judicially restricted to works of Malaysians or residents thereof.

In the Malaysia Patents Bill of 1983, in addition to patents for inventions that involve an "inventive step" and are "industrially applicable"[162] and meet the requirements that "such inventive steps would not have been obvious to a person having ordinary skill in the art",[163] a provision is made for petty patents that could have some significance for inventions embodying novel and industrially useful, but not non-obvious, software and programs. These petty patents are termed "utlitity innovations"[164] and carry a certificate of five years duration, with injunctive and damage relief. It is significant to the above that the exclusions from patentability do not specifically include computer software, but only scientific discoveries and mathematical methods, natural plant and animal varieties, methods of doing business and performing purely mental acts or playing games, and methods of medical treatment and diagnosis.[165] There are provisions for compulsory licenses after three years if there is no production, without legitimate reason, products are available only at unreasonably high prices or do not meet the public demand.[166]

A window for communicating ideas and establishing
ready interchanges with industrial, legal and university
groups in Malaysia is now provided by the formation, in
November of 1984, of a Malaysian chapter of the Academy
of Applied Science,[167] established to facilitate technology transfer and intellectual property law cooperation.
This chapter builds upon a model of technology transfer
activities with developing countries established by the
Academy at its first workshop held at Oxford University
in June-July of 1983.[168]

Returning to the new patent law of the Peoples Republic of China (PRC), regulations governing the operation
of which have been promulgated by the Patent Office of
the PRC on January 19, 1985, there is also provision for
both patents of invention, defined as "any new technical
solution relating to a product, a process or improvement
thereof"[169] and a lesser "utility model" defined as "any
new technical solution relating to the shape, the structure,
or their combination, of a product, which is fit for practical use". Should protection be sought either for an
invention or the lesser utility model, the novelty that
is to be claimed must be couched in terms of a preamble
setting followed by a specific characterization of "the
technical features...which, in combination with the features
stated in the preamble portion, it is desired to protect."[170]
Compulsory licensing may apply if the patent is not used
in China within three years of the grant, absent adequate
reasons for non-use. Insofar as inventions or utility
models embodying software may be concerned, it appears
that the patent law of the PRC is intended largely to track
the substance of the United States patent law.

There are thus exciting possibilities for international protection at least against close copying of whatever new contributions may be developed in the software area. But it is yet to be determined whether these shall be structured in some kind of copyright-like format or in a petty patent or utility model format;[171] though real inventions may still be subject to the normal patent laws, with their strengths and weaknesses, and the more limited contractural rights of confidentiality.

VIII. CONCLUSION

Determining which of the various aspects of intellectual property should be used to protect software can be a fairly complex task. The business aspects, the marketing plan, the particular nature of the software, its life, its novelty, etc. must all be considered by people who understand the advantages and disadvantages of utilizing the various types of intellectual property.

It is feasible to use a variety of intellectual property rights to protect a single piece of software. One might copyright the program and yet keep parts a trade secret which, while it seems to be an anomaly, can be done. One could also get a trademark on the program and, if appropriate, a patent on some novel aspect of it.

One of the most important items is to talk to knowledgeable people at any early time in the development of the software to make sure that no action is taken that will prohibit obtaining appropriate protection. A deliberate decision can be made not to obtain protection under patent, trademark or trade secret law. However, such a decision should be made only after knowledgeable people have looked into the matter and made such a decision.

IX. FOOTNOTES

1. The American Patent Law Association (APLA) has recently changed its name to the American Intellectual Property Law Association (AIPLA) to show others the AIPLA is involved in Trademarks, copyrights and trade secrets as well as patents.

2. Peter D. Rosenberg *Patent Law Fundamentals* 1-8.1, (2nd ed., 1984).

3. Nancy Blodgett, *Computer Law Quickbound*, 70 American Bar Journal 32-33 November 1984).

4. Numerous statements accepted by engineers and computer programmers to the effect that computer software is not patentable. Thus, often inventors will not realize they have made a patentable invention and will disclose it or use it commercially in such a way that prevents them from patenting it.

5. British Computer Society, *Proprietary Software Protection*, 6 Computer Law Services Reporter 1214 (R. Bigelow ed. 1979).

6. Current investment in the United States in software exceeded $100 billion in 1982; D. Bender, *The Licensing of Computer Software in Technology Licensing Volume Two* 36 (1982).

7. U.S. Const. Art. 1, §8.

8. 35 U.S.C. §101 (1976).

9. Kintner and Lahr, *An Intellectual Property Law Primer* 7 (2nd ed. 1982).

10. See Patent Study No. 15, 85th Congress, 2nd Session (1958).

11. *Sears, Roebuck & Co. v. Stiffel Co.*, 376 U.S. 225 (1964) and *Compco Corp. v. Daybright Lighting, Inc.*, 376 U.S. 234 (1964).

12. *United Shoe Machine Co. v. U.S.* 258 U.S. 451, 463 (1921); *Motion Picture Co. v. United Film Co.*, 243 U.S. 502, 510, (1916); *Bloomer v. Quewani*, 55 U.S. (14 How.) 539, 549 (1852).

13. 35 U.S.C. 271(a)(1976).

14. Homer O. Blair, *Understanding Patents, Trademarks and Other Proprietary Assets and Their Role in Technology Transfer and Licensing* 1 (1978); Peter D. Rosenberg *Patent Law Fundamentals* 1-9 (2nd ed., 1984); Tom Arnold and Frank S. Vaden, *Invention Protection for Practicing Engineers* 18-21 (1971).

15. *Supra* note 8.

16. 35 U.S.C. §100(b).

17. *In re Coleman*, 621 F.2d 1141 (C.C.P.A. 1980); *ex parte MacAdams*, 206 U.S.P.Q. 445 (P.T.O. Bd. App. 1980).

18. *Ex Parte Plaister*, 201 U.S.P.Q. 255 (P.T.O. Bd. App. 1976).

19. *Allegheny Drop Forge Co. v. Portec Inc.*, 541 F.2d 383 (3d Cir. 1976).

20. 35 U.S.C. §103 (1976).

21. Peter D. Rosenberg, *Patent Law Fundamentals* (1984); Donald S. Chisum, *Patents* (6 Vol. 1985) Ernest B. Lipscomb, *Deller's Walker on Patents* (9 Vol. 1984).

22. *Supra* note 8.

23. *Burr v. Duryee*, 68 U.S. (1 Wall.) 531, 570-71 (1863).

24. *Seymour v. Osborne*, 78 U.S. (11 Wall.) 516 (1870).

25. *Riter-Conley Mfg. Co. v. Aiken*, 203 Fed. 699 (3d. Cir. 1913).

26. U.S. Patent No. 223, 898, issued January 27, 1880.

27. 35 U.S.C. §102 (1976).

28. 35 U.S.C. §102 (a).

29. *Mast-Foos v. Stover*, 177 U.S. 485, 494 (1900); see also *Allegheny Drop Forge Co. v. Protec, Inc. supra* note 19, at 384.

30. 35 U.S.C. §102(b).

31. 35 U.S.C. §102(c).

32. *General Foods Corp. v. Unarco Industries, Inc.* 188 U.S.P.Q. 419, 428 (7th Cir. 1975).

33. 35 U.S.C. §102(d).

34. 35 U.S.C. §102(e).

35. 35 U.S.C. §102(f).

36. 35 U.S.C. §102(g).

37. *Supra* note 20.

38. As example, see John F. Witherspoon, *Nonobviousness, The Ultimate Condition of Patentability* (1980).

39. *Graham v. John Deere Co.*, 383 U.S. 1 (1966).

40. J. Soma, *Computer Technology and the Law*, 27-28 (1983).

41. *Cochrane v. Deener*, 94 U.S. 780 (1876).

42. *O'Reilly v. Morse*, 56 U.S. (15 Hous.) 62 (1853).

43. J. Soma, *Computer Technology and the Law* 29 (1983) citing *In re Abrams*, 188 F. 2d 165 (CCPA 1951).

44. 409 U.S. 63 (1972).

45. J. Soma, *Computer Technology and the Law*, (1983) citing *In re Comstock*, 178 U.S.P.Q. 486 (CCPA 1973) and *In re Knowlton*, 178 U.S.P.Q. 486 (CCPA 1973).

46. 573 F. 2d 1237 (CCPA 1978).

47. 437 U.S. 584 (1978).

48.   450 U.S. 175 (1981).

49.   450 U.S. 381 (1981).

50.   35 U.S.C. §101 *et. seq.* (1976).

51.   35 U.S.C. §101, *supra* note 8.

52.   *Supra* note 27.

53.   35 U.S.C. §103 *supra* note 20.

54.   35 U.S.C. §101, *supra* note 8, see also *Diamond v. Diehr*, 450 U.S. 175 (1981).

55.   *Diamond v. Bradley*, 450 U.S. 381 (1981). D. Davidson, *Protecting Computer Software, A Comprehensive Analysis* 19-25 (1982). Davidson suggests including the hardwired version of the software program in patent claims in order to circumvent a *Freeman* rejection. The doctrine of equivalents could be subsequently used to prevent the transaction and sale of any software versions of such apparatus.

56.   J. Soma, *supra* note 43, at 36.

57.   Internal Revenue Code, IRC §1235 (1983), permits royalties accruing to the inventor or qualified holder of an exclusive license for a patent to be considered long term capital gains and to be taxed at a lower rate than ordinary income.

58.   D. Bender, *The Licensing of Computer Software* in *Technology Licensing Volume Two* 45-49 (1982).

59.   *Computer Software and the Law* §9-4 Article 4, in *Computer Law Services* (R. Bigelow ed. 1979).

60.   35 U.S.C. §112 (1976).

61.   D. Davidson, *Protecting Computer Software, A Comprehensive Analysis* 69 (1982).

62.   B. Niblett, *Computer Software and the Law* §9-4 Article 4 in *Computer Law Service* (R. Bigelow ed. 1979).

63. WIPO, Report of the *Expert Group on the Legal Protetion of Computer Software, Nove.* 27-30, 1979, §9-4 Article 12 in *Computer Law Service* 1 (R. Bigelow ed. 1979).

64. *Id.* at 2.

65. U.S. Const. *supra* note 7.

66. Neil Boorstyn, *Copyright Law* 1 (1981).

67. 17 U.S.C. §1 *et. seq.*

68. P.L. 94-554, codified as 17 U.S.C. §101 *et. seq.*

69. 17 U.S.C. §301(a).

70. 17 U.S.C. §102(a).

71. Alfred Bell & Co. v. Catalda Fine Arts, Inc. 191 F. 2d 99 (CANY, 1951).

72. 17 U.S.C. §102(b).

73. Jon A. Baumgarten *Copyright and Computer Software, Data Bases and Chip Technology* appearing in Computer Software 1984-Protection and Marketing, Practicing Law Institute.

74. *Apple v. Franklin,* 7i4 F.2d 1240 (3d Cir. 1982).

75. 17 U.S.C. §102(a) provides that:

     (a) Copyright protection subsists, in accordance with this title, in original works or authorship fixed in any tangible medium of expression, now known or later developed, from which they can be preceived, reproduced, or otherwise communicated, either directly or with the aid of a machine or device.

76. *Apple v. Franklin, supra* citing H.R. Rep. No. 1476, 94th Congress.

77. Pub. L. No. 93-573 §201, 88 Stat. 1973 (1974).

78. *Coyright Registration for Computer Programs, Announcement from the Copyright Office,* 11 Bull. Copyright Socy 361 (1964).

79. *Id.* at 40 citing *National Commission on the New Technological uses of Copyrighted Works,* final report, July 31, 1978.

80. *Id.*

81. Pub. L. No. 96-517 §10, Dec. 12, 1980, 94 Stat. 3015, 3028.

82. See, dissent of John Hersey, CONTU Commissioner, *CONTU's Final Report and Recommendations* 56-76 (1980). Commissioner Hersey strenuously argued against the grant of copyright protection to programs which are addressed to machines and have no further purpose than to perform mechanical work. He reasoned that since the program instructions become an essential part of the machinery which produces the desired results, the grant of copyright would provide covert protection for the underlying mechanical ideas in the program. *Id.* at 63.

83. 480 F. Supp. 1063 (N.D. Ill. 1979), *aff'd* 628 F. 2d 1038 (7th Cir. 1980).

84. *Id.* at 1068.

85. 524 F. Supp. 171 (N.D. Cal. 1981).

86. *Williams Electronic Inc. v. Arctic International, Inc.,* 685 F. 2d 870 (3rd Cir. 1982).

87. *Apple v. Franklin, supra* note 74.

88. *Id.* at 24.

89. 17 U.S.C. §101 *et. seq.* 1976).

90. B. Niblett, *supra* note 61, at 5.

91. In the United States, the author's life plus 50 years adheres for all works created after January 1, 1978; 17 U.S.C. §301 (1976).

92. B. Niblett, *supra* note 61, at 6.

93. D. Davidson, *Protecting Computer Software: A Comprehensive Analysis* 69 (1982).

94.   *Id.* at 69.

95.   *Id.* at 75.

96.   *Id.* at 76.

97.   *Id.* at 77.

98.   The origin of trade secret is in state common law. Appropriateness of subject matter, secrecy, novelty and economic value must be met before such protection is afforded "trade secret" information. J. Soma, *supra* note 40, at 53-54.

99.   K. Payne, *Know-How Licensing - Definition, Duration and Deposition* in *Licensing Law Handbook* 36 (1981) [hereinafter cited as Know-How Licensing].

100.   Restatement of Torts §757 Comment (b) (1939).

101.   416 U.S. 470 (1974).

102.   *Id.* at 475-476.

103.   *Id.* at 475-476.

104.   Restatement of Torts §757, *supra* note 100.

105.   *Know-How Licensing, supra* note 51-52.

106.   Section 301 of the 1976 Copyright Act requires that any authorship which falls within a category of copyrightable subject matter is reviewed exclusively by the Copyright Act. 17 U.S.C. §301 (1976).

107.   *Warrington Assocs., Inc. v. Real-Time Engineering Systems, Inc.,* 522 F. Supp. 367 (N.D. Ill. 1981) as cited in *Technology Licensing Volume Two* 68 (1982).

108.   17 U.S.C. §102 (1976).

109.   *Trade Secret Protection for Computer Software,* D-13, 14 in the American Patent Law Association's *The Law of Computer-Related Technology* (1983), citing Melvin F. Jager, *Trade Secrets Law Handbook* 257-8 (1983).

110.   *Final Report of the National Commission on the New Technological Uses of Copyright Works* (July 31, 1978), Library of Congress (1979).

111.   H.R. Rep. No. 96-1307 96th Cong. 24 Sess., pp. 23-24 (1980).

112.   Notice of Inquiry - *Deposit of Computer Programs and Other Works Containing Trade Secrets*, Library of Congress, Copyright Office (1983).

113.   D. Davidson, *Protecting Computer Software: A Comprehensive Analysis* 70-71 (1982).

114.   *Id.* at 70.

115.   *Id.* at 71.

116.   Act of July 8, 1870.

117.   Trade-Mark Cases, 100 U.S. 82 (1879).

118.   U.S. Constitution, Article I, Section 8 (3).

119.   Act of Feb. 20, 1905.

120.   15 U.S.C. §1051 *et. seq.*

121.   For a complete discussion of the background and history of Trademarks see J. Thomas McCarthy, *Trademarks and Unfair Competition* 2nd Ed. (1984).

122.   *Hot Shoppes, Inc. v. Hot Shoppes, Inc.*, 203 F. Supp. 777 (N.C. Md. 1962).

123.   15 U.S.C. §1127.

124.   Processed Plastic Co. v. Warner Communications, Inc., 675 F.2d 852 (7th Cm. 1982).

125.   *Morendoz v. Holt*, 128 U.S. §514, 520 (1888).

126.   *Chemical Corp. of America v. Annheiser-Busch, Inc.*, 306 F.2d 433 (5th Cir. 1962).

127.   *American Automobile Assoc. v. Speigel*, 101 F. Supp. 185 (E.D.N.Y. 1951).

128.   *Ex Parte Haig and Haig, Ltd.* 118 U.S.P.Q. 299 (Com. of Pat. 1958).

129.   *In re Interstate Banking Corp.,*153 U.S.P.Q. 488 (TM Bd. 1967).

130.   *Jantzen Knitting Mills v. Spokane Knitting Mills, Inc.,*44 F. 2d. 656 (E.D. Wash. 1930).

131.   *CITC Indus., Inc. v. Levi Strauss & Co.,* 216 U.S.P.Q. 512, 516 (T.T. & App. Bd. 1982).

132.   *Visa Int'l Service Assoc. v. Visa Realtors,* 208 U.S.P.Q. 462, 463 (T.T. & App. Bd. 1980); *The Trademark Cases, supra* note 117; and *In re. Bookbinders Restaurant, Inc.* 240 F.2d 365 (C.C.P.A. 1957).

133.   15 U.S.C. §1052(f).

134.   15 U.S.C. §1052(a-d).

135.   Homer O. Blair, *Understanding Patents, Trademarks and Other Proprietary Assets and Their Role in Technology Transfer and Licensing* 11 (1978).

136.   *Blanchard v. Hill* 2 Ark 484, 26 Eng. Report 692 (1742).

137.   Rogers, *Goodwill, Trademarks and Unfair Trading* 50-52 (1914).

138.   *Levi Strauss & Co. v. Blue Bill, Inc.,* 632 F.2d 817 (9th Cir. Cal. 1980).

139.   *Car-Freshener Corporation v. Auto Aid Manuf. Corp.* 747, 750 (Dist. Ct, N.D., N.Y. 1977).

140.   17 U.S.C. §902 (1984).

141.   *Id.* at §902(a)(1).

142.   *Id.* at §902(a)(1)-(2).

143.   G.F. Fuller, Jr. *New Legislations Copyright Protection for Semiconductor Chip Masks,* 25 IDEA 4 (1985).

144.   *Supra* note 141.

145.   *Id.* at §902(b).

146.   *Id.* at §905.

147.   *Id.* at §906(a)(1).

148.   *Id.* at §907(a)(1).

149.   *Id.* at §914.

150.   (UNESCO/WIPO/GE/CLS/3 Prov.) Geneva, Feb. 25-March
         1, 1985 "Draft Report".

151.   *Id.*

152.   *Aims Towards Establishment of Legal Protection for Com-
         puter Software* (Interim Report), December 1, 1983,
         Information Industry Committee, Industrial Structure
         Council, Japan.

153.   *Id.*

154.   *Id.*

155.   Software Protection Workshop--"Study of Protection
         and Utilization of Computer Software and Information",
         October 22, 1984, Boston, Franklin Pierce Law Center
         PTC Research Foundation, Academy of Applied Science.
         "The Software Revolution and The protection of Intel-
         lectual Property", Workshop On Software Protection And
         A Planning Conference On Economic Development Of The
         Software Industry", March 7, 1985, Center For Entre-
         preneurial Development, Carnegie Mellon University
         in association with PTC Research Foundation and Ger-
         meshausen Center for Innovation and Entrepreneurship
         Law of the Franklin Pierce Law Center, Academy of Applied
         Science, National Inventors Council, American Bar As-
         sociation Technology Assessment Committee of Science
         and Technology Section.

156.   17 U.S.C. §115 "Compulsory license for making and dis-
         tributing phonorecords." (Earlier Act of March 4, 1909,
         as amended, Sec. 39).

157.   IACC Bulletin, Vol. 3-5, Aug./Sept./Oct./Nov., 1984,
         at 14.

158.   *Id.*

159.   Patent Law, Effective April 1, 1985, Peoples Republic
         of China. Patent Office Regulations (commencing China
         Daily, Feb. 1, 1985. p. 2) *Business China*, March 28,
         1984, Vol. X. No. 6, at 41.

160.   IACC, *supra* note 157.

161.   Patents Bill, 1983, Malaysia (Naskhah Sahih-Bahasa
         Malaysia).

162.   *Id*. at Part IV, Sec. 11.

163.   *Id*. at Part IV, Sec. 15.

164.   *Id*. at Part Iv, Sec. 17.

165.   *Id*. at Part IV, Sec. 13.

166.   *Id*. at Part X, Sec. 48-54.

167.   New Staits Times (Malaysia), November 6, 1984, p.
         10F, "Mind For Technology".

168.   "Transferring Tape and Label Technology To The Third
         World", *Adhesive Age*, September, 1983, p. 46-48.

169.   Patent Law, *supra* note 149, at Chapt. I, Rule 2 of
         Regulations.

170.   *Id*., at Chapter II, Rule 22.

171.   A bibliography of WIPO, UNESCO and other deliberations
         on the current protection of software include:

                  (UNESCO/WIPO/GE/CCS/2 Geneva, February 25 to March
                  1, 1985 "Legal Protection For Computer Programs:
                  A Survey And Analysis Of National Legislation And
                  Case Law, Document Submitted By the Secretariats
                  of Unesco and WIPO" (LPCS/II/INF/1) Second Session,
                  Geneva, June 13 to 17, 1983 "Summary Of the Replies
                  Received From Governments And International Organ-
                  izations To WIPO's Invitation To Present Observations
                  Concerning The Legal Protection Of Computer Software,
                  Memorandum By The International Bureau" (LPCS/
                  WGTQ/I/2) Canberra, April 2 to 6, 1984 "Technical
                  Questions Relating To The Legal Protection Of
                  Computer Software" (LPCS/II/5) Second Session,
                  Geneva, June 13 to 17, 1983 "Report Adopted By

The Committee Of Experts" (LPCS/II/4) Second Session, Geneva, June 13 to 17, 1983 "Protection of Integrated Circuits, Memorandum Prepared By The International Bureau" (LPCS/II/3) Second Session, Geneva, June 13 to 17, 1983 "Draft Treaty For The Protection Of Computer Software Prepared By The International Bureau" (LPCS/II/2) Second Session, Geneva, June 13 to 17, 1983 "Analysis Of the Results Of The Survey Concerning The Desirability And Feasibility Of A Treaty For The Protection Of Computer Software And/Or Other Possible Measures In The Field Of The Protection Or Deposit Of Computer Software" (LPCS/I/4) First Session, Geneva, November 27 to 30, 1979 "Report Adopted By The Expert Group" (LPCS/I/2) First Session, Geneva, November 27 to 30, 1979 "Measures To Enhance International Cooperation In The Field Of Legal Protection Of Computer Software" by the "Group Of Experts On The Copyright Aspects Of The Protection Of Computer Software".

Original research and prelminary writings by:

Homer O. Blair, B.S. Chemistry, B.S. Physics, J.D. University of Washington, formerly Vice President, Patents and Licensing for Itek Corporation and presently is a professor and Director of the Germeshausen Center for the Law of Innovation and Entrepreneurship of the Franklin Pierce Law Center.

Jennifer A. Tegfeldt, B.S. Biological Sciences, University of California, Davis, J.D. Franklin Pierce Law Center, registered patent agent, is presently a law clerk to the United States Court of Appeals for the Federal Circuit (1985-1987).

CHAPTER 3 - LICENSING OF COMPUTER TECHNOLOGY

I.   INTRODUCTION

Today, a computer-related business faces a baffling array of commercial and, as yet unclear, legal considerations in order to expand its computer software markets beyond national borders. Without significant legal precedent, such a business must look to established trade regulation and export procedure to determine guidelines for appropriate conduct. On the basis of these guidelines, agreements may be drafted both to protect the proprietary interests in the unique computer software technology and to allow for commercial expansion into foreign markets.

Within the United States, the development of software is limited by only technological initiative.[1] The term 'software' applies to any nonphysical component of the computer and may include programs, data bases or documentation. Software can be proprietarily protected by either patent or copyright, or retained as a trade secret by the creating entity.[2] However, economical benefit from the developed software can only be realized if the creator of the software exploits it or permits others to do so.

II.   LICENSING FROM THE UNITED STATES' PERSPECTIVE

For software developers who do not elect to exploit proprietarily protected software themselves, licenses offer an alternative. A license is an agreement by the owner of the software, the licensor, to permit another person, the licensee, to make, use or sell the protected software for a limited period or in a limited territory.[3] In the absence of statutory protection, trade secret licenses traditionally incorporate specific clauses which require the licensee to strictly guard the software as secret.

In international trade, the exchange of such high technology goods as software by license is subject to conflict between those governmental policies encouraging free trade and those restricting transfer of technology which might endanger national defense.[4] The focus of the policy dispute is not the act of exporting but rather the ingenuity which created the software. While the U.S. may have retained dominance in the computer field in the past, technology developments by other countries, particularly Japan, have usurped shares of markets held by the U.S. both domestically and abroad.[5] In order to maintain a competitive edge, a software developer must not only emphasize research and development to create new products, but also exploit the commercial goods of these products, particularly through licenses. Essential to the draft of the license is consideration of proprietary protection, United States government controls on exports, antitrust considerations, choice of law in determining jurisdiction over the drafted agreements, and each party's liabilities.

Before a license can be effectively exploited, expansion into a foreign market must be structured commercially. Depending on the structure of the foreign market and the requirements for effective distribution and sales, a software developer may elect to establish manufacturing subsidiaries in a specific market locale. While this decision may be based on certain incentives, such as tax privileges or government guarantees, the developer risks significant loss by way of confiscation of products or profit. A developer may opt to enter a foreign market

through joint venture manufacture and sale. For such
an investor, the negative aspects of partial control and
multiple division of profits may be more than offset by
joining an established, local partner-company familiar
with the national market and staffed with the personnel
necessary to effectively manufacture and market the technology. Finally, a software developer may elect to
license in exchange for royalties or for stock in lieu
of royalties.[6]

Such development of foreign markets is generally
accomplished by licensing. Licensing, as a means of ex-
ploiting markets and secondarily as a means of distributing the benefits of technological change through foreign
and domestic economies has been the subject of considerable governmental review.[7] A study prepared by the Yale
University Department of Economics, which analyzed corporate licensing trends, indicated a greater tendency
for U.S. firms to license technology internationally than
domestically.[8] Domestic corporations favored international licensing because of significant financial and
organizational constraints imposed on direct investment
overseas by foreign governments. International licensing
was also favored by firms seeking to maintain segmented
geographic markets by not licensing technology to domestic
competitors.[9] The Yale study did not address the likelihood that a licensee would become a direct competitor
of the licensor in the foreign geographic market after
the termination of the agreement.[10] The authors of the
study postulated, however, that the close relationship
between licensor and licensee built over the period of
the agreement would result in cooperative improvement
of licensed products and would provide a basis for future
partnerships.[11]

Small to medium-sized corporations[12] with limited resources use foreign licensing to transfer technology.[13] In order to overcome financial and organizational constraints on overseas expansion, a small licensor may elect to license to a large domestic corporation with foreign subsidiaries.[14] An established foreign sales network marketing licensed software, can offset owner concerns that multiple licensing agreements reduce the value of the technology to the owner through dilution. In essence, the small corporation trades a portion of the potential value of its software for the assurance of foreign markets already developed by larger corporations. Further, a small corporation may opt for stock interest in a foreign corporation in lieu of royalties. This permits a small corporation to develop foreign corporate ownership interests without significant risk or investment.

Basic to any licensing agreement is the identification of a qualified licensee, and the finalization of the intent of the parties within the terms of a written contract.[15] Licensing negotiations with non-English speaking licensees are complicated by both imprecise translation and ambiguous language. For example, a term of art of the computer field in the United States may not be translatable in the same meaning in a foreign language. If this term defines a particular proprietary feature of the licensed software or particularizes a duty assumed by one of the parties, ambiguous translation may render the agreement unenforceable. Therefore, experienced licensing parties tend to avoid idiomatic terms in favor of terms which are mutually explained and understood.[16]

III. GOVERNMENT CONTROLS ON THE EXPORT OF SOFTWARE

The export of computers and software is of particular interest to the Department of State and the Department of Commerce because of the role this technology plays in the economic and military development of a country. Export controls administered by the Department of State[17] and promulgated under the Mutual Security Act of 1954, and, later, under the Arms Export Control Act of 1976,[18] control commodities that constitute potential "arms, ammunition, and implements of war." Software, which may be used militarily against the United States, is considered in violation of International Traffic and Arms Regulations (ITAR) if exported without benefit of license.[19] Thus, technical data which may be used or adapted for use in munitions, as well as any technology which advances the state of the art or establishes new art relating to any controlled item on the "Munitions List",[20] is assigned a United States Security Classification.[21] The issuance of ITAR licenses to software so classified is allowed on a case-by-case basis if the export licensor provides written assurance that the software will not be disclosed to any party to whom such software could not be exported directly,[22] Nonetheless, the courts have held defendants guilty of exporting technical data without a license when such data was "significantly and directly related to specific articles on the Munitions List."[23] Proffered evidence that the defendant's technology was widely distributed in the United States has been held not to preclude government prohibition of export under the Mutual Security Act.

The authority of the Department of Commerce to regulate export of software derives from the Export Administration Act of 1969. [24] Under the Act, the President is authorized to control the export of technology in order to promote United States foreign policy, to preserve national security and to ensure the domestic availability of products in short supply. [25] The delegation of this authority to the Department of Commerce [26] prompted issuance of the Export Administration Regulations, administered by the Office of Export Administration (OEA) in the Bureau of Trade Regulation. [27]

All export of computer technology must be licensed by the Secretary of Commerce. [28] The Export Administration Regulations permit the issuance of a general license, a qualified general license or a validated license for exported technology.[29] A validated license is required for any commodity or destination listed on the Commodity Control List and may be obtained through submission of a written application to the Department of Commerce. [30] Such a license is further required only if the technology to be exported is 1) restricted by a multilateral agreement compelling approval of the parties for export, 2) sent to nations less technologically advanced than the United States, or 3) subject to a pending agreement sought by the United States which allows comparable controls on the technology from other suppliers. [31]

A Qualified General License (QGL) may be substituted for a validated license when multiple shipments are to be made to a specified consignee for a particular purpose. [32] Such a license may shorten the delay required for the license application process when, for example, a licensor exports a nonstrategic commodity to a controlled country. Nonetheless, the Secretary of Commerce retains broad discretion in determining the necessity for either a validated or a qualified general license. 33

For exports that do not require such licenses, a general license may conditionally and revocably be issued when the export conforms with all terms of the Export Administration Regulations. Through a commonly used general license, the G-DEST, a licensor is permitted to export technology on the Commodity Control List to any country where a validated license is not required. 34

The Commodity Control List requires the acquisition of a validated license for the export of most computer technology to all destinations except Canada. 35 To assist exporters in preparing license applications, the OEA has issued a guide which explains the requirements for a detailed description of the commodity to be exported, its value, content, end-user and end-use, and complete details of the business transaction. 36 Applications for export must also provide information on foreign availability of comparable technology and any previous approvals of applications for the same or comparable technology in order to justify the grant of a license.

All export license applications required for computer technology are transferred to the OEA. 37 The Operations Division of the OEA reviews the aplication for completeness then forwards it to the Licensing Computer Division, which recommends the level of review required for final action. The application is then sent to the OEA Policy Planning Division, which either recommends approval or refers the application to agencies for review. 38 All recommendations are sent back to the OEA for final decision. However, the President retains ultimate authority to

determine licensing issues. Any licensing recommendation made
by the Secretary of Defense pursuant to the Export Administration
Act that is overruled by the President must be explained in a
report to Congress.[39]

Tne powers of the Export Administration Act to promote
foreign policy, to protect national security and to limit export
of products in short supply have been amended to include specific
limitaions. Licensure is no longer determined solely on a
country's Communist or non-Communist status but rather on the
country's present and potential relationship to the United States
and the country's ability and willingness to control retransfers
of United States export technology in accordance with United
States policy.[40] The Act also does not permit the President
to control the export of commodities available from sources outside the United States, unless the absence of such controls would
endanger national security.[41]

Congress has further sought to improve the process of
licensing by requiring the Department of Commerce to consult
with industry representatives.[42] These Technical Advisory Committees (TACs) must be consulted on issues of licensing procedure
and on technical aspects of controlled commodities and their
world wide availability.[43] The extent to which the Department
of Commerce uses TAC must be reported to Congress.[44] While a
number of TACs have been established in the computer industry,
the extent of their influence on computer licensing policies
is unclear.[45] Thus, until the Department of Commerce classifies
the recommendations, licensors must abide by established
regulations and decisions controlling the export of licensed
technology.

IV.   ANTITRUST CONSIDERATIONS

The nature of the obligations, formalized by an agreement, between licensors and licensees shapes national and international commerce. [46]   In order to encourage the continuing growth of computer capability and use through innovation and competitive cost, these agreements must reflect a commitment to free competition.   Through antitrust and trade regulation laws designed to prevent coercive practices and aggregation of economic power by unfair means, restraints may be imposed to assure that agreement obligations allow a fairly waged competitive struggle. [47]

While the antitrust laws have no jurisdiction in foreign commerce, a licensor must nonetheless meet United States statutory requirements for fair business practice to export technology when such transactions affect domestic commerce.   Under Section 1 of the Sherman Act, every contract, combination or conspiracy in restraint of trade with foreign nations is declared illegal. [48]   Such determination applies regardless of whether the restraint on trade is undertaken in the United States or in a foreign jurisdiction. [49]   Section 2 of the Sherman Act further requires that "[e]very person who shall monopolize, or attempt to monopolize, or combine or conspire with any other person or persons, to monopolize any part of the trade or commerce...with foreign nations, shall be deemed guilty of a felony" [50]

Activities tending to lessen competition and to create a monopoly in a line of commerce, such as activity resulting from mergers and acquisitions, are further deemed illegal under the Clayton Act. [51]   This Act is applicable to both horizontal and vertical merger circumstances. [52]

Horizontal mergers, in which competitors join to concentrate a larger percentage of the available market, are presumptively illegal since the effect of such a merger produces an undue percentage share of the relevant market. Vertical mergers between manufacturers and suppliers, for example, are also illegal when the effect substantially reduces competition and creates monopoly, which substantially lessens competition. Section 3 of the Act holds as illegal any leases, sale or contract to sell products, conditioned on the requirement not to use or sell products of a competitor. Such agreement is held illegal regardless of whether or not the technology is patented.[53] Similarly, Section 7 prohibits conduct in mergers and acquisitions that will lead to restraints on competition. Mergers, especially between large organizations, that have the potential to create a monopoly, must be reported to the Justice Department and the Federal Trade Commission prior to such mergers. [54]

American businesses are further bound by Section 5(a)(1) of the Federal Trade Commission Act (FTC Act) which states that "[u]nfair methods of competition in or affecting commerce, and unfair or deceptive acts or practices in or affecting commerce are declared unlawful." [55] Conduct that is technically beyond the standards of proof required for actions under the Sherman and Clayton Acts may be prosecuted under the FTC Act in order to "stop in their incipiency acts and practices which, when full blown, would violate" the Sherman and Clayton Acts. [56] Thus, activities that would be illegal under the Sherman Act, for example, only if there was an actual deleterious effect on the market, can be held to violate the FTC Act if such an effect would be a probable result from continued practice.

Once the Justice Department determines that the licensing restraint is subject to United States antitrust laws, a separate analysis follows to discern whether the restraint is reasonably within the scope of a lawful patent monopoly, or whether it is a restraint ancillary to lawful contract. If the Justice Department concludes that the restraint is anticompetitive, the licensor may invoke the application of the antitrust "rule of reason" as a defense. Under this rule, contract limitations that are ancillary to the lawful purpose of the contract, of a scope that is not substantially greater than necessary to achieve the purpose of the contract, and otherwise reasonable under the circumstances are not held to extend beyond the fair protection of the contracting parties. Similarly, a licensor granted a patent for his software product is bound not to grant more than is reasonably within the scope of the award of his patent.[57] Such considerations are particularly compelling in view of the natural monopoly created in a new software product. Until competitors develop a comparable product or reverse engineer the new product, the licensor retains over his competitors significant leverage in market lead time. The application of the rule of reason permits businesses to actively compete but restricts the grant of rights under contract to that which is reasonably earned and deserved.

Despite such statutory guidance, difficulty remains in distinguishing reasonable restraints from those which are part of a conspiracy to monopolize markets. A study completed by the American Bar Association Antitrust Section established a series of questions based on factors relevant in making such a distinction.[58] Affirmative responses to any or all of these questions would indicate a potential for antitrust violation:

1. Does the restraint exceed the scope of the patent grant in time or subject matter?

2. Do the licenses grant reciprocal rights?

3. Is the restraint part of a larger plan for competitive restriction?

4. Are the licensor and licensee actual or potential competitors such that a restrictive license covenant would effectively inhibit competition?

5. Is a territorial restraint based on technology of insufficient value to justify it?

6. Is the time period of the restraint unreasonable-based on commercial circumstances?

In contrast, particular agreements or practices are considered per se unreasonable, without further inquiry, if they have a noxious effect on competition. Among these are price fixing,[59] division of markets,[60] group boycott,[61] and tying arrangements.[62] Clauses which may violate antitrust principles, yet are fairly drafted to protect the interests of the contracting parties, are subject to analysis by the antitrust rule of reason. Such clauses include territorial restrictions, field of use restrictions and grant backs.

A territorial restraint in a licensing agreement allows a licensor to preclude a licensee from competing in a licensor's home market.[63] The rule of reason is applied when the pattern of conduct includes the transfer of rights in some areas and a reservation of rights in others. In the case of a Westinghouse license to two Japanese companies to make, use or sell products under Westinghouse patents anywhere except in the United States, with reciprocal licensure of Westinghouse excluding Japan, such conduct was regarded by the court as permissible under antitrust principles.[64] The court reasoned that the failure of the Japanese companies to enter the U.S. market for fear of infringing Westinghouse's patent negated the inference of illegal market division. This decision was further premised on the assumption that the licensors are free to license foreign patents while reserving the rights to domestic ones.[65] Such actions were held not to give rise to antitrust violations in view of the reasonable use of the grant of monopoly through patent.

Field of use restrictions are drafted to exclude from the license at least one other possible use of the licensed software.[66] Such restrictions do not merit United States antitrust concern until a substantial effect on competition in American domestic or international commerce can be shown. Further analysis for antitrust violation requires the conclusion that the license was granted upon conditions not consistent with the grant of the patent.[67] Although a field of use restriction may be lawfully used to restrict the sale of the patented product from non-licensed sources, and to limit the licensee's right to make, use or sell the patented product, further restrictions are not permitted. Clauses that limit the sources or markets for ancillary products not directly protected under the patent are specifically unlawful and unenforceable. Moreover, clauses that would, in effect, divide fields of use among licensees who would otherwise be in competition are also unlawful.[68] As an exception to this reasoning, a licensee may lawfully retain for personal exploitation and development a specific field of use. Antitrust common law permits a patent licensor to divide his statutory rights to make, use or sell his product among several licensees so long as such a division is within his statutory grant. [69] Thus, as in *United States v. Ciba-Ceigy Corp.*, a patentee was permitted to retain the rights of manufacture and production of a bulk form of drug and to license the rights of packaging the drug in dosage form. [70]

Grant back clauses in a license agreement grant to the licensor the rights to any software the licensee may invent, discover or acquire in the future. Such a clause grants a licensor access to improvements on the licensed subject developed by the licensee. [71] As in the antitrust analysis of field of use restrictions, United States antitrust laws will not apply to a grant back provision unless a substantial effect is demonstrated on national commerce. Once an "adverse economic consequence arising from the grant backs" is shown, the grant back clause is analyzed against the principles of United States antitrust law. [72] Grant back clauses are summarily invalidated if they perpetuate the control of the licensor over an industry after the patent expires or are part of a cumulative anti-competitive effort to monopolize a market. [73]

In determining the legality of grant back clauses, the courts have particularly examined the degree of exclusivity achieved by the licensor. While it is arguable that exclusive grant backs deny to licensees who invent improvements the right to exploit them, such a clause may be reasonably justified. A provision that would permit the licensor exclusivity in only one field of use and would allow the licensee to exploit all other fields, might not be considered as inhibiting innovation.[74] Alternatively, a licensor may lawfully limit licenses to a specific field of use and retain exclusive rights to all other fields. Illegality arises when the licensor divides the market in a plurality of fields, which grant more to each licensee than would otherwise be granted if the patent rights were licensed to one licensee.

The grant back clause, however, may not have the same life as the patent. Under patent law, once the life of the licensed patent expires, the licensee is permitted to exploit any product improvements in competition with the licensor. A clause that is narrow in scope, limited to immediate improvements on the licensed software, or broad in scope, including all related improvements, may not be considered anticompetitive if rights are not extended beyond the scope of the basic patent.[75] If there are alternatives to the licensed product available to the consumer, exclusive grant back clauses will most likely be recognized as having little effect on the competitive market.[76]

In the software industry, the practice of providing programs in a package has the potential for illegal exploitation of the patent monopoly when customers are required to concurrently purchase unpatented rights.[77] Such a tie-in is illegal under the Sherman and Clayton Acts where two products are involved, the seller retains economic power over the "tying product," and the tied product may only be obtained through purchase of the tying

product.[78]   Tying arrangements that serve no other purpose than to suppress or distort competition are "vig-
ilantly" struck down by the courts as exclusionary conduct.[79]

If software is protected by trade secret, the potential
for duplication by competitors diminishes the liklihood
that the program would be a source of economic power
sufficient to characterize it as a tying product. Under
patent or copyright protection, however, the program is
presumed to possess economic value by virtue of the statutory grant.[80]   In order to avoid the potential for coercive tie-ins, a licensor must offer his programs individually as well as in a package.[81]   An exception to
this prohibition is a demonstration that a tie-in clause
was necessary to preserve the good will of the licensor.
Such a defense has been narrowly construed by the Supreme
Court to apply to circumstances only where a substitute
"tied" product could not be practicably obtained.[82]
Clearly, a commercially indispensible program protected
by the economic power of a patent or copyright will merit
sufficient concern of the court, in preserving free competition, to require vigorous application of antitrust
laws.

V.   CHOICE OF LAW IN DRAFTING LICENSING AGREEMENTS

It is well established in the law of the United
States that when a court concludes there has been a breach
of contract, it will afford remedies to the aggrieved
party in order to compensate expectation interests   or
claims to damages.[83]   In international agreements, determination of the nature of the remedy available, source

for redress, and the law and procedural rules governing relief in the event of breach is compounded by the differences in legal environment, language and customs of the contracting parties. A solution is to incorporate a choice of law clause in international agreements such that parties stipulate the forum in which to adjudicate a dispute. Such applicable law may be 1) the laws of the United States, 2) the laws of the place of residence of the foreign licensee, 3) the laws of the country where the license was granted, 4) the law of the forum if stipulated in the agreement, or 5) the law of a neutral country.[84]

By determining the proper law of the contract under a choice of law clause, parties are assured of the certainty and predictability of rights under the contract, and achieve a permanent record of these intentions.[85] In the event of dispute, such a clause removes the need for a forum to apply its own choice of law rules in deciding applicable law.[86] In drafting such a clause, however, contracting parties should use the terms "applicable law" or "proper law" to designate the law controlling the duties and rights of the parties under the proposed contract. Different terminology should be used for other aspects of law affecting the transaction.[87]

While most legal systems recognize the freedom to stipulate choice of law in a contract, courts may refuse to recognize such clauses if the contract is not between two parties who are, in fact, international.[88] The chosen law will be ignored in some jurisdictions if it is repugnant to the public policy of the forum or if it is so unfamiliar to the court that a fair adjudication would not be possible. Lastly, a forum will decline to apply a choice of law clause when its own conflict of laws rules require the application of the law of another country. [89]

While the choice of U.S. law may be favored as the law most familiar to licensing corporations and attendant attorneys, and the law most highly developed to resolve contractual disputes, such a choice may have an unexpected negative effect on foreign business relations. A foreign court may refuse to recognize such a clause when the election of U.S. law is construed as an attempt to intrude into and influence local policy.[90] Even if the court recognizes the choice of U.S. law, the results may be unpredictable and unappealable based on the foreign juris- diction's understanding of applicable U.S. law. A foreign court may construe such an election of choice of law as a lack of trust in its legal system, hindering present and future business transactions.[91]

Alternatively, the election of foreign law may permit a corporation to receive local tax benefits or to avoid applicable U.S. antitrust laws.[92] Such a selection may also provide a beneficial bargaining chip, exemplifying good will in negotiations. In a jurisdiction unlikely to recognize any other law than its own, foreign law may be preferred when proceedings must be brought in that forum. However, such an election must be weighed against the potential that the foreign law may be unable to resolve the dispute for lack of precedent, the foreign judgment may be difficult to enforce, or the court may not be able to apply the chosen law effectively.[93]

Clearly, the appropriate choice of law ultimately rests with the jurisdiction most likely to recognize such a clause. In Great Britain and France, a choice of law clause will be readily recognized if the parties are international and the clause does not contravene public policy.[94] In contrast, West German courts rarely apply any law other than their own.[95] While the usefulness and enforceability of such clauses have been debated, especially in view of the natural bias of courts to apply the laws of their own country in event of dispute,[96] stipulation of the parties as to applicable law nonetheless elimates uncertainly where the choice is honored.[97]

VI. TAXATION AND CUSTOMS DUTIES APPLICABLE TO LICENSING AGREEMENTS

The imposition of United States federal income tax on all income, regardless of its foreign or domestic source, requires the planning of a license agreement to include analysis of tax liabilities.[98] A licensor must also consider foreign customs duties levied on agreements which license software in a foreign jurisdiction.

All income derived from licensing agreements is taxed as ordinary income to the licensor unless the licensed property rights are sufficiently divested to qualify for capital gains treatment.[99] The significantly lower tax rate levied on long term capital gains is applied to license payments if such payments fulfill three criteria.[100] Specifically, the property must be used in a trade or business,[101] a product of a sale or exchange,[102] and held for at least one year prior to the transaction in order to justify capital gains characterization.[103]

According to this analysis, statutory capital gains treatment has been held applicable to patents and trade secrets when such property has been recognized as either a capital asset or depreciable property of a business.[104] Identification of a "sale or exchange"[105] or a "transfer of all substantial rights"[106], as required under the statute, has been held to be dependent on the restrictive clauses of the license agreement. If such clauses transfer significant interest in these rights, captial gains characterization will apply. The last requirement for capital gains characterization under the statute, the requisite holding period, has been held particularly in the case of patents, to be the date from which the invention was first reduced to practice.[107]

Under taxation principles, licensing agreements are permitted to include certain restrictive clauses without preventing the royalty payments from being treated as capital gains. Thus, a licensor may retain the right of termination if the licensee fails to meet the royalty obligation or is declared insolvent. Similarly, agreements that permit breach of contract by the licensor for conditions which occur after the grant and which were beyond the licensor's control have been approved for favorable tax treatment.[108] However, clauses which limit the license to less than the life of the patent, impose geographical restrictions to one area, limit the field of use, or fail to grant all the rights under the patent to "make, use or sell" have been denied any capital gains characterization.[109]

Licensed software protected under copyright is denied capital gains characterization if the benefits from those rights remain within the control of the originator. [110] For subsequent successors-in-interest acquiring the copyright for consideration, however, capital gains treatment may be applied to license payments if statutory requirements are met. [111] For a transfer of interests other than a sale or exchange of patent rights, characterization as interest may be applied. [112] While the Internal Revenue Code provides that no gain or loss will be recognized for the transfer of property interest in exchange for stock sufficient to control the transferee corporation at the time of transfer, [113] such tax-free benefits do no extend to the sale or transfer of interests to foreign subsidiaries in which the transferor corporation holds more than 50 percent of the voting stock. [114]

Irrespective of whether license royalties are taxed as ordinary income or capital gains, the U.S. licensor is granted a credit against federal income tax for foreign income tax paid. [115] Such credit is calculated based on the division of taxable income from a foreign source by total taxable income and multiplication by the U.S. tax rate. [116] Where the United States is a member of a foreign tax convention, any income derived through treaty obligation requirements is excluded from federal income tax.

Exports into the European market are subject to the customs administration procedures of the Customs Co-Operation Council (CCC). [117] While valuation of hardware is relatively simple, the value of software has, historically, been determined by the value of the media on which it was recorded. [118] In a study entitled "Dutiable Value of Computers and Program Media" issued in 1979, the CCC recognized the impracticable nature of this policy and suggested valuation to distinguish between hardware-related software and user application programming. Under this plan, any software relating to hardware would be included in the value of that hardware. If the seller bundles hardware and software together at a standard rate, the value of programs not produced with that hardware, would be deducted from the invoice price in order to determine customs duty.[119]

Programs that are not essential to computer function would be considered within the category of application programs. For custom programs developed for the user, valuation would be based on the sum of 1) the price of the medium on which the program is recorded, 2) operations cost up to and including the completion of the program for recording on the medium, 3) the cost of recording the program on the medium, and 4) profit. Any associated services provided by the vendor to the user are to be excluded from the dutiable value. For packaged programs, value would be determined at invoice price.[120]

Exporters are also subject to the tariff barriers of each country into which software is exported. Under the General Agreement on Tariff and Trade (GATT), member countries have sought to reduce barries to trade and to encourage trade in a nondiscriminatory environment by negotiating tariff rates.[121] Agreements under GATT are drafted between governments and establish trade policies to be followed. Such agreements, however, are nonbinding and have no independent force of law.[122] While the treaty, itself, has not been ratified by Congress, the Trade Agreement Act of 1979[123] encompasses many of the aspects of the GATT treaty. Institution of a multilateral reduction in customs and tariff rates would correspond well with the adoption of a uniform approach to valuation. The increasing likelihood of a single valuation system based on the price of goods at open sale on the import market would most certainly strengthen efforts by nations to develop software resources.[124]

VII. SPECIAL CONSIDERATIONS IN LICENSING TO JAPAN

The enactment of the "Law on Foreign Capital" in 1950 stimulated energetic efforts on the part of Japanese businesses to import technology from the United States and Europe.[125] Japanese public policy considered the "purchase" of technology both as a means to establish domestic innovation and manufacture as well as a method to attain the level of technological sophisticaion held by industrially advanced nations. During this period of technology importation, the Japanese government provided the guidance and support of industry necessary to create a capital- and technology-intensive economy.[126] Based on continuous government-industry cooperation, Japanese businesses have been able to vigorously compete with the technical achievements of international competitors.[127] Of particular interest to software licensors is the recognition by the Japanese government that computers "form the nucleus of the 'information' age...(and serve) as a nerve center of the advancing modern society and economy."[128] Such a conclusion clearly represents the potential for a significant import market in software technology in Japan.

As a response to increased trade throughout the last 20 years, the Japanese government has liberalized its restrictive trade practices to avoid trade imbalance and to preserve its ability to compete in the world market.[129] Through amendments enacted in December of 1979 and 1980, The Foreign Exchange and Foreign Trade Control Act reflect the objective of assuring "freedom of external transactions" while providing minimum necessary controls.[130] Thus, while the old Foreign Exchange Law and Foreign Investment Law prohibited all technological inflow unless validated, the new law encourages inflow and requires a license for any outflow of technology.

License agreements that include the transfer of rights relating to technology, the grant of licenses for such rights, or the transfer of technology relating to enterprise management are subject to reporting requirements. Software licensing agreements drafted between a foreign licensor and a resident Japanese licensee in which the resident is granted rights under the license must be reported to the Ministry of Finance through the Bank of Japan. [131]

Once the report notice is received, the Minister of Finance may direct amendment of the agreement or its suspension if the agreement would adversely affect the objectives of the Foreign Exchange and Foreign Trade Control Act.[132] Such circumstances would include transactions that might adversely affect the Japanese or international money market, the business activities of Japanese industry, or the performance of treaties such that international security or public order would be disturbed.[133]

For transactions directly involving the import of a product, the Ministry of International Trade and Industry (MITI) applies a similar analysis in determining the requirement for issuance of a license. [134] Under the new law, licensing contracts are generally approved within 30 days of submission of notice. [135]

After the agreement is reviewed by Japanese government agencies, the Fair Trade Commission (FTC) examines it for antitrust violations. Patterned after the Sherman-Clayton Acts, the Fair Trade Commission Act encourages fair competition by prohibiting anti-competitive conduct such as private monopolizations and unreasonable restraint of trade. [136] According to this law, Japanese corporations which conclude international agreements must file a report with the FTC within 30 days after the agreement is executed. Unfair business practices resulting from license agreements are further analyzed under the Anti-Monopoly Act guidelines for international agreements issued by the FTC on May 24, 1968. [137] By promulgating specific regulations against "unfair trade restraints and unfair trade practices," the FTC clarified the examination standards strictly enforced by the Commission. [138]

International jurisdictional disputes arising from antimonopoly cases involving foreign companies have been resolved through implementation of an international "Notification System." [139] Once an agreement is considered in violation of antitrust, a member nation of the Committee of Experts on Restrictive Business Practices (RBP Committee), Organization of Economic Cooperation and Develpment (OECD), notifies the other member country of pending antitrust violations against its domestic companies.

While participation in the "Notification System" is voluntary, amicable resolution of complex jurisdictional issues has been documented as satisfactory in the pre- servation of international trading relationships.[140]

In recognizing the sigificant commercial value in "intangible" software and the potential for infringement, the Japanese have sought to establish statutory protection that would stimulate innovation and protect the software investment while promoting the dissemination of programming. In 1971, MITI held a meeting of the Software Legal Pro- tection Investigation Committe which recommended the introduction of a registration system for program outlines and the publication of the outlines after registration.[141] This system would further provide compensatory damages and injunctions for any infringement by reproduction.[142] Though recognized as experimental, this system would benefit the foreign licensor by affording software protection under the national objective of stimulating program dis- semination.[143] Acknowledgement of the Japanese goals in techological development would, therefore, permit the licensor in a Japanese market to enjoy the commerical advantage in software technology, despite the formidable level of competition offered by the Japanese.

VIII. SPECIAL CONSIDERATIONS IN LICENSING TO THE EUROPEAN ECONOMIC COMMUNITY (EEC)

Intellectual and industrial property rights provide the vehicle for sovereign states to convert innovation into economic power. Yet, the grant of these rights, enabling an inventor to exclude or limit the use of the invented technology for a limited time, inhibits competition. In countries such as Japan or the United States, intellectual and industrial property interests are balanced against these antitrust considerations to motivate innovation. Licensors exporting software to the EEC, however, must draft agreements in view of the integrated European antitrust policy, and the individual application of sovereign laws which provide statutory protection to technology. [144]

The Treaty of Rome, enacted in 1957, created a homogenous market by reconciling industrial property rights with free competition, movement of goods, and market integration. [145] Although barriers to trade were removed, separate national industrial property laws remained intact. To resolve antitrust issues, the Treaty created the Court of Justice of the European Communities as an adjudicatory body, and the European Commission as a legislative body. Nonetheless, uncertainty remains in the analysis of antitrust considerations of industrial property rights due to national inexperience in operating under the Treaty, bias of individual member states toward their own industrial property laws, and the sensitivity of the Court and the Commission to political influence. [146]

License agreements which export software to the EEC must conform to the goals of the Treaty as stated in Article 2: "to promote throughout the Community a harmonious development of economic activities, a continuous and balanced expansion, an increase in stability, an accelerated raising of the standard of living and closer relations between the States belonging to it." [147] Article 2 resolved the tension between the exercise of industrial property rights within national borders and the expressed treaty principles of encouraging free movement of goods across national boundaries and competition within the Community by requiring that "this treaty shall in no way prejudice the rules in Member States governing the system of property ownership."[148] Licensors who apply for statutory protection for their software among the members of the EEC are permitted such rights when exercised within national boundaries, under the authority of Article 2. Limitations in the exercise of statutory rights are only invoked when Treaty principles are violated.[149]

International licensing agreements are primarily governed under Articles 85 and 86 of the Treaty. Article 85(1) prohibits "agreements," "concerted practices," and "decisions by associations of undertakings"[150] which distort trade among EEC members and which restrict competition.[151] This article is similar to the Sherman Act, Section 1 in prohibiting, as anti-competitive, agreement practices which affect two or more Member states, and which restrict trade, such as pricefixing, product limitation, market sharing, and tie-ins.

Article 85(2) declares an agreement in violation of Article 85(1) as automatically void unless an "exception" is requested pursuant to Article 85(3).[152] To qualify for the grant of an exception, the agreement must 1) contribute to the production of goods or to the promotion of economic or technical progress, 2) allow customers to share fairly in the resulting benefit, 3) impose no restrictions on any undertakings other than those necessary to obtain the objectives in 1 and 2, and 4) prohibit undertakings to eliminate competition "in respect of a substantial part of the products in question."[153] The Commission may grant an exception on an individual basis, after receipt of notification of the agreement from the parties. A block exemption may also be granted for agreements exempted by category. Individual notification filed for each agreement within the specified category thereby becomes unnecessary. [154]

Article 86 prohibits the distortion of competition resulting from abusive behavior by an enterprise in a dominant position. [155] While Article 86 resembles Section 2 of the Sherman Act, it does not proscribe against attempts to monopolize. Thus, it is only when there has been an abuse of monopoly through business conduct that the Commission may impose a fine for violations. Unlike Article 85, conduct prohibited under Article 86 does not automatically render the agreement void. [156]

For practices that potentially violate Article 86, a "negative clearance" may be obtained under Regulation 17/62. [157] Once a registration is submitted and evaluated by the Commission, the granted "negative clearance" indicates that, based on available information in the requisite registration, grounds are not present to merit Commission intervention. [158] This regulation further establishes the requirements for notification necessary to receive an Article 85(3) exemption for any action subject to Article 85(1). [159]

Based on Articles 85 and 86, exclusive licenses are generally prohibited. [160] An Article 85(3) exemption may be granted, however, when exclusion of a third party enhances the competitiveness of the matter, or produces more trade than would otherwise have resulted. [161] To acquire such an exemption, the licensee must also have committed a large part of its investment resources in order to exploit the licensed technology. [162] Once formal notice has been served and the factual circumstances meet the Article 85(3) requirements for exemption, the Commission is empowered to grant an exemption.[163] Generally, however, the Commission draws a distinction between exclusive manufacturing rights and exclusive sales rights and is more likely to grant an exemption for a former.[164]

In order to facilitate the approval of valid agreements, the Commission has drafted a proposed block exemption for license agreements based on a patent grant.[165] By the terms of the draft regulation, automatic exemption would be granted if the parties conclude the agreement would meet with Commission approval. If exemption is uncertain, the parties have to notify the Commission and request an exemption under Article 85(3). Clauses which unreasonably extend the grant of a patent would necessarily be denied automatic exemption. [166]

Since its introduction in 1977, the block exemption proposal has undergone numerous drafts, each expressing the concern of the European Economic Community with the legality of dividing the Common Market according to patent licenses. The latest draft, and the one most likely to become law in early 1985, permits a degree of exclusivity within different parts of the Common Market.

In contrast to the terms of earlier drafts, the new regulation would permit a licensor to restrict the freedom of the licensee to manufacture or sell under two sets of circumstances. Under the first, a licensor who manufactures within the Common Market could contractually prohibit the licensee from selling the product within the territory of the licensor. Such a prohibition would apply in both active sales, in which the vendor solicits customers, and passive sales, in which the purchaser requests a sale of goods from the vendor.[167] In the second set of circumstances, as outlined in the proposed statute, a licensor could exclude a licensee from making active sales within the territory of another licensee but could not prohibit any passive sales the licensee might enjoy. Analysts within the United Kingdom believe this change, permitting passive sales, will ensure equalization of prices through competition in the Common Market.[168] Therefore, licensors may incorporate a restriction in a license agreement only if they hold patent rights in the Common Market countries where they have established exclusive manufacturing licenses.

Another amendment which reflected the change in approach taken in the latest draft limits restrictions in the use of licensed know-how. By eliminating articles 3(10) and 3(11) of the 1979 draft, the new proposal allows a licensee to use know-how under trade secret even after license expiration. A licensee may be restricted, however, to use this know-how in a specific field of use.[169]

During the seven years since the introduction of the proposal, license agreements have been drafted with uncertainty as to the law which ultimately would control them. Should the proposal be approved within the short time projected, licensors and licensees will need to renegotiate their agreements in order to conform to the new laws.[170] Until the promulgation of such a draft regulation, licensing agreements whose exclusivity does not grant absolute territorial protection may be exempted under the block exemption of Regulation 67/67.[171]

Because the balance of trade in information technology products has been declining for Europe since the late 1970s, the EEF created the European Strategic Programme on Research in Information Technology (ESPRIT).[172] Similar to MITI in Japan, and the Microelectronics and Computer Technology Corporation (MCC) in the United States, ESPRIT represents a partnership between companies, academic re-search facilities, and government agencies. However, because ESPRIT was created to afford all of Europe a stronger technology base, EEC members cooperate in the contribution of both research and funding.[173]

Long-range plans for research designed to reverse Europe's decline in competitiveness include development in software technology.[174] ESPRIT's projects will be primarily aimed at improving software engineering techniques so that, for example, individual software modules may be reused in other contexts where the same functions are necessary.[175]

The basis for ESPRIT, in providing a building block for improving the use of European research and development, differs from MITI in its limitation to precompetitive research. By encouraging participating companies to develop products based on the information gained, ESPRIT reinforces national research and development programs.[176] The EEC's recognition that high technology industries are essential to economic growth, combined with the emphasis on develop-ment of a strong technology, offer significant opportunities for license agreements which conform with Common Market principles.

IX.   CONCLUSION

Licensure of software technology ensures the dissemination of information to countries seeking to improve
their standard of technology sophistication as well as
providing substantial potential for economic gain for
the licensing companies. Domestic companies which export
such technology, therefore, would require that the technological information enter a free and competitive market.

Licensors seeking to export software technology from
the United States must meet domestic export requirements
as well as foreign market import requirements. In addition
to considerations of domestic statutory protection,
necessary to preserve the "home" market, the transfer or
export of technology is subject to federal government
controls intended to preserve the interests of national
security. License agreements must also conform to federal
antitrust provisions which assure that the "monopoly" offered
to statutorily protected technology is not abused through
anti-competitive practices. By proper implementation
of choice of law clauses, a licensor may determine the
law that will be applied in the event of dispute. Finally,
taxation provisions and required customs duties for any
international licensing agreement determine the monetary
liability to licensors seeking to expand their markets
abroad.

In addition to markets within the United States,
Japan and the EEC offer significant and ready markets
for the licensure of software. The transfer of such technology through license, as a fundamental basis for development, serves a dual nature. The exportation of software
technology to a foreign entity represents a factor of

domination over the entity when a single country or
company has a monopoly or possesses the exclusive means
for applied research and development on the innovation.
However, this technology transfer also represents a
means for dissemination of innovation related information that is encouraged by foreign governments even
when access to a market is incomplete. This aspect
of market independence enables foreign nations to
strengthen their technical and economical potential,
and in turn supports the international free market in
technology.

X.   FOOTNOTES

1.   Wright, *Technology Policy and Policy Making in the United States*, in *Technology and International Affairs* 129 (J. Szyliowcz ed. 1981).

2.   Statutory authority includes 35 U.S.C. §101 *et. seq.* (1976) (patent), and 17 U.S.C. §101 *et. seq.* (1976) (copyright).   Trade secrets are not statutorily protected.

3.   Black's Law Dictionary 829 (rev. 5th. ed. 1979).

4.   Wright, *supra* note 1, at 129.

5.   J. Soma, *Computer Technology and the Law* 369 (1983).

6.   T. Arnold, *Basic Considerations in Licensing* in *Technology Licensing*, Vol. I at 11 (1982).

7.   R. Wilson, *The Sale of Technology Through Licensing*, (1975).

8.   *Id.* at 173.

9.   *Id.* at 177.

10.   Pollzien, *Introductory Remarks about International Licensing Agreements* 3 (1973).

11.   *Id.* at 3.

12.   R. Wilson, *supra* note 7, at 178, describing small firms as those with less than $50 million in annual sales.

13.   *Id.* at 178.   Compare with results of a survey of corporate licensing showing a tendency for U.S. corporations with sales between $10 million and $500 million to enter licensing agreements more frequently with domestic companies, Rostoker, *PTC Research Report*, *A Survey of Corporate Licensing*, 24 Idea 2 (1983).

14. Franklin Pierce Law Center Annual Entreprenurial Workshop, *Buying and Selling Technology Based Companies*, October 29, 1983, Massachusetts Institute of Technology.

15. Pollzien, *supra* note 10 at 6-7.

16. *Id.* at 7.

17. Munition Control Regulations, 22 C.F.R. §121-128, as cited at Zaucha and Swennen, *Department of Commerce Controls on the Export of Computers* §9-3§ Article 2 in *Computer Law Service*, (R. Bigelow ed., (1979). [hereinafter cited as Controls].

18. 22. U.S.C. §1934 (repealed 1776) and replaced with Arms Export Control Act of 1976, 22 U.S.C. §2751.

19. 22. C.F.R. §121, Subchapter M.

20. 15. C.F.R. §370, Supp. 2. See also 45 Fed. Reg. 43010 (1980).

21. 22 C.F.R. §125.02.

22. J. Conner, *An Introduction to U.S. Government Controls on Export of Technology* in *Current International Legal Aspects of Licensing and Intellectual Property* 195 (1980).

23. *U.S. v. Edler Industries, Inc.* 479 F. 2d 516 (1980).

24. 50 U.S.C. §§2401-2413 (1976 Supp. V. 1981), amended by Pub. L. No. 96-72, 93 Stat. 503 (1979) codified at 50 U.S.C. §2401-2419.

25. 50 U.S.C. §2402(2)(c), (1976 and Sup. V. 1981).

26. Executive Order No. 12002, July 7, 1977, and Executive Order No. 12214, May 2, 1980.

27. 15 C.F.R. §368 *et. seq.*

28.   Controls, supra note 17, at 2.

29.   A general license allows the export of technology
        without the need for individual license. A general
        qualified license permits multiple exports on
        approval of an application. Validated licenses
        only authorize the export of a specific item upon
        acceptance of an application. Export Adminis-
        tration Act of 1979, 50 U.S.C. §§2403(a), Evrard,
        *The Export Administration Act of 1979: Analysis
        of its Major Provisions and Potential Impact on
        United States Exporters*, 12 Cal. W.L. Rev. 19 (1982).

30.   15 C.F.R. §371.

31.   Evrard, *supra* note 29, at 20 citing 50 U.S.C. §2404
        (e) (2).

32.   *Id.* at 20.

33.   *Id.* at 21.

34.   15 C.F.R. §371.3.

35.   15 C.F.R. §379.2.

36.   *Guide For Exporters of Computer and Computer
        Related Equipment* as cited in Controls, *supra* note
        17, at 5. The guide specifically deals with ap-
        plications to countries most highly scrutinized
        by export regulations. For commodity control
        list categories not controlled by the OEA, see
        15 U.S.C. §370.10 (1976 and Supp. V. 1981).

37.   15 C.F.R. §782.9.

38.   Controls, *supra* note 17, at 6-7. Zaucha and
        Swennen advise that the OEA policy Planning
        Division may seek recommendations from other
        agencies regarding a license application in the
        following ways: Formal referral to an agency,
        referral to the Operating Committe (OC) of the
        Advisory Committee on Export Policy (ACEP), or
        informal referral to agencies through a "waiver
        memo." Licenses required to be reviewed by the
        Defense Department under the Export Administration
        Act are formally referred by the OEA.

39.   50 U.S.C. §2403-1(c) (1976 and Supp. V. 1981); an example of the exercise of the President's authority is the denial of a license to Sperry Univac for export of a computer to the U.S.S.R, as cited in *Controls, supra* note 17, at 7, footnote 15.

40.   50 U.S.C. §2404(b) (1976 and Supp. V. 1981). See also Evrard *supra* note 29, at 28.

41.   50 U.S.C. §2403(c) and 50 U.S.C. §2404(f), (1976 and Supp. V. 1981).

42.   50 U.S.C. §2404(h) (1976 and Supp. V. 1981).

43.   50 U.S.C. §2404(h)(2) (1976 and Supp. V. 1981).

44.   50 U.S.C. §2413 (A) (10) (1976 and Supp. V. 1981), the Department of Commerce, however, is not required to justify to the TAC's any failure to adopt their advice, H.R. Rep. No. 95-190, 95th Congress 1st Sess. 16 (1977).

45.   *Controls, supra* note 17, at 9.

46.   E. Kintner and M. Joelson, *An International Antitrust Primer* 91 (1974).

47.   *Id.* at 8.

48.   15 U.S.C. §1 (1976).

49.   Conduct resulting in restraint of trade must have a direct and substantial effect on United States commerce. *United States v. Aluminum Co. of America,* 148 F. 2d 416 (2d Cir. 1945).

50.   15 U.S.C. §2 (1976)

51.   15 U.S.C. §§12-27 (1976).

52.   E. Kintner and M. Joelson, *supra* note 46, at 17.

53.   15 U.S.C. §14 (1976).

54.   U.S.C. §18 (1976). Note: One option involves

contacting the FTC and the Justice Department to determine the threshold size of companies for reporting purposes since this factor is especially uncertain for international businesses. J. Soma, *supra* note 5, at 373, footnote 21.

55. 15 U.S.C. 45(a)(1) (1979).

56. F.T.C. Act Section 5, Act of September 26, 1914, 38 Stat. 717, 15 U.S.C. §§41-51.

57. Brunsvold and O'Reilley, *Outline: The Impact of the Antitrust Laws on Patent and Know-How Licening 1981* Licensing Law Handbook 247-248 (1981). [hereinafter cited as Brunsvold and O'Reilley].

58. ABA Antitrust Section, Monograph No. 6, *U.S. Antitrust Law in International Patent and Know-How Licensing* 18-25 (1981) [hereinafter cited as ABA Monograph].

59. *United States v. Socony-Vacuum Oil Co.,* 310 U.S. 150 (1940).

60. *United States v. Addyston Pipe & Steel Co.,* 85 F. 271 (6th Cir. Tenn. 1899), aff'd, 175 U.S. 211 (1899).

61. *Fashion Originators' Guild v. Federal Trade Comm'n,* 310 U.S. 457 (1941).

62. *International Salt Co. v. United States,* 332 U.S. 392. (1947).

63. ABA Monograph *supra* note 58, at 11-31.

64. *United States v. Westinghouse Electric Corp.,* 471 F. Supp. 532 (N.D. Cal. 1973).

65. ABA Monograph *supra* note 58, at 31; see also *SCM Corp. v. Xerox Corp.* 745 F. 2d 1195 (2nd Cir. 1981) and Hammond and Medlock, *Lessons Learned from Recent Licensing Cases in Technology Licensing Volume Two* 171 (1982).

66. ABA Monograph, *supra* note 58, at 40.

67.   *General Talking Pictures Corp. v. Western Electric Co.*, 304 U.S. 175 (1938), *aff'd on reh*, 305 U.S. 124 (1938), *reh denied* 305 U.S. 675 (1939).

68.   ABA Monograph, *supra* note 58, at 47-48 cautions that the grant of exclusive licenses which insulate each licensee from competition may be upheld, while exclusive licenses that have the effect of inhibiting research and development in the field of the licensed subject may be held as an unreasonable restraint of trade.

69.   *United States v. General Electric Co.*, 272 U.S. 476 (1926).

70.   *United States v. Ciba Geigy Corp.* 508 F. Supp. 1118 (D.N.S. 1976); see also *General Talking Pictures v. Western Electric Co.*, 305 U.S. 124 (1983).

71.   ABA Monograph, *supra* note 58.

72.   *Sperry Products, Inc. v. Aluminum Co. of America*, 171 F. Supp. 901 (N.D. Ohio 1959).

73.   *Id.* at 56.

74.   *Id.* at 59.

75.   *Id.* at 60.

76.   *Id.* at 61.

77.   E. Kintner and M. Joelson, *supra* note 46, at 154.

78.   D. Baker, *Antitrust Aspects of the Software Issue* §7-1 Article 1 in *Computer Law Service* (R. Bigelow ed. 1979).

79.   *International Salt Co. v. United States*, 332 U.S. 392 (1947).

80.   *United States v. Lowe's, Inc.*, 371 U.S. 38 (1962).

81.   D. Baker, *supra* note 78, at 7.

82.   *Id.*

83.   Restatement of Contracts, 2d §§344, 346.

84.   B. Brunsvold and D. Jeffrey, *Choice of Law and Selection of a Forum for International License Disputes* in 1981 *Licensing Law Handbook* 327.

85.   *Id*. at 321.

86.   *Id*.

87.   Modiano, *International Patent Licensing Agreements and Conflict of Laws*, 2 NW J. Int'l L. & Bus. 17 (1980).

88.   G. Pollzien, *Introductory Remarks About International Licensing* in 1981 *Licensing Law Handbook* 14 (1981).

89.   B. Brunsvold and D. Jeffrey, *supra* note 84, at 321.

90.   *Id*. at 326.

91.   *Id*. at 327.

92.   *Id*. at 328.

93.   *Id*. at 329.

94.   *Id*. at 326.

95.   *Id*.

96.   M. Finnegan, *International Patent and Know-How Licensing: The Rules of the Game in Current Trends in Domestic and Secrets*, Know-How and Industrial Property 1975 193 (1974).

97.   G. Pollzien, *supra* note 88, at 14.

98.   IRC §§11 and 61 (1954); see also R. Goldscheider, *International Licensing from the American Point of View* in *International Licensing* **Agreements** **469** (1973) [hereinafter cited as Goldscheider]. Note: Readers are advised to update tax information yearly. 1984 legislation permits a portion of taxable income attributable to foreign trading gross receipts to be elligible for an exemption from U.S. Federal Income Tax; see IRC §§922-927 (1984).

99. *Technical Requirements and Definitions Under the New Foreign Sales Corporation Legislation*, The Computer Lawyer, Vol. 1, No. 1, at 469, August 1984.

100. Economic Recovery Tax Act; Pub. L. No. 97-34, 95 Stat. 172 (1981), see also T. Smegal, *Tax Considerations Relevant to Domestic and International Transferfer of Industrial Property Rights in Technology Licensing Volume Two* 559-568 (1982).

101. IRC §§1221,1231, (1983).

102. IRC §1222, (1983).

103. IRC §§1222, 1223, (1983).

104. Goldscheider, *supra* note 98, at 469.

105. IRC §1221, (1983).

106. IRC §1235, (1983).

107. Goldscheider, *supra* note 98, at 470.

108. *Id.*

109. 35 U.S.C. §101 (1976).

110. IRC §1221(3), (1983).

111. *Supra* note 101.

112. IRC §483, (1983).

113. IRC §351, (1983).

114. IRC §1249 capital gains similarly denied. See also T. Smegal, *supra* note 100, at 464.

115. IRC §901 (1983).

116. T. Smegal, *supra* note 100, at 566.

117. The Customers Co-Operation Council (CCC) was established to harmonize customs administration pro-

cedures in 80 member countries. Not all members have agreed to be bound by all decisions to the CCC, and the United States has not agreed to the decisions of the CCC's Valuation Comittee. However, trade agreements ratified by Congress, Trade Agreements Act of 1979, Pub. L. No. 96-97, July 26, 1979, seem to indicate development of a uniform approach to valuation. R. Bigelow, *Customers Duties §9-2.3* in *Computer Law Service* (Revised, January 1980, R. Bigelow ed. 1979).

118.   Based on a study completed by its Valuation Committee "Dutiable Value of Computers and Program Media," separate rules were created for hardware. The use to which the computer is to be put is considered unimportant, in its valuation. If an entire system is imported, valuation is based on its actual sale price. Hardware related software essential to computer function is included in the value of the hardware. R. Bigelow, *supra* note 117, citing App. 9-2.3a 4.

119.   *Id.* at 3-4.

120.   *Id.* at 4.

121.   General Agreement on Tariff and Trade, Oct. 30, 1947 55 UNTS 194, TIAS No. 1700. See also Presidential Proclamation No. 4707, Dec. 11, 1979, 44 Fed. Reg. 72348, and Present and Projected US Tariff Rates and Duties at 6.

122.   J. Soma, *supra* notes, 5 at 384.

123.   Trade Agreements Act of 1979, Pub. L. No. 96-39, July 26, 1979.

124.   R. Bigelow, *supra* note 117.

125.   K. Kobayashi, *Technology Transfer in Japan, In Introduction to the Current State of Japanese Industry,* in *Technology Transfer in Industrial Countries* 27 (S. Gee ed. 1979).

126.   *Id.* at 28.

127.   *Id.*

128.   MITI, *A Registration and Certification Type of System to Protect Computer Programs*, 9-4 Article 3 in Computer Law Service 2 (R. Bigelow ed. 1979).

129.   D. Nikaido, *Recent Changes in the Japanese Law - Is It Now Easier to Obtain Agreements with Japanese Companies* in *Recent Developments in Licensing* 27 [hereinafter cited as Recent Changes].

130.   *Id.* at 231 citing Article 1 of the Foreign Exchange and Foreign Trade Control Law.

131.   M. Sharp, *Japanese Licensing Environment* in *Technology Licensing Volume Two* 244 (1982).

132.   Recent Changes *supra* note 129 at 232.

133.   Article 23 of the Foreign Exchange and Foreign Trade Control.

134.   Article 24 of the Foreign Exchange and Foreign Trade Control Law.

135.   Recent Changes, *supra* note 129, at 232.

136.   Law relating to Prohibition of Private Monopoly and Methods of Preserving Fair Trade, Law No. 54 of 1947.

137.   Y. Sakamoto, *Licensing in Japan* in *International Licensing Agreements* 278 (1973). The Anti-Monopoly Act Guidelines for International Licensing Agreements, May 24, 1968 as issued by the Fair Trade Commission are cited, in traslation at pp. 281-282.

138.   *Id.* at 278, 281.

139.   M. Ariga, *Regulation of International Licensing Agreement Under the Japanese Antimonopoly Law* in *Patent and Know-How Licensing in Japan and the United States* 308-309 (1977).

140.   *Id.* at 309.

141.   MITI, *supra* note 128, at 1.

142. *Id.*

143. *Id.* at 6. The MITI report noted, however, that this form of protection for software would provide interim protection until the passage of new legislation. In view of the indefinite status of foreign legislative protection for software, the report did not predict rapid enactment of any such new legislation.

144. K. Payne and J. Bagarazzi, *Effect of the EEC Rules of Competition on Industrial Property Rights and Technology Transfer* in *Recent Developments in Licensing* 245 (1981). [hereinafter cited as EEC Rules].

145. D. Guy and G. Leigh, *The EEC and Intellectual Property* 3-4 (1981). The Treaty of Rome was originally signed by Belgium, the Federal Republic of Germany, France, Italy, Luxembourg and the Netherlands on March 25, 1957 and came into effect January 1, 1958. Denmark, Ireland and the United Kingdom joined on January 1, 1973 and Greece joined on January 1, 1981.

146. *Id.* at 246.

147. *Id.* at 247.

148. D. Guy and G. Leigh, *supra* note 145, at 8.

149. Articles 30 and 34 prohibit all quantitative restrictions on trade between member States which are asserted based on industrial property rights. Article 36 offers protection from these Articles when restrictions are justified on grounds of protecting industrial and commercial property. Such "grounds" are the current center of debate for the Court and Commission.

150. The term "undertaking," while not defined by the Court or Commission, applies to private and public commercial exploitations, and to state owned corporations.

151. EEC Rules, *supra* note 144, at 248. See also, D. Guy and G. Leigh, *supra* note 145, at 41.

152.   The Commission may also levy substantial fines on infringing agreements unless an Article 85(3) exemption is filed.

153.   EEC Rules, *supra* note 144, at 248.

154.   The Commission must seek specific authorization to issue a block exemption from the Council of Ministers, Article 87, Treaty of Rome.

155.   Abuse is defined under Article 86 as:

"(a) directly or indirectly imposing unfair purchase or selling prices or other unfair trading conditions;

(b) limiting production, markets, or technical development to the prejudice of consumers;

(c) applying dissimilar conditions to equivalent transactions with other trading parties, thereby placing them at a competitive disadvantage;

(d) making the conclusion of contracts subject to acceptance by the other parties of supplementary obligations which, by their nature or according to commercial usage, have no connection with the subject of such contracts."

156.   EEC Rules, *supra* note 144, at 248.

157.   EEC Rules, *id.* at 249.

158.   K. Newes, *Licensing Agreements Under the Antitrust Rules of Common Market* in *International Licensing Agreements* 547 (1973).

159.   EEC Rules, *supra* note 144, at 249.

160.   D. Guy and G. Leigh, *supra* note 145, at 174-175.

161.   EEC Rules, *supra* note 144, at 251. See also D. Guy and G. Leigh *supra* note 145, at 174-178.

162.   *Id.*

163.   *Id.*

164.   D. Guy and G. Leigh, *supra* note 145, at 177.

165.   EEC Rules, *supra* note 144, at 257.

166.   Such clauses would include:

      1) No Challenge Clause, Article 3(1)
      2) Undue Extension of Terms, Articles 3(2) and 3 (4)
      3) Mandatory Packaging, Article 3 (14)
      4) Agreements not to Compete, Article 3(3)
      5) Royalties on Non-Patented Items, Article 3(4)a
      6) Price fixing, Article 3(7)
      7) Grantback Assignments, Article 3(12)
      8) Production Limitations, Article 3(6)
      9) Restrictions beyond Technical Scope of the Patent, Article 3(8)
     10) Exclusive Territorial Restrictions for Manufacture or Use, Article 3(13)
     11) Exclusive Sales Restrictions
     12) Clauses creating Quasi-Patents.

167.   Burnside, *New EEC Licensing Regulation*, Les Nouvelles, September 1984, at 154.

168.   *Id.* at 154.

169.   *Id.*

170.   *Id.* at 154-155.

171.   D. Guy and G. Leigh, *supra* note 145, at 321. For the complete text of the regulations see Appexdix 6, Commission Regulation 67/67, March 22, 1967.

172.   Nasko, *European Common Market*, Spectrum, November 1983, at 71.

173.   *Id.*

174.   *Id.* Other research areas include advanced microelectronics, advanced information processing, office automation, and computer-integrated flexible manufacturing.

175.   *Id.* at 72.

176.   *Id.*

Original research and preliminary writings by:

Jennifer A. Tegfeldt, B.S. Biological Sciences, University of California, Davis, J.D. Franklin Pierce Law Center, registered patent agent, is presently a law clerk to the United States Court of Appeals for the Federal Circuit (1985-1987).

CHAPTER 4 - COMPUTER CONTRACTS

I   INTRODUCTION

Computer equipment, products and services comprise a market that has grown from one percent of the gross national product (GNP) in 1970 to five percent a decade later.[1] Coupled with this increase were the necessary contracts drafted for the procurement of computer systems. In the early development of computer technology, users seeking to acquire a computer system were limited to the contractual obligations drawn by a small number of vendors. The subsequent rise in the number of firms competing in the computer technology market has given users the opportunity to choose products and services on other than a take-it-or-leave-it basis. The success of the acquisition, however, depends on the user's comprehensive analysis and plan for his needs.

Procurement of a computer system can take the form of a purchase, lease or rental. A user has the option of acquiring software as a bundled package with the hardware. Alternatively, the user may negotiate with a multitude of software and hardware vendors to create a custom-designed system of compatible components which best meet the user's particular needs. Such options are limited, however, by the functional characteristics of the hardware. For example, operational programs which cause the machinery to perform basic functions may best be obtained from hardware manufacturers familiar with the particular hardware's circuitry design. In contrast, application programs which facilitate customer use of the system, can be purchased from a number of software suppliers. Because these programs are written in a non-English computer language, a user must have or acquire technical expertise in order to make cost and efficiency comparisons among such software packages. None-the-less, the presence of these programs on the market increases the possibilities for system design beyond those conceived by the manufacturer.[2]

Non-custom application or consumer software can also be obtained for a computer system. Such software is specifically designed to be 'user-friendly' and, as such, has simplified instructions often written in English. With this type of software the user has access to such diverse services as word processing, inventory control and literature research. Originally, these programs could only be purchased from the hardware manufacturer or developed by the user himself. However, independent suppliers of this software now commonly license the software rather than selling the software package. In exchange for a license to use the proprietary software, the user agrees to maintain its secrecy and integrity by limiting distribution. Software suppliers may also develop a specific (custom) program suited to the needs of the user. Software development agreements, in turn, provide the software developer the benefit of having another product to enter on the market after an agreed upon time.[3]

The basis for procurement of any computer system is a contract. This document integrates the agreement of the parties and determines the management of the acquisition or development. If the contract is based on an agreement by a software developer to create software for a user, the document can specify which of the parties retains ownership of the proprietary interests in the software. A contract can also specify damages in event of breach.

Contract terms can be drafted at the negotiations table or derived from standard user or vendor procurement forms. The General Services Administration of the U.S. Government negotiates each year the most established of the user-created contracts. This contract is necessarily general in its terms since it encompasses both small and large system acquisitions. Because it comprises the terms, requirements and expectations of a purchaser with considerable negotiating power, it can be used as a basis for other user-vendor contracts, with modifications for specific needs appended.[4]

While procurement contracts can take as many forms as required by user needs, every contract shares the esential role of risk-allocation. Regardless of how carefully a contract is drafted, it is not a guarantee that the system will be installed and will function without problems. To properly allocate liability for system failure or improper operation, a comprehensive anaylsis of all possible elements of risk is a requirement.[5] The system may be damaged or destroyed by natural hazards such as fire, flood or earthquake. Risk should also be allocated for unplanned events such as bankruptcy, non performance, failure to maintain or lack of responsiveness.[6] Lastly, planned acts of sabotage, misappropriation or computer fraud should be included in a risk analysis.[7] In contract negotiations, each party should create an ordered priority of risks, the order being ranked by a factor of the probability that each risk element might occur times the loss due to the occurrence of each risk element. The resulting contract clauses will then reflect a mutual understanding of risk-taking and risk avoidance by the user and the vendor. Other related issues to be dealt with in a contract would include maintenance, software updates, training costs, *etc.*

In addition to allocating risk, a contract is a tool to protect proprietary rights. Considering the case of reproducing software, and the difficulty of tracing the source of unauthorized copies, disclosure of the elements of a software package to a user, even under a confidentiality agreement, creates the possibility for destruction of the value of the package to the software suppliers. As a result, vendors will often deliver to the user a program in a language which may be directly loaded into the hardware, as object code. The vendor retains, as secret, the source code language which must be compiled prior to being executed by the hardware. While *this method* certainly assures the vendor control over his proprietary property, there are some instances for which the user should have a copy of the source code particularly when the software is essential to the user's business. The user may want a copy of the source code to avoid relying on the vendor should the system fail.[8] Similarly, should the vendor go bankrupt, the user may be precluded from maintaining the system without access to the source code. Lastly, auditors seeking to audit the user's accounts may require access to the source code to determine what algorithm or procedure is being used to produce the output, or for the vendor to deposit the source code with an escrow agent, such as a bank. Upon bankruptcy of the vendor, or notice of audit, the agent is authorized to disclose the source code. If the procurement agreement permits the user to have a copy of the source code for maintenance purposes, the contract should have a confidentiality clause protecting the secrecy of the software.[9]

If the software is protected by copyright or patent, the contract may include a clause to protect the user from infringement claims. Without such a clause, the user may be required not only to surrender the purchase but to pay damages to the holder of the copyright or patent. Under the patent laws, specifically 35 U.S.C.§ 287 (1976), an innocent infringer of a patented article without notice of patent is not liable for damages to the patentee. The patent holder may recover damages from an infringer of a non-noticed patented article only if the patent holder proves the infringer was "notified of the infringement and continued to infringe thereafter."[10] Under the copyright laws, which protect only "original works of authorship fixed in any tangible medium of expression,"[11] innocent infringers may avoid liability if it is proven that the copyright notice had been omitted by the copyrighter,[12] However, if the innocent infringers who acquired pirated copyrighted copies have reasons to believe are legitmate, they may still be laible for statutory damages for infringement, though these damages may be reduced by the court.[13] Since much of the software available for purchase is copyrighted, the user should incorporate an indemnification clause in the event that the vendor sues the user for infringement of the software. From the vender's perspective, the sale of hardware or software diminishes the vendor's control over proprietarily protected property. By electing to lease or rent the property, a vendor may control the use of the product to allow vendor enforcement

of rights to the product, particularly for products constituting trade secret. A user may be permitted only
limited control over the product and may be required to
conform to stringent confidentiality standards. While
such restrictions might appear to be prohibitive to a
user the benefits are significant. By leasing, a user
is not required to pay the full purchase price of the
product. If the lease agreement permits the user to
terminate prior to the end of the lease, the user further
avoids the risk of the equipment becoming obsolete.[14]

II   CONTRACT FORMATION

The procurement contract expresses mutual agreement
as to terms and conditions between the parties, and the
exchange of consideration. As with other contracts, they
are construed as a whole and written forms are generally
preferred over oral. If a contract is contested and a
court cannot determine the essential terms of the contract
or its incident liabilities, the court will not construe
a meeting of the minds. Thus, in *Data Central Corp.*,[15]
a contract dispute with the U.S. Government because the
private contractor intended to supply a computer system
meeting only standard specification, and the government
intended to accept only a system complying with government
specifications, the court could not find mutual intent
between the parties. The court further explained that
a purchaser's notice of fraud which fails to conform to
a vendor's proposal does not constitute a contract until
the vendor accepts the terms.[16]

Written contracts are generally preferred over oral agreements because of the simplified task of construing memorialized terms in the event of a dispute.[17] However, if the court can determine that the parties have agreed on the essential terms of the procurement, and the remaining terms and conditions may be ascertained from the surrounding circumstances, the court may find a binding agreement, even in the absence of a formally executed document.[18] Depending on the particular requirements under the statute of frauds of the state in which the procurement contract is drafted, an oral agreement may be enforced if followed by a written momorandum of agreement. Such a memorandum must include all the essential elements of the agreement to be enforceable. In *Ancom, Inc. v. E.R. Squibb & Sons, Inc.*, the Eighth Circuit Court of Appeals held an oral contract of procurement of an audiovisual client education system unenforceable because a subsequent letter between the parties failed to include an essential exclusivity feature.[19] Similarly, in *Computer Servicenters, Inc. v. Beacon Manufacturing Co,Inc.*, the District court in South Carolina could not construe an orally created contract for data processing services because the only memoranda were a collection of corporate minutes. Thus, without the submission of an offer, as embodied within the minutes, the court reasoned that there could not be an acceptance by the seller giving rise to a contract.[20]

It is well established in contract law that a merger or integration clause incorporated in an agreement ensures that the agreement is final and complete.[21] Any oral terms discussed prior to the execution of this agreement which are not consistent with the written terms are excluded at trial as parol evidence. In *IBM v. Catamore Enters, Inc.*, the First Circuit Court of Appeals held that a written agreement bars evidence of preceding oral agreements when the written agreement purports to supersede all prior oral and written proposals and communications between the parties.[22]

Parol evidence has been admitted, however, when the contract document is ambiguous. In *Carl Beasley Ford, Inc. v. Burroughs Corp.*, a Pennsylvania District Court held that oral agreements for programming to accompany a written hardware sale agreement must be admitted when defendants conceded that the equipment without programming was worthless.[23] The court concluded that these admissions supported the argument that the writing did not encompass the entire agreement. The Pennsylvania District Court applied similar reasoning in *Diversified Environments, Inc. v. Olivetti Corp.* holding that the parol evidence rule is applicable when the only memorandum supporting a lease for an accounting system is a written proposal and a customer software acceptance.[24] Since neither document completely embodied the agreement between the parties, the court required the defendant to perform the services to which it had orally agreed.

Liability for ambiguity in a contract is applied against the drafter. In a factual situation common to many users, a manufacturer, Burroughs Corp., presented its form agreement as the basis for the sales agreement to the user, Chesapeake Petroleum and Supply Co., Inc.[25]

When a dispute arose between these parties, the court prohibited Burroughs from enforcing a standardized disclaimer of warranties clause located on the reverse of the contract when the requisite spaces on the contract were left blank. The ambiguity as to intent of the parties caused by a document that could serve as a sales contract or security agreement could, therefore, only be "resolved against the sale draftsman of the instrument."[26] In order to avoid the mixed legal effects of an integration clause, the user may insist that all sales brochures, functional specifications and other vendors literature be incorporated in the agreement.[27] Such an action would integrate the expectations of the buyer and the functional capabilities of the vendor's product into the agreement and would render the standard merger clause irrelevant.[28]

Use of clear terminology is essential to the contract's expression of the intent of the parties. The contract should identify the names of the contracting parties and respective states of incorporation if the parties are corporations.[29] The expectations of the parties, as expressed by technical phrases, should be defined. Where contracting parties do not define terms, a court is often willing. For example, the court in *Triangle Underwriters, Inc. v. Honeywell, Inc.*[30] defined software as "programming created for use in connection with" hardware. The court further defined a turnkey system as one capable of performance upon completion of installation. Moreover, even where the terms defined by the court were even incorporated into the written contract, the court considered such to be governing concepts with which the written contract was consistent, and applied them to the parties' contractual relationship.

The court will add or construe necessary terms
in the procurement contract "in their ordinary and popular
sense as a man of average intelligence and experience
would understand them."[31] In *Teamsters Security Fund of
Northern California, Inc. v. Sperry Rand Corp.*, the court
interpreted the phrase, "ready to use" as meaning capable
of performing useful work.[32] To construe any other meaning
would permit Sperry Rand to install equipment capable
of performing only isolated tasks, thus contravening the
intent of the contract. Moreover, terms such as "up and
running" are evaluated as terms of the trade. Thus in
Chatlos Systems, Inc. v. National Cash Register Corp., the
district court in New Jersey defined "up and running"
as a trade term indicating a fully functional system which
performs the tasks for which it was intended.[33] This
was an attempt to consider the term as it was intended
by the parties so as not to destroy the essence of the
contract.

A definition of clear project goals and required
performance is of equal importance to the expression of
the meeting of the minds between parties. Before seeking
proposals from vendors, the user must structure a plan
for his own computer system needs. If the user does not
have a processing staff, a consulting firm may assess
the user's needs.[34] The resulting document is a request
for proposal RFD , which includes a statement of the
computational task and a request for proposed solutions
from vendors. The document should also include an evaluation of the tasks the system will undertake upon installation and anticipated changes in needs which might
affect the capabilities of the acquired system.[35]

A carefully prepared RFD establishes the user's intent to create a binding relationship. The proposal should request technical specifications, such as reliability, capacity, and upgrades, to enable the user to objectively compare vendor offers.[36] Copies of draft contract forms, as written by the user, should be attached to the RFD to allow a vendor to specify unacceptable provisions.[37] A vendor should similarly attach to its response a form contract indicating which terms are non-negotiable.[38] Lastly, the RFD should require vendor responses to be in writing, and that the responses become part of the final contract at the user's option.[39]

Based on an RFD, a procurement contract can be designed in terms of functional performance, so that the organization's functional needs are matched to the specific functional capabilities of the proposed computer system. As noted computer law author and practitioner, Duncan Davidson advises, vendor contracts typically promise delivery of electronic components which function within published specifications. By negotiating the contract from the perspective of systems analysis, the user has a higher likelihood of achieving the desired functional performance from the acquired system.[40] Functional specifications clarify the contractual responsibilities of the parties and establish performance criteria. Hardware and software components to be interfaced must be specified to ensure that current and further use may be accomodated. For example, the hardware's memory capacity, capability to handle multiple terminals and ability to handle simultaneous users and ability to be upgraded are characteristics critical to the user's choice in procuring a system that will not become obsolete before the end of its useful life.[41] The functional specific- ations must also include an estimated useful life of the system. Functional specifications must also account for compatibility between new equipment and that already in place. A failure to assess functional compatibility be- tween permutations of new and old software and hardware can cost the user much more than simply the cost of the upgrade or rental of the current system.[42] While uni- formity in products would alleviate the problem of in- compatibility, it is unlikely that the market for computer products would remain static long enough to provide such uniformity. With manufacturers continually seeking to meet user demands for greater capabilties, users should request information on compatibility prior to the formation of a procurement contract.[43]

Obtaining modular system components provides an alternative to retrograde fitting of system sections. Such a modular approach to equipment construction permits the user to purchase individual computer components that may be upgraded or altered later.[44] Modularity has the advantages of:

    1) avoiding replacement of in-house equipment
        by horizontally extending its capabilities;

    2) adding new components to a system already
        in existence, and

    3) permitting the replacement of a component
        of different performance level without destroy-
        ing compatibility.[45]

In order to include requirements for modularity in the procurement contract, the user should require that

sales documents describing modularity be integrated into
the contract. Further, to ensure that the vendor ful-
fills its commitment of modularity, the user should incorporate the following concepts into the final contract:

1) specifications for future equipment options
   should be as precise as those describing the
   acquired equipment;

2) each option should state whether factory
   installation is required;

3) the maximum number of options allowed for
   the system should be specified;

4) hardware options should specify the extent
   of software and maintenance support included;

5) software options must indicate any limitations
   on hardware configuration; and

6) the manufacturer should specify the time during
   which the options are available.46

The negotiation of these concepts may be difficult,
however, because they impose an open-ended commitment
on a vendor who desires to continually upgrade a product
line. As a compromise, the vendor may agree to offer
options for a specified period of time if the user agrees
to buy before that date.47

By incorporating each of these elements into the
contract negotiations, the user is forced to evaluate
the impact of the procurement on its other business and
data processing activities.48 The user should be educated
in the capabilities and intended uses of the system prior
to its acquisition to facilitate the installation of a
functional system. Moreover, the vendor benefits from
such detailed specifications if the user requests sub-
modifications, usually requiring an adjustment of the
time and payment terms.49

A systems analysis approach to contracting further requires specification of delivery and acceptance testing standards. The contract must clearly indicate delivery dates and testing completion dates. Delivery should not be considered complete until all the components of the system are received from the vendor,[50] and the system is ready for use. If delivery is imperative by a specific date, the contract should specify that "time is of the essence."[51] The failure to include a delivery date in the contract nonetheless requires that the delivery occur within a reasonable time. Because reasonable delivery depends on the nature of the software and hardware, the parties' intentions as expressed in the contract, and the transportation conditions, a user may be able to sue for breach of contract for unreasonably late delivery even if the contract lacks a delivery date.[52]

Acceptance tests determine whether the user in fact has received the system it wants. Computer systems, unlike household appliances, cannot be plugged in to be rendered fully functional. Acceptance testing standards requiring full user satisfaction can be very powerful leverage over the vendor if the user exercises good faith.[53] However, termination of the agreement may not be in the user's best interest, particularly if much time and capital were invested in the acquired system. By basing the acceptance standards on the functional specifications stated in the procurement contract, the user may negotiate for a strong standard of compliance.[54] This standard is typically that of substantial compliance. Experienced contract negotiators caution users to apply this standard for a period of time equal to the normal cycle time for the tasks to be performed on the system. Similarly, the user should allow sufficient time to become familiar with a system, expecially a new system, before determining whether the system is acceptable.[55]

Acceptance testing clauses should define delivery dates, specify what documentation and training should be provided, and what technical support is necessary for system start up. If the system includes custom-designed software, extra time should be allowed for debugging, or locating and correcting software malfunctions, before the package is deemed acceptable or unacceptable. Acceptance provisions must define what level of satisfaction must be achieved before the system is rejected. Vague definitions of satisfaction may preclude a vendor from ever curing system defects sufficiently to meet user demand.

For software, acceptance testing should be run on both sample data and live data. Sample data should be run on machinery already installed in-house so that the results accurately reflect the normal function of the system.[56] This data should be independently derived to avoid any bias in the results. Software should not be accepted until the package is tested in conjunction with all other load programs and with normal to heavy processing loads.[57]

Upon delivery, hardware can develop several problems unacceptable to a user. First, the delivered hardware may never function. In that case, a user's determination of unacceptability is easy. Second, the hardware may function for only a short time before it is rendered unusable. If the user has anticipated a burn-in period[58] system failure will occur before the user accepts the system. Lastly, the delivered hardware may fail during its useful life and require maintenance. Failure due to poor system design and manufacture can be anticipated by user investigation prior to procurement.[59] By incorporating a maintenance clause in the agreement, a user can be assured that a vendor will repair normal system failures within a reasonable time.

Contract terms for payment should be conditioned upon sucessful completion of acceptance testing, and final acceptance of equipment. Vendor contracts typically require payment within a specified time after installation of hardware or completion of software.[60] Such terms leave the user without any effective economic leverage over the vendor if the system or software should prove unusable. From the user's perspective, an ideal payment schedule would allow partial payment after satisfactory performance of software, a large payment upon completion of the system acceptance test, and a small final payment after completion of training, provision of documentation and correction of any small problems.[61] Aside from avoiding a lump sum payment, a payment schedule has a clear benefit in establishing a good working relationship between user and vendor. A user's partial payment prior to the completion of any acceptance testing expresses the user's good faith intentions towards the procurement agreement. Such an expression may actually benefit the user by providing the incentive to the vendor to complete a task, such as software development, ahead of the schedule. Moreover, acquisition of the entire system ahead of projected delivery dates provides the user with the economic benefit of using a system on-line sooner than projected.[62]

More important to the acquisition of a computer system than delivery dates is the provision for update and maintenance terms.[63] Proper maintenance of the acquired equipment has a direct impact on the total running time for the machinery and its useful life. Therefore, a user should insist on a maintenance plan in the acquisition contract since few vendor sales forms include such a plan. The user should also negotiate long-term maintenance at the time of contract formation. Failure to do so leaves the user in the uncomfortable position of having no negotiating leverage and being forced to choose a vendor-proposed maintenance plan or to undertake all maintenance in-house.[64]

Regardless of whether the user contracts with the vendor or a third party for maintenance service, maintenance terms should specify reliability standards, response time, repair time, and any guarantees for limited 'down-time' of the system.[65] Under the GSA contracts, for example, reliability is quantified by an equation that requires a 90 percent effectiveness level:

$$\text{effectiveness level} = \frac{(\text{available time per month}) - (\text{down-time per month})}{\text{available time per month}} \times 100$$

Available time per month is agreed, under the contract, to so many hours. Similarly, down-time per month is specified as those hours of available time per month during which the equipment is unusable to the user less any hours lost due to the fault of the user.[66]

By clearly specifying the reliability standards required for the system, the user obtains a commitment from the manufacturer to provide a useful system and to be responsible for remedies should the system continually fail.

Evaluation of the overall performance of the system should not only include the statistical mean time between failures (MTBF) but also the mean time to repair (MTTR).[67] This factor is of particular importance in an environment where a user's credibility and capability to do business are dependent on a reliable system. Thus, a system which maintains long periods between breakdowns but which requires lengthy repair time is clearly unacceptable to a user who may never be able to recover business losses during the repair down-time. Computer components, by nature, are complex combinations of electro-mechanical machinery and circuitry, exhibiting a profound lack of graceful degradation. Repeated, lengthy, down-time events most often involve a poorly designed component.

In addition to carefully studying the vendor literature and design diagrams, to assure functional integrity, a user should specify, in the maintenance terms, maximum down-time limits for individual components, as well as the entire system.[68] When inevitable hardware failures do occur, a specification requiring response time of maintenance personnel within two hours, for example, will further mitigate a user's losses.[69]

Vendor agreements for maintenance typically include clauses which excuse the vendor's failure to perform.[70] These clauses permit a vendor to avoid the responsibility set by performance on the basis of unforeseeable "acts of God." Such clauses should be carefully scrutinized by a user and amended if necessary. Short of requiring costly litigation for breach, a user can incorporate clauses allowing speedy arbitration, liquidated damages or credits for losses accrued through unforseen circumstances.[71]

If the user has leased the equipment, credits may be applied against the entire amount due under the lease. The user should foil vendor attempts to base credits on an average loss period over a month or a quarter or against the average loss periods of similar systems.[72] Such clauses leave the user with little recourse if a poorly operating system is to be averaged against one with superior performance. A user should also not discount bonus credits earned by a vendor during consistent periods of superior performance. As a negotiating chip, a user may agree to the award of bonus credits in exchange for down-time credits and for assuring rapid vendor response to maintenance calls.[73] However, users should be aware that such credits are calculated linearly while actual losses due to down-time may multiply geometrically. In an environment where down-time seriously affects the user's business reputation, credits may prevent the user from ever rectifying the damage.[74] Therefore it may be to the user's best interest to seek guaranteed limits of down-time or accelerated response times, at an added cost, rather than credits. To businesses whose livelihood rests on a reliable system, the value of such clauses may outweigh the increased costs charged.[75]

Users must also be cautious of refurbishment clauses.[76] These clauses, aimed at substandard equipment which constantly requires repair, permit the vendor to determine when it may cease efforts to repair and must replace the equipment. While it would appear economically beneficial to the vendor to replace equipment it is constantly repairing, the invocation of the refurbishment right allows the vendor to charge the cost of repair to the user. Consequently, maintenance terms should specify those failures in excess of normal which would require replacement of the equipment. The contract terms should also limit rights of refurbishment so that the user is not liable for costs of repair on a defective system.[77]

In acknowledging that maintenance costs often exceed the purchase price, users can lessen the financial burden by training in-house personnel to do the maintenance.[78] Requiring the vendor to provide replacement parts within a few hours of the system breakdown may be the most efficient way of dealing with maintenance problems.[79] If the system is irreparable without outside assistance, the user may require, in the contract maintenance terms, that the vendor provide a fully compatible back-up system.[80] The cost of the additional rental equipment during down-time can be outweighed by the actual losses achieved if no computer support was available.

III. BREACH OF CONTRACT

The restatement of contracts describes contract terms as 'reasonably certain' if the terms provide a basis for determining the existence of a breach and for giving an appropriate remedy.[81] All terms need not be certain, but all essential terms must be sufficiently definite to create a contract.[82] Based on definite terms, breach of contract occurs when there is a non-performance of a duty due under the contract.[83] Such a breach can be total or partial. Total breach exists when non-performance is so material as to justify the injured party to consider the transaction at an end. This party may then maintain an action against the non-performing party for damages. Partial breach occurs when the non-performance is not critical to the completion of the agreement. Under conditions of partial breach, the injured party must continue to perform its contractual duties or be liable for breach and damages.[84]

In contracts for the procurement of computer products and services, disputes that arise between user and vendor may not be accounted for in the agreement or may not have contractual remedies appropriate to the circumstances of the dispute. Litigation of a dispute based on a breach of contractor is, by nature, protracted and expensive. Unless parties carefully frame the issues and discovery, a desired resolution may not be realized even after judgment is rendered. Acquisition of computer products and services is rarely accomplished through a single contract. Analysis of the dispute, then, must begin with consideration of the nature of the transaction and the interaction of multiples of transactions entered into throughout the acquisition process.[85]

Analysis of a dispute must also include a determination of culpable parties. Such parties as consultants, vendors, manufacturers, software developers or individual sales people may be direct or indirect participants in the agreement.[86] Regardless of the combination of parties chosen as defendants in a law suit, for a judgment to be rendered, each may be liable, in some way, for nonperformance under the contract.

Of equal importance to dispute resolution is the discovery of dispute-related information from a multiple of sources. This information is critical in determining appropriate means for resolving the dispute. Discovery complexities can easily arise if the data processing

or accounting personnel are the only staff with full understanding of the ramifications of a computer disruption.
Moreover, the bargaining position taken by management
during dispute settlement negotiations may be seriously
hindered by the failure of in-house personnel to take
actions which would lessen the delay or otherwise mitigate
the damages.[87]

In addition to interviews with management and staff,
discovery must include disclosure of documentation, both
technical and business. Such documentation, including
logs and printouts demonstrating errors in the program
routine, are key to determining the nature and scope of
the dispute and to evaluating an appropriate resolution.
Documents exchanged early in the contractual relationship
should be included in the analysis since these may best
reflect the intention of the parties in creating the contract.[88]

The role of legal counsel in the initial stages
of dispute litigation is not only in protecting the legal
interests of the injured party but also in providing an
objective analysis of the magnitude of the dispute. Counsel
has the further, more important, role of mediating a
practical resolution to the dispute.

The economic effect, on a user, of computer down-
time can be extensive. By introducing counsel into the
resolution process, a user has the benefit of both assuring
the determination of an appropriate course of action and
of objectively assessing the costs incurred by system
failure.[89]

There are a number of approaches an injured party in a contract dispute can use to recover damages. The lead case in litigation prompted by users is *Clements Avro Supply Co. v. Service Bureau Corp.* In 1961, Clements, an automobile supply wholesaler, sought to improve its inventory control system with computerization. Various data processing experts advised Clements of the impossibility of such a plan. In 1963, the defendant promised to program and implement its new computer to provide Clements with reports on inventory and sales activity. During the next four years, Clements never received an accurate computer-generated report. In addition, keypunch operators fell behind schedule and were never able to produce hard copy invoices intended to accompany shipments. Finally, Clemets determined from expert advisors that an inventory control system could be computerized and sued the defendant in 1967.

Clements proceeded on five legal theories: Reformation and recission of contract, breach of implied warranty, breach of contract and the tort of fraud and misrepresentation. Reformation and recission of contract was denied by the Minnesota District Court based on a lack of factual finding that mistake had occurred. Breach of implied warranty was also held inapplicable since contract language specifically disclaimed implied warranties. The court similarly held that breach of contract was inapplicable because the contract contained none of the representations of the proposal. Further, the contract limited the liability of the defendant for breach of contract.[90]

While breach of contract or breach of warranty, as a cause of action, was unsuccessful, based on the facts in *Clements* , users have been able to successfully recover in other cases based on these theories. In *Chesapeake Pe - troleum and Supply Co. v. Burroughs Corp.* the circuit court for Montgomery County, Maryland, held the defendant answerable for breach of contract and breach of warranty when specific contract terms were not met.[91] A Pennsylvania district court applied similar reasoning in *Diversi - fied Environments, Inc. v. Olivetti Corp.,* in holding that the failure of the defendant to provide the services particularized in oral and written agreements justified the imposition of liability.[92]

As a defense to cause of action arising under contract law, vendors have alleged impossibility of performance. Thus , a vendor may be precluded from performing its part of contract in installing a useful system if the user fails to prepare the site according to the needs of the system. A vendor may also profess inability to provide the training necessary for a user to effectively implement the system, if the user does not produce the appropriate personnel. However, as held in *Diversified Envi - ronments, Inc. v. Olivetti Corp.,* the vendor will not be excused from performance based on impossibility if the facts support full cooperation by the user in implementing installation and training of personnel. A user's reasonable refusal to permit such installation and training after repeated unsuccessful attempts by the vendor to provide a working system is not considered by the courts as material interference with the obligations of the vendor.[93]

Clements finally won its suit by using the legal theory of intentional tort, fraud and misrepresentation. The Eighth Circuit Court of Appeals enumerated the essential elements of a fraud action in Minnesota as follows:

1) there must be a representation;

2) the representation is false;

3) the representation has to do with past or present fact;

4) that fact is material;

5) the fact must be susceptible to knowledge;

6) the representer must know the fact to be false, or must assert it as his own knowledge without knowing whether it is true or false;

7) the representer must intend to have the other person induced to act, or justified in acting upon it;

8) that person must be so induced to act or so justified in acting;

9) that person's action must be in reliance upon the representation;

10) that person must suffer damages; and

11) that damage must be proximately caused by the misrepresentation.94

Both the district court and the Eighth Circuit Court of Appeals found that the service bureau corporation had made an actionable misrepresentation in proposing a data processing system which would, when fully implemented, be capable of supplying Clements with suf- information to constitute an effective and efficient tool in inventory control.[95] While the law in Minnesota did not require proof of an active intent to deceive, the courts relied on clear evidence of the Service Bureau Corporation's superior expertise in the computer field to find that Clements reasonably relied on the representations made. Presentation of testimony which directly connected the misrepresentations to the ultimate failure of the system justified the court in holding Service Bureau Corporation liable for damages under tort.

In *Clements*, the court allowed recovery of damages for fraud based on innocent misrepresentation. While some jurisdictions may require proof of actual knowleged by the vendor of the falsity of the statements, recklessness or even the lack of a reasonable basis for the statement will justify a finding of scienter.[96]

The extent to which a misrepresentation theory will be accepted by a court is tempered by the actions of the user. A buyer who has little or no expertise in computerization must exercise good business judgment where it is reasonable to do so. A user who fails to use sound judgment will have great difficulty in convincing a court of his reasonable reliance on vendor proposals if such proposals are clearly sales-puffing.[97] Using outside technical expertise early in the negotiations process establishes a record of good faith reliance by the user on vendor representations and would measure in favor of the user should litigation ensue.

A user may also seek to ground a suit for damages in the tort of negligence. The basic elements of negligence include a duty to perform as recognized by law, a breach of that duty, proximate cause between the conduct and the injury, and actual loss.[98] Negligent performance of a contract, however, imposes liability for damages for breach of that contract but not for tortious negligence.[99]

A negligence theory may realize more success if it is considered under the doctrine of a *res ipsa loquitur* . This doctrine, which shifts the burden of proof to the party most capable of proving the occurrence of negligent conduct, coincides theoretically with the complexities of advanced computer technology. Thus, a plaintiff raising *res ipsa loquitur* may argue that he is unable to prove that negligence has occurred because of the immense technical difficulties in proving negligent dissemination of information. Also, security systems designed to protect data processing systems can arguably be designed to prevent unauthorized dissemination in the absence of negligence. Based on such arguments, the courts may use the doctrine of *res ipsa loquitur* to allocate burdens of proof among the parties in order to reach an equitable result.

Robert Bigelow, an acknowledged expert on computer law, warns that users may not always prevail in lawsuits over vendors or manufacturers.[100] He cited *Honeywell, Inc.v. Lithonia Clothing, Inc.* as an example of a case in which a court denied damages to a user whose equipment malfunctioned through no action or fault of the vendor.[101] The user in *Fruit Industries Research Foundation v. National Cash Register Co.* was dismissed from both district and appellate courts when evidence established that the user's own agent was fully appraised of the same technical limitations on which the complaint was based.[102] Finally,

Bigelow cited *National Cash Register Co. V. Marshall Savings and Loan Association* for the proposition that users may not recover when the contract terms and actual delivery of equipment are never rejected or disputed.[103] Oral promises by the user to forward payment only serve to support the conclusion that the transaction was completed successfully. In light of these examples, Bigelow advised users to institute legal action only when they are sure that the breach of contract was the fault of the manufacturer and the computer system.[104]

IV.   REMEDIES

For every breach of contractual duty, the court provides a remedy in contract disputes. This remedy is often the award of compensatory damages. According to the restatement of contracts, in a claim for total breach, damages are based on all of the injured party's remaining rights to performance.[105] Damages for partial breach are based on the rights of the injured party to remaining performance.[106] Each violation of the contract terms should specify its own remedy and should provide for notice to the opposing party to cure the defect, if possible.

Damages recoverable in user-vendor disputes can take three forms: direct, incidental and consequential. Direct damages, such as return of the purchase price, are available to the user when the equipment fails to meet contract specifications and is rejected. When a user shows the court that defective equipment has been returned to the vendor, incidental damages comprising the cost of shipment, preparation of space to accomodate the equipment, and storage costs may be recovered. Consequential damages are recoverable when damages result as a consequence of the failure of the equipment. For example, the expense of completing accounting procedures through outside consulting services would be recoverable as a consequential damage of the system failure. Such damages are typically larger than incidental damages but are more difficult to recover. Incidental and consequential damages are also frequently limited by vendors to repair and replacement of parts. While courts are reluctant to rewrite a contract, they will consider limitations on damages as having failed if repairs or replacements according to contract provision do not render the equipment operable. Under these circumstances, a limitation on damages clause will not preclude the recovery of incidental or consequential damages.[107]

In a user-vendor dispute, the value of a system may not only be assessed according to the contract purchase price but also on the value of the system as promised. In *Chatlos Systems Inc. v. National Cash Register Corp* ., the Third Circuit Court of Appeals granted the user damages equivalent to the difference between the fair market value of the goods accepted and the value they would have had if installed as promised.[108] Because the user contracted for a system with specific capabilities which the vendor was unable to supply, the court did not limit consideration of damages to the fair market value of the system as delivered. As a result of the judgment, the user was only liable to pay $46,000 for a system worth $202,000 once it performed as warrantied by the vendor.

In *Chatlos*, the user was also able to recover labor costs which would have been saved by implementation of the computer system. Since this labor savings was acknowledged as a major reason for entering the transaction; the court awarded the salaries as consequential damages. Similarly, executive salaries expended outside of initial contract negotiations were considered by the court as reasonable to include in the damage award.[109]

Losses in profits resulting from excesses and and deficiencies in inventory due to computer error were also included as consequential damages. Moreover, the cost of a manual inventory system, which did not function as well as the computer system should have, was added into the cost profit figure.

Lastly, the cost of supplies purchased in trying to make the computer function were assessed against the vendor. The rental cost for the space occupied by the non-functioning machine was also considered as reasonable to include in vendor liability. In *Convoy Corp. v. Sperry Rand Corp.*, the user recovered rental costs for additional equipment necessary to allow the faulty system to function when a vendor failed to provide the system contracted. Such rental costs would be reasonably foreseeable at the time of contract formation. As such, these direct damages would not be susceptible to limitation of liability clauses which exclude incidental or consequential damages.[110] *Convoy Corp.* is further cited as support for remuneration of the user for site preparation. In *Convoy*, the user constructed a new building addition to house the computer system. Based on the breach of contract, the court held that such costs could be reasonably included in the judgment.[111]

According to the precedent set by *Clements* , expenditures made for the maintenance of equipment are recoverable from the vendor whether or not such equipment is faulty in performance or fails to fulfill contract specifications.[112] Other efforts by the user to mitigate his losses are similarly assessed against the vendor as damages. Thus, in both *Convoy*[113] and *Chesapeake Petroleum and Supply Co. v. Burroughs Corp.*,[114] the cost of using outside consultants to render the computer system operable was included in the damages award.

J.T. Westermeier, an expert in user litigation, has recommended that users include interest payments on financing and costs of borrowing in claims for damages.[115] The question of interest, particularly prejudgment interest, can be problematic if state jurisdictions do not find that the dates and amounts of expenditures are easily ascertainable. In *Clements*, the court relied upon the laws of Minnesota to deny the award of prejudgment interest. Thus, when claims could not be readily ascertained by computation or referenced to recognized standards, and were dependent upon the discretion of the jury, interest could not be reliably calculated. However, interest was allowed on the payments made between the time the initial contract was signed and the time that Clements was fully aware of the problems in the system so that it stopped relying on the defendant's representations. Interest was also allowed for the lease of peripheral equipment and the cost of its maintenance during this time frame.[116]

The rule that interest could only be awarded when the exact amount of damages is readily ascertainable was

applied in *Convoy* . The court found that neither the underlying facts nor the fundamental issues rendered damages
uncertain. Thus, the award of prejudgment interest and
an award of interest on out-of-pocket expenses experienced
by the user as a result of breach was not held unreasonable
or unwarranted under Oregon law.[117]

Contract remedies, as specified in the final agreement, provide a simple and effective means for allocating
risk of failure to perform without relying on court intervention. Such remedies vary according to the nature of
the contract, value of each remedy, and the bargaining
strength of the parties. A remedy should be drafted for
each technical aspect of the contract and should be
activated by either partial or total failures.[118]

In response to the high cost incurred when equipment is not delivered on time, the General Services Administration Incorporated a liquidated damages clause
in its procurement contracts. Such clauses, which place
a linear value relative to the cost of the equipment on
failure to deliver, permit the user to fund replacement
equipment until the contract equipment arrives.[119] A
liquidated damages clause can be based on the effectiveness
level formula discussed previously.[120]

Liquidated damages clauses are useful for minimizing
risks between parties but may eliminate the availability
of other remedies. Thus, a user may have contractually
agreed to a linear analysis of loss when the circumstances
result in a significantly greater loss. A vendor may
be reluctant to agree to liquidated damages clauses when
the equipment contracted for is experimental. The high

cost charged for liquidated damages for new equipment is unlikely to be acceptable to a buyer. By agreeing to liquidated damages clauses, a user may be limited to the recovery amount provided for, in derogation of other possible remedies.[121] Nonetheless such damages will not be allowed where they are so unreasonable as to be punitive.[122]

Parties are free to limit damages by contract, subject to review by a court. For example, users may agree to an exclusive remedy to repair and replace but the agreement must reflect a minimum reasonable remedy. In *Chatlos Systems, Inc. v. National Cash Register Corp.*[123] the repair and replace remedy was considered to have failed when the equipment was inoperable even after repeated attempts to repair. The vendor was thus held liable for damages without respect to any limitations on liability agreed upon in the contract.

The courts will similarly disallow a total exclusion of remedies when a minimum reasonable remedy is not pro-vided.[124] Implementation of back-stop provisions, which trigger a new remedy when the first one fails, prevent a court conclusion that no minimum reasonable remedy is available.[125] The courts, however, are reluctant to re-write contracts when the parties are assumed to be sophisticated businessmen. Thus, parties familiar with contracting law outside of the computer field are pre-sumed to understand limitations or exclusions on direct, incidental or consequential damages. If the facts support a conclusion that a user did not knowledgeably waive rights to damages, the courts will disallow the clause as un-conscionable. In *Chesapeake Petroleum and Supply Co. v.*

Burroughs Corp., the court found a limitations clause unconscionable to enforce when the clause appeared in fine print on the reverse of the contract and did not appear to have applicability to the contract aside from a security agreement.[126]

V.   ALTERNATIVES TO LITIGATION

For young business with limited working capital, litigation is a luxury both in time and expense. Protracted litigation may be avoided by incorporating project controls within the procurement contract. Such controls ensure that both parties actively participate to create the system desired.

Duncan Davidson views the contract as a mechanism to ensure that buyers receive what they desire.[127] Clauses incorporated in the contract regulate implementation. Therefore, the performance concepts sought by the buyer must be specified by the functional specifications. A project timetable particularizing the major components of the system and their respective due dates fix the obligation of the vendor for each major task. Such a timetable specifies indicia for the declaration of failure of contract terms constituting breach. However, project timetables that are too detailed with minute tasks may render the vendor's performance impossible.[128]

Project controls, as specified in the contract, must include complete and adequate acceptance testing for each component and for the entire system. Standards for performance and requirements for maintenance support assure the user continued service consistent with functional specifications for the computer system even after delivery.[129]   Software development contracts require functional specifications to be as precise as possible. The provision of precise specifications require the developer to accurately estimate the time and capital necessary to create the desired software. A user thereby avoids the trap of open/time and cost agreements that may never produce the necessary software.[130]

When unexpected problems arise to justify time delays and price increases, a user may incorporate a rolling estoppel clause in the agreement. Rolling estoppel requires that notice be sent regularly to the user in the form of project reports. These reports not only describe the problems but also propose remedies. When a developer fails to report a problem within the reporting period, the rolling estoppel clause prevents the developer from excusing delay or price increase based on unanticipated problems.[131]

Under a rolling payment clause, payment is established up to a maximum price for each task unless justified by notice of unforeseen problems. As opposed to forwarding payment upon completion of the entire project, a user may use rolling payments to encourage the developer to produce the desired software on time. A user should withhold portions of the payments until final acceptance since new problems may arise in the total system which were not obvious in individual component-testing.[132]

The project may be further controlled by designing each component as a discreat deliverable item under the contract. Such a designation permits the user to seek new vendors should the original vendor fail to provide discreet operable software. Components critical to system operation should also be scheduled for delivery at staggered times throughout the development period. Such planning avoids locking the user into a single supplier who has failed, at the last minute, to provide operable software. Moreover, each deliverable must be subject to independent approval. Inclusion of a rolling acceptance clause will prevent a developer from considering the development task complete until after all components are both delivered and accepted. [133]

Should an alternate software developer be needed to assume unfulfilled development duties, a user must be able to supply documentation on that software already completed and delivered. This documentation would readily assist the new developer in completing the software system in progress.

Davidson advises that, in implementing project controls, both parties should govern their contractual relationship by business sense standards. These standards require the user to make good faith requests, reasonable in view of the agreement and its circumstances. The vendor must also be responsive to the concerns of the user in acquiring the desired system. In negotiating the agreement, concepts should be emphasized over clause language. While such advice is seemingly obvious, many user-vendor agreements fail from the beginning when the contract does not convey the intent or desires of the parties in procuring a system. Flexibility and creativity in applying business judgment to negotiations assure that the user concepts coincide with the needs and problems of the vendor attempting to achieve them. [134]

VI. WARRANTIES IN COMPUTER ACQUISITIONS

The United States Congress has not enacted the Uniform Commercial Code (UCC) as part of the federal statutory law, but the UCC has become state law in all jurisdictions except Louisiana.[135] Although most of the states have adopted the model code of the UCC without change, some have modified sections of it.[136] "The purpose and policies of the UCC are to simplify, clarify and modernize the law governing commercial transactions, and to permit the continued expansion of commercial practices through custom, usage and agreement of the parties."[137] Further, the Code is to "be liberally construed and applied to promote its underlying purposes and policies."[138]

Article 2 of the Uniform Commercial Code embraces the law of sales. Its scope applies to "transactions in goods."[139] The Code defines a "sale" as "the passing of title from the seller to the buyer for a price,"[140] and "goods" to "mean all things (including specially manufactured goods) which are moveable at the time of identification in the contract for sale."[141] The sale of computer equipment falls within the scope of Article 2.[142]

A. Express Warranties

Warranties that are discussed in this section arise in connection with the sale of computer equipment, and software bundled with the equipment. The various courts have not reached concensus as to whether a computer program is a good or service as defined under the UCC. Such detailed analysis of the various theories is not necessary for a clear understanding of protectable warranties.

The UCC does not expressly define the term 'warranty.' However, a warranty can be thought of as a form of promise by one party to the contract that certain facts about the goods are true or that certain events will occur as promised.[143] An *express* warranty is a promise or affirmation of fact that becomes the basis of the bargain.[144] The express warranties are a statutorily mandated integral portion of any contract under the scope of the UCC. As such, they go clearly to the 'essence' of the contract as would any negotiated aspects of the bargain.[145] An express warranty can be not only an affirmation of fact by the seller but also a description of the goods or exhibitions of samples. If any of these aspects are made part of the bargain, no specific intention to make a warranty is necessary.[146] The seller does not have to use formal words like "warrant" or "guarantee" to create an express warranty.[147]

The applicability of the UCC to acquisition contracts arises in the disclaimer of warranties cases. In offering hardware or software for sale, the vendor is bound to provide a product that will perform comparably to the sample product. Statements of fact regarding the product, performance and descriptions of the product create express warranties that the product will conform to the specifications of the demonstrated sample.[148] A buyer may also reasonably assume that the vendor has title to the computer product and that the vendor may convey that title for consideration.[149]

Disclaimers of express warranties, which typically appear in form contracts, are not favored under the UCC. Such clauses will not be honored by a court if the terms are inconsistent with express warranties which form the basis of the agreement. The UCC does not consider a writing to be final on all matters that were agreed upon. Thus, a vendor is held liable not only for representations expressly made by using the words "warrant" or "warranties" but also for any statements made to the buyer which formed the basis of the bargain.

Sales and promotional literature as well as advertising can provide the basis for an express warranty.[150] To the extent that specifications are incorporated by reference into the contract, they may create the basis for express warranties. Statements that are clearly the seller's opinion or recommendation do not constitute warranties.[151]

An example of how courts deal with express warranties and attempts to disclaim them is *Consolidated Data Terminals v. Applied Digital Data Systems.*[152] In this case a distributor of computer terminals sued the manufacturer for breach of warranty. There was no substantial dispute that the terminals were poorly designed and failed to perform according to specifications. The specifications represented that the computer would operate at a speed of 19,200 baud. These specifications constituted an express warranty because the distributor relied on them when ordering the terminals. None of the terminals ever operated at 19,200 baud, and the specification on the terminal was ultimately reduced to 1,900 baud, less than one-tenth the speed originally promised.

The manufacturer contended that even if the computer failed to perform as promised, the warranty disclaimer clause incorporated into each contract negated any other promise contained in oral or written descriptions of the goods or in promotional literature. The court concluded that the disclaimer cannot be permitted to override the highly particularized warranty created by the specifications.[153]

Where a contract includes both specific warranty language and a general disclaimer of warranty liability, the former prevails when the two cannot be reasonably reconciled.[154] An attempt to both warrant and refuse to warrant goods creates an ambiguity which can only be resolved by making one term yield to the other.[155]

Since descriptions and performance specifications which are included in the agreement usually qualify as express warranties, the purchaser can usually obtain greater contract protection if sales literature describing the system, the vendor's proposal, and technical specifications comprising the request for proposal are incorporated in the contract. Form contracts which disclaim all warranties and substitute a repair or replacement clause are useless to users who have executed maintenance agreements ancillary to the procurement contract. To avoid creation of a limited warranty resulting from a disclaimer of warranties, users should obtain or incorporate by reference in the final agreement as many of the preliminary documents or statements as possible which formed the basis of agreement and insist that all substantial documents which describe the commitments of the parties be made an express part of the agreement. If the goods or services do not conform to the express warranty, the vendor may be liable for breach of the warranty.

On occasion, the question may arise as to whether the seller's statement was 'puffing' or an express war- ranty.[156] The answer is based on whether the statement formed part of the basis of the bargain.[157] The law recognizes that some sellers' statements are only puffing, and not express warranties.[158] Section 2-313 of the UCC provides that "[a]n affirmation merely of the value of the goods or a statement purporting to be merely the seller's opinion or commendation of the goods does not create a warranty."[159]

When a contract has been reduced to a writing which the parties intend to be a complete statement of their agreement, this contract may not be contradicted by a prior or contemporaneous agreement.[160] However, the court may admit evidence, intended to show course of dealing,[161] usage of trade,[162] course of performance,[163] or to explain or supplement the terms of the contract of the vendor and buyer, so that the true understanding of the parties may be reached. This is called the parol evidence rule and is important in computer acquisitions since it relates to the problems of establishing express warranties or other terms not specifically covered by the language of the agreement.[164]

Under the Uniform Commercial Code, vendors can protect themselves against warranty liability that can arise from implied warranties and express warranties.[165] However, *Carl Beasley Ford, Inc. v. Burroughs Corporation* [166] illustrates the extent to which the courts will go to ensure a fair trial. In this case the cause of action was based upon a breach of contract of an oral agreement by Burroughs Corporation for failing to supply to Carl Beasley Ford adequate software for a minicomputer system designed to handle the accounting functions for Carl Beasley.[167] The court based its decision upon a jury finding that a salesperson's promise, even if made orally, can be binding when it is made to clarify vagueness or generalities in the contract.

This case is of significant importance to the entire data processing industry, because, despite the presence of express disclaimer in the written contract, parol evidence was admitted to show an agreement for programming services, and consequential damages were allowed.[168]

B.   Implied Warranties

In the realities of computer contract procurement, it is not unusual for a contract to fail to reflect the essential representations of the vendor which the user relied upon in entering the contractual relationship. In the absence of express warranties, including these representations, a user may rely on implied warranties when considering the product unsatisfactory. An "implied" warranty is a promise arising by operation of law. It means that the goods delivered by a merchant in a given trade must be of a quality comparable to that generally acceptable in that line of trade.[169]

The warranty of merchantability is an implied affirmation that the goods are fit for the ordinary purposes for which they were purchased.[170] Breaches of the warranty of merchantability occur when defects in the goods purchased prevent their proper operation.[171] The breach of warranty of merchantability is a first cousin to product liability cases and strict tort liability.[172]

Under section 2-314 of the UCC a warranty of merchantability will be implied in a. contract for the sale of goods when the seller is a merchant.[173] Moreover, a warranty of merchantability under this section must be at least such as:

1) pass without objection in the trade under the contract description; and

2) in the case of fungible goods, are of fair average quality within the description; and

3) are fit for the ordinary purposes for which such goods are used; and

4) run, within the variations permitted by the agreement, of even kind, quality and quantity within each unit and among all units involved; and

5) are adequately contained, packaged, and labled as the agreement may require; and

6) conform to the promise or affirmations of fact made on the container or label if any. [174]

In contrast to an express warranty, a user need not prove reliance on vendor representations in order to allege a breach of the implied warranty of merchan-

ability.[175] However, when user dissatisfaction arises
from a lack of timely performance of the computer system,
as opposed to a total failure of the system, the warranty
of merchantability is of limited use in user-vendor
litigation.[176]

A more significant tool in resolving user-vendor
disputes is the implied warranty of fitness for a particular purpose.[177] These implied warranties do not rest
on the agreed upon aspects of the individual bargain but
rather on common factual situations or sets of conditions
which do not require particular language or actions to
evidence them.[178] Breach of this implied warranty occurs
when the vendor has reason to know the user's particular
purpose, that the user is relying on the vendor's skill
and judgment in furnishing the appropriate goods, and
that the user will in fact rely on the vendor's skill
and judgment.[179] It is not necessary that the user provide
actual knowledge to the vendor of the intended purpose
for the system in data processing situations. The vendor
may become aware of the user's intent through submitted
requests for proposal.

A particular purpose differs from an ordinary purpose in that it envisages a specific application by user
which is peculiar to the nature of the user's business.[180]
Ordinary purposes are those envisaged in the concept
of "merchantability" and relate to uses which are custom-
arily made of the goods in question.[181] As an example
of the distinction, under UCC section 2-315, the official
comment cites shoes, which are generally used for the

purpose of walking on ordinary ground, but which a seller may know are selected to be used for climbing mountains, jogging, or some other special purpose.[182] While reliance is not difficult to prove, a user must show actual dependence on the skill and judgment of the vendor in order to raise claims against the vendor based on implied warranty of fitness.[183]

The significance of the implied warranty of fitness is best illustrated in *Sperry Rand Corporation v. Industrial Supply Corporation.*[184] Industrial Supply Corp. (ISC) brought an action for the recision of its purchase of a record-keeping system and equipment. ISC is engaged in the business of selling and distributing steel, pipe, equipment, tools, and hardware. Its customers are industrial and agricultural users doing a large volume of business. Sperry Rand is in the business of manufacturing, selling and installing business systems, including automatic electronic data processing equipment. Industrial Supply, wanting to improve the efficiency of its record keeping system, invited several makers of electronic processing equipment to make surveys and recommendations. Conferences were held between representatives of Sperry Rand and Industrial Supply. Sperry Rand through its Univac division made the following recommendations:

> 1. We recommend the use of [Remington Rand Univac] as the one best suited to a tailor made job for your organization.

> 2. We have demonstrated the fact that through the use of RRU punched card procedures and exclusive equipment features, we can produce your records and reports more economically, faster and accurate [sic] than your present operation. [185]

The district court found that Sperry Rand's statements were representations and not merely the opinions of salesmen and that the equipment was not reasonably fit for the purpose and use for which it was intended and had been recommended. The *Sperry Rand* court traced the development of implied warranty of fitness for a disclosed purpose. The court stated that at common law the doctrine of caveat emptor applies to all sales unless there is an express warranty of the seller or a warranty is implied by operation of law. More specifically,

> [W]here a person contracts to supply an article in which he deals for a particular purpose, knowing the purpose for which he supplies it and that the purchaser has no opportunity to inspect the article, but relies upon the judgment of the seller, there is an implied condition or "warranty" as it is called, that the article is fit for the purpose to which it is to be applied.[186]

The court stressed the requirements that the seller be possessed of a superior knowledge of the articles sold, that the seller know of the particular purpose for which the articles are required, that the buyer relies upon the skill and judgment of the seller, and that the seller is aware of such reliance by the buyer.

In addition to warranties of merchantability and fitness, a user can raise usage of trade in a claim against a vendor.[187] Usage of trade pertains to business practice regularity to justify an expectation that it will continue.[188] While this warranty provides an avenue of recourse to a disgruntled user who has agreed to exclusion of the warranties of merchantability and fitness for a particular purpose, usage of trade considerations are subject to express disclaimer.

Form contracts characteristically include general disclaimer of warranties. An example of such a provision reads:

> THE WARRANTIES STATED IN THIS AGREEMENT ARE EXCLUSIVE AND IN LIEU OF ALL OTHER WARRANTIES, EXPRESS, IM-PLIED OR STATUTORY, INCLUDING, BUT NOT LIMITED TO, ANY WARRANTY OF MERCHANTABILITY OR FITNESS FOR A PARTICULAR PURPOSE.

This provision applies to modifications as well as exclusions of implied warranties.[189] Any written disclaimer must be conspicuous. The warranty of fitness can be disclaimed only in writing but not necessarily in bold face type.[190]

Section 2-316 of the Uniform Commercial Code explicitly requires that, subject to subsection (3), any disclaimer of the warranty of merchantability must mention the word "merchantability". Comment 4 of the UCC states that the implied warranty of fitness for a particular purpose may be excluded by general language.[191] For example, the following language is sufficient to negate this warranty: "The warranties and guaranties herein set forth are made by us and accepted by you in lieu of all statutory or implied warranties or guaranties, other than title".[192]

W.R. Weaver Company v. Burroughs Corporation is a case that deals with express and implied warranties and attempts by the vendor to disclaim those warranties.[193] W.R. Weaver leased a computer that was designed to perform certain accounting procedures. At the same time, Burroughs, in a separate contract, agreed to provide and sell to Weaver's automated sales accounting, finished goods inventory control, payroll and related reports, accounts receivable with aging, and accounts payable. Burroughs, in addition to the lease agreement and the sales contract, executed and delivered to Weaver the following documents:

> Burroughs Corp. will, as provided in the cost of software programming, include the services of our district systems analyst to completely define your accounting needs and design a working system to meet your specific requirements. You will also receive the complete support of our local force in training your staff both prior to and after completion of the installation.

> Burroughs Corp. further agrees that software, as listed in addendum for application software support, will be operable prior to installation.

The original agreement was that all accounting programs, with the exception of the accounts payable, would be operable at the time of installation. During the first year of the computer's use, only the payroll program was in normal operation. Weaver discontinued the use of the equipment and the programs and filed suit. Weaver alleged a breach of an express warranty and implied warranties of fitness and merchantability.

Burroughs, as a lessor in the lease agreement and seller in the equipment sales contract, argued that the written contract between the parties specifically excluded any warranty, express or implied, of merchantability or of fitness for a particular purpose and, therefore, no such warranties existed.

The court stated that a warranty that is implied from the existence of a written contract is as much a part of the writing as the express terms of the contract. The court further held that if there is any ambiguity concerning the combined effect of an expressed warranty and a warranty exclusion, the doubt will be resolved in favor of the express warranty.[194]

In summary, if a seller's statement created an express warranty, words disclaiming that warranty will have no effect. The disclaiming language is inherently inconsistent. Most attempts are made to disclaim the implied warranties of merchantability and fitness for a particular purpose. Any written disclaimer must be conspicuous. The warranty of fitness can be disclaimed only in writing, while the implied warranty of merchantability must specifically mention the word 'merchantability.' However, standard form contracts are now being used by vendors who sell computer equipment that contain blanket disclaimers of any express or implied warranties. If the end result is unfair, courts may strike down such provisions or the contract entirely.

VII.   TAX PLANNING IN COMPUTER ACQUISITIONS

After making the decision to purchase or up-grade a computer system, the user should determine, before any commitments are made, what the financial consequences of a lease or a purchase would be to the business operation. If the user elects a straight rental or lease, the lease payment can be treated as a business expense.[195] If the user chooses an outright purchase, the equipment may be depreciated under the Acelerated Cost Recovery System (ACRS) and the Investment Tax Credit (ITC). The rule as to who is entitled to the tax benefits associated with ownership of property focus on the economic substance of the transaction, not its form. If the user decides to lease the equipment, the person claiming ownership for federal tax purposes must show sufficient economic indicia of ownership to claim the tax benefits.

In most contracting situations, the purchaser or lessee is responsible for all taxes imposed as a result of the transaction. These taxes may include federal, state and municipal as well as excise, sales use, property, or occupational taxes.

A.   Purchase

The choice of whether to lease or purchase requires a full consideration of the tax consequences and alternatives of both.[196] Before making any decisions regarding the acquisition of computer equipment, the buyer should evaluate three tax considerations: 1) The Accelerated

Cost Recovery System (ACSR)[197] 2) the Investment Tax Credit,[198] and 3) equipment leasing under the Economic Recovery Tax Act of 1981 (ERTA).[199]

Accelerated Cost Recovery System

For property placed in service after December 31, 1980, the Economic Tax Recovery Act of 1981 (ERTA) imposed an accelerated cost recovery system (ACRS).[200] Prior to 1981, the taxpayer could choose to use a straight line method, declining balance, or the sum of the years digit method to compute depreciation.[201] ERTA replaced this prior depreciation system with a new mandatory cost recovery system in which eligible property is recovered over a period of 3, 5, 10, 15 or 18 years.[202] ACRS radically altered the depreciation of property. Part of the alteration was in the use of terminology. The word "depreciation" was replaced by "cost recovery", and property that applied under the new rules was termed "recovery property".[203] The term "recovery property" means tangible property that is subject to the allowance for depreciation that is used in a trade or business or held for the production of income.[204] Almost all computer hardware, and software bundled with the acquisition of hardware, will qualify as recovery property under ACRS.[205]

ACRS permits a taxpayer to depreciate qualifying property on an accelerated basis over relatively short periods. Under ACRS most property, which includes computer equipment, is given a five-year 'write-off' period regardless of the useful life of the equipment.[206] However, the taxpayer may elect a recovery period of 5, 12, or 25 years using a straight line method over the recovery period chosen.[207] Whatever method the taxpayer chooses, recovery is on a property-to-property basis.[208] The entire cost of the depreciable property is recovered under the prescribed statutory period, and the salvage value of the equipment is not used to reduce the basis upon which the ACRS is computed.[209]

Gain or loss is recognized on the sale or other disposition of computer equipment unless other provisions specify that non-recognition treatment is applicable.[210] Generally, all depreciation taken on personal property is subject to recapture at the time of its sale or disposition.[211] When a computer system is sold or disposed of, any gain on the disposition is taxable as ordinary income to the extent of the ACRS depreciation already taken.[212] If computer equipment is transferred to a new or controlled corporation, the transferor may recognize a taxable gain if the adjusted basis of the computer assets is less than the amount of liabilities to which the assets are subject, plus any other liabilities assumed by the transferee in the transaction.[213]

Investment Tax Credit

The Investment Tax Credit (ITC) permits a taxpayer to reduce tax liability by a percentage of the investment in statutorily defined eligible property. The purpose for the credit is to encourage taxpayers to invest in eligible equipment and, in turn, to stimulate the economy. The ITC is governed by sections 46-50 of the Internal Revenue Code. Section 46 stipulates that a credit against income tax is allowed for qualified investment in certain property.[214]

Property which qualifies for the credit allowed is known as section 38 property.[215] The Tax Reform Act of 1984 (TRA) repealed the old section 38 that originally enabled the taxpayer to take the investment tax credit. Section 46(a) still grants the credit, and section 48(a) defines qualifying property as section 38 property, a designation which has become a term of art.

Section 38 property refers to property that is subject to depreciation, has an estimated life of three years or more (determined as of the time property is placed in service), and is tangible personal property, or any other tangible property used as an integral part of manufacturing, production, extraction, or electrical energy, gas, water, or sewage disposal services.[216] If hardware and software are bundled as a single acquisition item, the ITC will generally be available for the entire acquisition.

The Investment Tax Credit rate is ten percent of the investment in section 38 property.[217] This is applied to qualifying property placed in service during the tax year. For ACRS recovery property, the qualified investment is 60 percent for three-year property.[218]

If the taxpayer sells or disposes of the property before the end of the three-year recovery period, part of the tax credit must be recaptured.[219] Thus, the taxpayer must increase tax liability by a portion of the credit taken.[220] A taxpayer who has any unused investment tax credit may carry back the unused credit three years, and carry forward the unused credit up to 15 years.[221]

B. Lease

Tax considerations and obsolesence are often significant in determining whether to buy or lease computer equipment.[222] Leasing minimizes cash outlay, spreading cash requirements over several years. Also, lessors may take advantage of their credit ratings and the consequent lower interest costs. However, with leasing, the advantages of ownership may be lost.

Whether a transaction is treated as a purchase or a lease for tax purposes is important in determining who is entitled to the investment tax credit and such business-expenses as depreciation, rent, and interest payments. Under the Internal Revenue Code's special rules for leases, the lessor is deemed to have entered into the lease in the course of carrying on a trade or business and is allowed the ACRS deduction and the Investment Tax Credit on the leased property. In this way the depreciation deduction and Investment Tax Credit can be transferred to a taxpayer who might not otherwise qualify to claim the deductions and credits. However, there is a 50 percent limit on the amount that lessors can reduce their income tax liability. The finance lease tax benefits are for property placed in service after 1983 and before October 1, 1985.

With the lease of computer equipment, tax benefits may be transferred from the potential lessee to the corporate lessor. If the user wishes to acquire computer equipment under a lease, the equipment must be finance-lease property.[223] Such property is recovery property subject to a qualified agreement and, if acquired by the lessee, would have been new section 38 property having a useful life of three years or more.[224]

The qualified agreement between the lessor and lessee must meet the following guidelines: 1) the computer equipment must be leased within three months of acquisition;[225] 2) the lessor must be a corporation other than a subchapter S corporation or a personal holding company; 3) the lessor and lessee must characterize the agreemet as a lease; and 4) the agreement must allow the lessee to purchase the property at a fixed price which is not less than ten percent of the original cost of the property to the lessor (such property may qualify as recovery property even if it is not readily usable by any person other than lessee). Under such guidelines, the agreement would be treated as a lease, and the lessor under the agreement would be treated as the owner of the property.[226] The rules generally apply to lease agreements entered into after December 31, 1983.

As an illustration of how tax benefits may be transferred from a potential lessee to a corporate lessor, suppose a first corporation wishes to acquire a $2 million computer system which is finance-lease property with an eight-year economic life and falling within the five-year ACRS class. A second corporation is a 'person' meeting the requirement of being neither a subchapter S corporation nor a personal holding company and wishes to be the owner of the computer system for federal tax law purposes.

Both corporations enter into an agreement that is characterized as a lease. The agreement provides that the second corporation has the right to purchase the property for $200,000. Because of the special software that was developed for the first corporation as part of this lease, the computer equipment is of a type not readily usable by any person other than the first corporation. The second corporation purchases the equipment from the manufacturer for $2 million.

The time and amount of the rental payments required of the first corporation (as the lessee-user) under the lease will be exactly equal to the timing and amount of the principal and interest payments that the second corporation (the lessor) must make to the bank for the purchase money note. Under these circumstances the second corporation is treated as the owner and lessor of the property for federal tax law purposes and is entitled to the investment tax credit and the ACRS deductions on the property. The second corporation must report the rent as income and is entitled to deduct the interest on the purchase money note.[227]

The lessee of computer equipment may negotiate with the lessor for the credit pass-through as part of the contract agreement.[228] Lessors may elect to transfer the investment tax credit for the new section 38 property to the lessee of the computer equipment.[229] The pass-through is subject to statutorally mandated conditions. The conditions used to decide whether a transaction is a lease or a purchase require the IRS to look to the intent of the parties as the controlling factor.[230] To determine intent, the IRS examines whether the following factors exist: 1) the rental payments are credited against the option price; 2) automatic passage of the title occurs at end of the lease; 3) the rental payments exceed the fair rental value; 4) total payments are equal to the purchase price plus interest; 5) there are high front end payments; 6) a nominal purchase option is available; and 7) portions of the payments are iden- tifiable as interest.[231] Clearly, the IRS determination of the transaction as lease or purchase has significant financial implications relative to the tax imposed on the user in acquiring the computer equipment.

VIII. SPECIAL CONSIDERSATIONS IN SOFTWARE DEVELOPMENT CONTRACTS

A user may acquire software that is compatible with the computer hardware by either purchasing already developed packages or contracting for a custom-written package. Software, as the sales product upon which development companies are based, is necessarily protected as proprietary. Such software is furnished by a vendor through a non-exclusive, non-transferrable license. Software not protected by patent is licensed with strict provisions to preserve its confidentiality.[232]

While machine readable object code is freely available to the user, source code intelligible to human readers is typically restricted from release. Such restrictions, essential to the continuing commercial life of the software developer, create serious problems for the user in accessing the software if the developer ceases to provide maintenance services or goes bankrupt. Contract provisions which allow a user access to the source code under these circumstances may prove ineffective if courts seize the code as property to offset bankruptcy debts. Purchase agreements for software should therefore include provision for an escrow agent who holds the source code for release. Criteria under which the escrow agent may release a copy of the source code are:

1) written notification by the software vendor;

2) liquidation by the software vendor;

3) appointment of a trustee in bankruptcy for the software vendor;

4) dissolution of the software vendor;

5)   insolvency of the software vendor; and

6)   an agreed-upon failure of the vendor to service the software. 233

For software classified as trade secret, the purchase agreement will include stringent limits on distribution. Thus, a vendor may contractually limit the use of the program to specified processors and may restrict the generation of any copies. However, if a user modifies such programs or purchases a new program, the original vendor may not maintain a claim that such software infringes upon trade secret information. 234

The purchase agreement must also specify title in the software. The retainer of residual or proprietary rights by either vendor or buyer, including rights to license to a third party, should be carefully described. 235 The title to improvements made on the software package should be partitioned at the agreement negotiation stage to avoid subsequent protracted litigation. Should ownership remain with the software developer, the purchaser should seek to include indemnity clauses for infringement suits based on copyright or patent. 236

Software development and service agreements raise a different set of problems in contracting. Circumstances affecting the contract include variables such as:

1)   knowledge and experience of the buyer;

2)   nature of the code furnished, whether object of source code;

3)   value of the contract;

4)   nature of the contract exposure;

5)   distribution of the software;

6) nature of the contract itself as fixed price development or time and materials or a combination or a shop contract;

7) software with or without custom features;

8) additional services bundled or unbundled with the software; or

9) the vendor as a specialist versus a generalist. [237]

In view of the effect of these variables on otherwise standardized contracts, a development contract must define functional specifications to establish common understanding of purpose between user and developer.

A common misunderstanding arises in expectation of time to effect delivery and to debug errors. Such a misunderstanding is complicated by user changes in functional requirements after the work has commenced. The user may, for instance, decide that more memory or faster mechines are necessary in order to obtain the desired quality of service. These changes radically affect the perspective of the developer in creating the software package.[238]

Software developers may also be delayed by the unavailability of hardware for testing. The absence of necessary programmers further hampers development efforts. Lastly, the development project may be delayed by a gross underestimate of the amount of work necessary to create an operable system. [239]

Users, disgruntled by seemingly unnecessary delays, may be precluded from transferring the contract to another software developer by the nature of the software.

Characteristically, software development is nearly impossible to pick up midstream. However, by breaking payment into at least two portions, the user retains the option of seeking help from other vendors. For example, if 15 percent of the payment is rendered at the software definition stage and the remainder paid on completion, the user can break contractual relations on the basis of dissatisfaction. Implementation of the second stage may proceed either with the same or an alternate vendor.[240]

Control of software, as a valuable property right, depends on the allocation of proprietary rights. Copyright attaches proprietary rights to works rendered in tangible form. For software created under a development contract, the user will be considered the author unless otherwise specifically agreed.[241] Thus, it will be user rather than the software developer who retains the right to license the developed software. [242]

Trade secret is characteristically effective only where distribution may be restricted. Software protected as trade secret realizes no statutory protection against infringement. As such, a software developer insured by trade secret appropriation is limited in a court action to injunctive relief and damages.[243]

In allocating the rights in software, the vendor is concerned with maintaining his rights to continue to program in a specific industry. Development agreements should not transfer all rights in a software package to the user, lest they have the effect of contractually precluding the developer from ever continuing in the trade. Rights which should be retained by the vendor include the right to use or authorize others to use software that is not specific to the initial purchaser. Developers should also be able to develop functionally similar software for in-house use or for third parties. Rights to all vendor-furnished software tools should vest in the vendor. 244

Developers may further be precluded from a software market by programmers who leave their employment with the programming in hand. Developers may circumvent this problem by requesting an agreement from the programmer not to engage in a directly competing business for a reasonable period of time. However, when the programmer is the one person most familiar with the developers software package, developers may best be able to meet the users needs for updates by having the programmer agree to continue to work on the program on a limited basis. 245

In view of significant investments made by users to obtain a desired software package, the distribution of proprietary rights is of prime concern to users. Under the development contract, users should retain sufficient rights to permit normal corporate reorganizations without destroying the license agreement. Access to the software by third parties such as programmers, auditors or consultants necessary to normal user business practice should not constitute a license violation. The user should also be able to perform normal data processing operations and maintenance without breaching the agreement with the vendor. 246

Essential to the creation of any development contract is the recognition that the document embodies the working relationship between the parties. For example, a vendor may not be held liable for failing to repair a problem in the software if the user does not document the circumstances which led to that problem. A development contract requires the active participation of both parties. Therefore, in accurately describing the allocation of responsibility between each of the parties, the intent of the parties in creating a useful software package may be fulfilled. [247]

IX. CONCLUSION

The basis for a procurement contract is the allocation of risk. Where the technology is known, contract terms reflect the intent of the parties in distributing risk for untimely delivery or for nonperformance. However, where the technology contracted for is unknown, an undeveloped allocation of risk for failure or technological innovation is problematic. As held in the 1966 case, *United States v. Wegematic Corp.*, the promotion of an electronic system as a revolutionary breakthrough supports the conclusion that the system was already in existence. [248] Thus there was no basis to justify placing the risk of the revolution's occurrence on the purchaser. Because the contract specified delivery of a particular computer system, rather than development of that system, the risk had to fall upon the vendor. [249]

The plaintiff in *United States v. Wegematic* alleges misrepresentation of the benefits to be derived from the new technology. The vendor assumes the risk of failure

when an inexperienced computer user relies on the representations of the state of the art by more knowledgeable
parties. However, when the parties are relatively sophisticated, the question of allocation of risk is not
so clear. In analyzing risk distribution for new technology, it may be more equitable to assign risk or loss
to the party most capable to bear economic loss. Moreover, the party with the decision-making power throughout the development process should assume the responsibility for potential loss.[250] Of equal importance to risk
allocation is the determination of the state of the art
and of the nature of the innovation. The extent to which
representations are considered inaccurate will depend
on the standard of knowledge of the mythical person who
is skilled in the art.

Until common law and statutory regulation establish standards for professional regulation and licensing,
risk allocation will rest on the sophistication of contract
negotiation.[251] Contracts to procure innovative products
must be matched with equal flexibility and creativity in
draftsmanship.

X. FOOTNOTES

1. J.T. Westermeier, *Practical Considerations in Contracting for Computer Equipment Products and Services/Litigating Computer-Related Disputes* 2 (1983) [hereinafter cited as Westermeier].

2. Freed, *Negotiating For a Computer Without Negotiating Trouble.* Computer Law Service §3-2 Art. 1 at 7-9.

3. *Id.*

4. D. Brandon & S. Segelstein, *Data Processing Contracts Structure, Contents, and Negotiation* 5 (1976)

5. Westermeier, *supra* note 1, at 7.

6. *Id.* at 7.

7. *Id.* at 7.

8. J. Soma, *Computer Technology and the Law* 83 (1985) [hereinafter cited as Soma].

9. *Id.* at 84.

10. 35 U.S.C. §287 (1976).

11. 17 U.S.C. §102 (1976).

12. 17 U.S.C. §405(b) (1976).

13. 17 U.S.C. §504(c)(2) (1976); this section states that the copyright owner may elect, prior to final judgment, to recover actual damages and profits or statutory damages for all infringements. In the event that an infringer proves he was unaware or had no reason to believe that his acts constituted infringement, the court may reduce statutory damages to a sum not less than $100.

14.   R. Bigelow, *Contract Caveats*, Computer Law Service §3-1 Art. 3 at 5 (1979).

15.   7 CLSR 953 (Army Service Board of Contract Appeals 1976).

16.   *Id.* at 968.

17.   *IBM v. Catamore Enters, Inc.* 548 F.2d 1065 (1st Cir. 1976).

18.   See note 18, *supra* at 967 citing *Penn-Ohio Steel Corp. v. United States,* 173 S.Ct. 1. 1064.

19.   658 F. 2d 650 (8th Cir. 1981).

20.   328 F. Supp. 653 (D. South Carolina 1970).

21.   Restatement (Second) of contracts §209 (1979).

22.   *Supra* note 20, at 1074.

23.   361 F. Supp. 325, 333 (E.D. Penn. 1973).

24.   461 F. Supp. 286, 7 CLSR72, 79, 80, (M.D. Penn, 1978).

25.   *Burroughs Corp. v. Chesapeake Petroleum and Supply Co., Inc.* 282 Md. 406, 384 A.2d 734, 6 CLSR 782 (Ct. of App. 1978).

26.   6 CLSR at 786.

27.   Soma, *supra* note 8, at 83.

28.   *Id.* at 83.

29.   Westermeier, *supra* note 1, at 8.

30.   604 F. 2d 737 (2nd Cir. 1979).

31.   *Teamsters Security Fund of Northern California, Inc. v. Sperry Rand Corp.,* 6 CLSR 951, 975 (N.D. Ca. 1977).

213

32.   *Id.*

33.   479 F. Supp. 738, 7 CLSR 388 (D.N.Y. 1979).

34.   G. Adam, M. Gordon, S. Starr, Contractual, Financial, and Tax Issues in Major Procurements, Computer Law Journal Vol. 10 465, 479 (1983) [hereinafter cited as Adam, Gordon and Starr].

35.   Soma, *supra* note 8, at 77.

36.   Adam, Gordon & Starr, *supra* note 34, at 479.

37.   *Id.* at 479.

38.   *Id.* at 479.

39.   *Id.* at 479.

40.   Davidson, *Project Controls in Computer Contracting,* Computer Law Journal 133, 142. [hereinafter cited as Project Controls].

41.   Adam, Gordon & Starr, *supra* note 34, at 481.

42.   R. Bernacchi, G. Larsen, *Data Processing Contracts and the Law,* 85-90 (1974) [hereinafter cited as Bernacchi & Larsen]

43.   *Id.* at 91.

44.   *Id.* at 98.

45.   *Id.* at 99.

46.   *Id.* at 103.

47.   *Id.* at 106.

48.   Project controls, *supra* note 40, at 143.

49.   *Id.* at 144.

50. Adam, Gordon & Starr, *supra* note 34, at 480.

51. Westermeier, *supra* note 1, at 20.

52. *Id.*

53. Project Controls, *supra* note 40, at 144.

54. *Id.* at 144.

55. *Id.* at 145.

56. *Id.* at 145.

57. *Id.* at 145.

58. Burn-in is defined as sufficient active time to determine component reliability.

59. Project controls, *supra* note 40, at 146.

60. Adam, Gordon & Starr, *supra* note 34, at 482.

61. Davidson, *Negotiating Procurements*, III Computer Law Journal 385, 392. [hereinafter cited as Negotiating Procurements]

62. Adam, Gordon & Starr, supra note 34, at 482.

63. Negotiating Procurements, *supra* note 61, at 392.

64. D. Myers, *More Seen to Contracts than Price, Delivery*, Computer World, Nov. 14, 1983 at 23.

65. Project controls, *supra* note 40, at 153.

66. Westermeier, *supra* note 1, at 18.

67. *Supra* note 42, at 574 to 586.

68. *Supra* note 40, at 154; Duncan Davidson advises a user to determine and have a vendor agree to an objective standard for determining up-time. For example, up-time percentages may be agreed to apply to critical components, and overall up-time agreed for the entire system.

69.   *Supra* note 61 at 394.

70.   *Id.*

71.   *Id.*

72.   *Supra* note 40 at 155-156.

73.   *Id.* at 156.

74.   *Id.*

75.   Negotiating Procurements, *supra* note 61 at 394.

76.   *Id.* at 395.

77.   *Id.* at 394-5.

78.   *Id.* at 395.

79.   *Supra* note 1, at 23.

80.   *Id.*

81.   Restatement of contracts 2d §33(2).

82.   *Id.* §34(a).

83.   *Id.* §235(2).

84.   4 A. Corbin, Corbin on Contracts §946(1951 & Supp. 1971).

85.   Adam, Gordon and Starr, *supra* note 34, at 509.

86.   *Id.*

87.   *Id.*

88.   *Id.*

89.   *Id.*

90.   *Clements Auto Co. v. Service Bureau Corp.*, 444 F.
       2d. 169 (8th Cir. 1971) [hereinafter cited as Clem-
       ents].

91. *Chesapeake Petroleum And Supply Co., v. Burroughs Corp.* **6** CLSR768 (Cir. Ct. Md. 1977).

92. *Diversified Environments, Inc. v. Olivetti Corp.,* 461 F. Supp. 286 (D. Pa. 1978).

93. *Id.* at 80-81.

94. Clements, *supra* note 90 at 175.

95. *Id.*

96. *Data Processing Contracts, supra* note 45, at 162-163.

97. *Id.* at 162-163.

98. *Id.* at 165.

99. *Supra* note 8, at 101.

100. R. Bigelow, Contract Disputes and Litigation, Introduction in Computer Law Service §3-5 at 1 (1981) [hereinafter Contract Dispute Introduction].

101. *Honeywell, Inc. v. Lithonia Lighting, Inc.* 317 F. Supp. 406, 2 CLSR 894 (NDGa. 1970).

102. *Fruit Industries Research Foundation v. National Cash Register Co.* 406 F.2d 546, 2 CLSR 92 (9th Cir. 1969).

103. *National Cash Register Co. v. Marshall Savings & Loan Ass'n,* 415 F.2d 1131, 2 CLSR 332 (7th Cir. 1969).

104. Contract Dispute Introduction, *supra* note 100, at 2.

105. Restatement of Contracts 2d §236(1).

106. *Id.* at §236(2).

107. J. Greenfield, *Computers: How to Protect Your Rights Rights When You Buy One,* Architectural Record 43-45 (April 1983).

108. *Chatlos Systems, Inc. v. National Cash Register Corp.* 670 F.2d 1304, 1306 (2nd. Cir. 1982).

109. *Id.* at 400-401.

110. *Convoy Corp. v. Sperry Rand Corp.*, 672 F.2d 781 (9th Cir. 1981), see also *Huntington Beach v. Continental Info. Sys.*, 621 F.2d 353 (9th Cir. 1980).

111. *Id.* at 783.

112. Clements, *supra* note 90, at 189.

113. Convoy, *supra* note 110, at 783 citing same case at 601 F.2d at 386-8.

114. *Chesapeake Petroleum And Supply Co. v. Burroughs Corp.*, 6 CLSR 768 (Cir. Ct. Md. 1977).

115. J.T. Westermeier, *supra* note 1, at 14.

116. Clements, *supra* note 90, at 191.

117. Convoy, *supra* note 110, at 785.

118. Data Processing Contracts, *supra* note 42, at 181.

119. *Id.* at 182-183.

120. Westermeier, *supra* note 1, at 18.

121. Data Processing Contracts, *supra* note 45, at 183.

122. Westermeier, *supra* note 1, at 18. See UCC section 2-718.

123. Chatlos, *supra* note 108. Facts derived from district court opinions cited at 479 F. Supp. 738. (D.N.J. 1979).

124. Westermeier, *supra* note 1, at 16.

125. See Convoy, *supra* note 110, and discussion of facts in district court, 7 CLSR 1021 (D. Ore. 1977).

126. Chesapeake, *supra* note 114, at 769.

127. Project Controls, *supra* note 30, at 147-148.

128. *Id.* at 149-150.

129. *Id.* at 148.

130. *Id.* at 150.

131. *Id.* at 150-151.

132. *Id.* at 151-152

133. *Id.* at 151-152.

134. *Id.* at 157-158.

135. J. White & R. Summers, *Handbook of the Law Under the Uniform Tax Cote* [1] [hereinafter cited as White & Summers].

136. R. Bernacchi & G. Larsen, *Data Processing Contracts and the law* 138 (1974) [hereinafter cited as Bernachi].

137. U.C.C. §1-102(2)(a)(b)(1978).

138. U.C.C. §1-102(1).

139. U.C.C. §2-102.

140. U.C.C. §2-106(1).

141. U.C.C. §2-105(1).

142. The application of Article 2 of the Uniform Commercial Code to computer products has, itself, been extensively analyzed. Section 2-102 (transactions in goods), section 2-105(1)(goods are those things moveable at the time of identification to the contract for sale), and section 2-106(1)(sale is passing

of title for a price) apply to transactions of computer goods. Article 2 is also applicable to transactions such as leases, bailments, distributorship agreements, and service contracts. See, Mc-Gonigal, *Application of Uniform Commercial Code to Software Contracts*, Computer Law Service section 3-3 Art. 4 at 1 (1978).

143. Bernacchi, *supra* note 41, at 140.

144. U.C.C. §2-313(1)(a).

145. U.C.C. §2-313, comment 1.

146. U.C.C. §2-313, comment 3.

147. U.C.C. 2-313(2).

148. U.C.C. §2-312.

149. Section 2-313 of the Uniform Commercial Code reads in full:

(1) Express warranties by the seller are created as follows:

(a) Any affirmation of fact or promise made by the seller to the buyer which relates to the goods and becomes part of the basis of the bargain creates an express warranty that the goods shall conform to the affirmation or promise.

(b) Any description of the goods which is made part of the basis of the bargain creates an express warranty that the goods shall conform to the description.

(c) Any sample or model which is made part of the basis of the bargain creates an express warranty that the whole of the goods shall conform to the sample or model.

(2) It is not necessary to the creation of an express warranty that the seller use formal words such as "warrant" or "guarantee" or that he have intention to make a warranty, but an affirmation merely of the value of the goods or a statement purporting to be merely the seller's opinion or commendation of the goods does not create a warranty.

150. Marcellino, Nycum, Sherry, *Warranties, Limitation of Remedies and Limitation of Actions,* Annual Computer Law Institute: Current Issues in Computer Contract Law 258 (1983) [hereinafter cited as Marcellino].

151. *Id.* at 259.

152. 708 F.2d 385 (9th Cir. 1985).

153. *Id.* at 391.

154. U.C.C. §2-316 provides:

> Words or conduct relevant to the creation of an express warranty and words or conduct tending to negate or limit warranty shall be construed wherever reasonable as consistent with each other; but subject to the provisions of this Article on parol or extrinsic evidence negation or limitation if inoperative to the extent that such construction is unreasonable.

155. Wilson Trading Corp. v. David Ferguson Ltd.

156. White & Summers, *supra* note 135, at 430.

157. *Id.* at 328.

158. *Id.* at 329.

159. U.C.C. §2-313(2).

160. U.C.C. §2-202.

161. U.C.C. §1-205(1) course of dealing-relates a sequence of previous dealings between the parties on similar transactions prior to the making of the contract. This is a common basis of understanding for interpreting their expressions and other conduct.

162. U.C.C. §1-205(2)-usage of trade-is a practice or method of dealing, having such regularity of observance in a place, vocation or trade as to justify an expectation that it will be observed in a place, vocation or trade as to justify an expectation that it will be observed with respect to the transaction in question.

163. U.C.C. §2-208(1) - course of performance-where the contract for sale involves repeated occasions for performance by either party with knowledge of the nature of the performance and opportunity for objection to it by either party.

164. Bernacchi, *supra* note 136, at 144.

165. U.C.C. §2-316(1) Exclusion or Modification of Warranties (1) Words or conduct relevant to the creation of an express warranty and words or conduct tending to negate or limit warranty shall be construed whever reasonable as consistent with each other; but subject to the provisions of this Article on parol or extrinsic evidence negation or limitation is inoperative to the extent that such construction is unreasonable.
(2)...Lauguage to exclude all implied warranties of fitness is sufficient if it states for example, that "There are no warranties which extend beyond the description on the face hereof."
(3)(a) unless the circumstances indicate otherwise, all implied warranties are excluded by expressions like "as is", with all faults" or other language which in common understsanding calls the buyer's attention to the exclusion of warranties and makes plain that there is no implied warranty.

166. 361 F. Supp. 325, Affd. without published opinion 493 F.2d 1400 (1974).

167. Bernacchi, *supra* note 136, at 707 no. 1-162.

168. R. Raysman, *Warranty Disclaimer in the Data Processing Contract*, 6 Journal of Computer and Law 265, 269.

169. U.C.C. §2-314, Comment 2.

170. J.T. Westermeier, Jr., *Practical Considerations in Contracting for Computer Equipment Products and Services/Litigating Computer-Related Dispute* 11 Nov. 3, 1983) (unpublished)[hereinafter cited as J.T. Westermeier]

171. *Id.*

172. White & Summers, *supra* note 135, at 343.

173. One can be a merchant by "dealing in goods" or "otherwise by his occupation" holding himself out as having knowledge or skill peculiar to the practice or goods involved.

174. U.C.C. §2-314.

175. *Id.*

176. Bernacchi, *supra* note 136, at 146-147.

177. U.C.C. 2-315.

178. Marcellino, *supra* note 150, at 259.

179. J.T. Westermeier, *supra* note 170, at 12.

180. Marcellino, *supra* note 150, at 260.

181. *Id.*

182. *Id.*

183. Bernacchi, *supra* note 136, at 150-151.

184. 337 F.2d. 363(5th Cir. 1964).

185. *Id.* at 366.

186. *Id.* at 369.

187. U.C.C. §2-314(3).

188. Bernacchi, *supra* note 136, citing U.C.C. 1-205(1).

189. White & Summers, *supra* note 135, at 438.

190. *Id.*

191. *Id.* at 439.

192. *Id.*

193. *W R. Weaner Company v. Burroughs Corporation* **580** S.W. 2d 76 (Tex. Cir. App. 1979).

194. *Id.* at 80 & 81.

195. I.R.C. §162(a)(1984).

196. Soma, *supra* note 8, at 114.

197. I.R.C. §168(1984).

198. I.R.C. §46 (1984).

199. I.R.C. §168(8)(F)(1984).

200. A. Rosenberg, *Tax Shelters* 409 (R. Schapiro 3rd. ed. 1983)[hereinafter cited as Tax Shelters].

201. I.R.C. §167 (1984).

202. I.R.C. §168 (1984).

203. Tax Shelters, *supra* note 200, at 409.

204. I.R.C. §168(c)(1)(A)&(B)(1984).

205. Rev. Rul. 71-177.

206. I.R.C. §168(c)(2)(B)(f)(1984).

207. I.R.C. §168(b)(3)(g)(1984).

208. I.R.C. §168(b)(3)(B)(ii)(1984).

209. I.R.C. §168(f)(9)(h)(1984).

210. I.R.C. §1001(c)(1984).

211. I.R.C. §1245 (1984).

212. Stand. Fed. Tax Rep. (CCH) 11 55.037.

213. I.R.C. §357(c)(1) I.R.C. 357(c)(1)(1984).

214. Stand. Fed. Tax Rep. (CCH) 11 509 (1984).

215. Treas. Reg. § 1.48-1(b).

216. *Id.*

217. I.R.C. §46(a)(1) & 46(b)(1984).

218. I.R.C. §46(c)(7)(B)(1984).

219. I.R.C. §47(a)(1)(1984).

220. I.R.C. §47(a)(3)(B)(1984).

221. I.R.C. §39(a)(1)(A)&(B)(1984).

222. R. Bernacchi, *Financial Aspects of Computer Contracting, Third Annual Computer Law Institute: Current Issues in Computer Contract Law* 59 (1983) [hereinafter cited as R. Bernacchi].

223. I.R.C. §168(f)(8)(A)(1984).

224. I.R.C. §48(b)(1984).

225. I.R.C. §168(f)(8)(B)(i)(1984).

226. I.R.C. §168(f)(8)(C),(i),(ii),(iii),(iv)(p)(1984).

227. I.R.C. §5c. 168(f)(8)-1(e)(1984).

228. I.R.C. §48(d).

229. *Id.*

230. R. Bernacchi, *supra* note 222, at 70.

231. Rev. Ruling 55-540 in Bernacchi, *supra* note 222, at 7c.

232. Westermeier, *supra*, note 1, at 24.

233. *Id.* at 25.

234. *Id.* at 25-26.

235.   R. McGonigal, *Software Contracts*,   Computers and the Law 174 (1981).

236.   Westermeier, *supra* note 1, at 26.

237.   P. Hoffman, *Software Development and Service Agreements*,   24 Jurimetrics 58-59 (1983) [hereinafter cited as Hoffman].

238.   *Id.* at 60.

239.   *Id.*

240.   *Id.* at 61.

241.   17 U.S.C. §201(b) (1976).

242.   Hoffman, *supra* note 145, at 61.

243.   *Id.* at 61-62..

244.   *Id.* at 62-63.

245.   R. Bigelow, *Programming Contracts*, Computer Law Service §3-4, Art. 3 at 2 (1976).

246.   Hoffman, *supra* note 145, at 63.

247.   *Id.* at 63.

248.   *United States v. Wegematic Corp.*, 360 F.2d 674, 676 (2d Cir. 1966).

249.   *Id.* at 676.

250.   L. Boorin, *Who Should Pay for Risk of Revolution in New Technologies?*, Computer Law Service §3-5 Art. 1 at 5 (1976).

251.   *Id.* at 6.

Independent research and preliminary writing by:

Arlene C. Halliday, B.A. Political Science, Merrimack College, J.D. Franklin Pierce Law Center has been an independent businesswoman and is presently in private practice.

Jennifer A. Tegfeldt, B.S. Biological Science, University of California, Davis, J.D. Franklin Pierce Law Center, registered patent agent, is presently a law clerk to the United States Court of Appeals for the Federal Circuit (1985-1987).

CHAPTER 5 - COMPUTERS AND PRIVACY

I.   INTRODUCTION

> On each landing, opposite the lift shaft, the
> poster with the enormous face gazed from the
> wall. It was one of those pictures which are
> so contrived that the eyes follow you about when
> you move. BIG BROTHER IS WATCHING YOU, the caption
> beneath it reads. . . . [In his apartment], the
> telescreen which could not be shut off, received
> and transmitted simultaneously. Any sound that
> Winston made . . . would be picked up by it;
> moreover, so long as he remained within the field
> of vision which the metal plaque commanded, he
> would be seen as well as heard . . . There was
> of course no way of knowing whether you were
> being watched at any given moment.[1]

These excerpts from George Orwell's novel, *1984*, portray the "anti-utopian" society "Oceania", in which the government kept every activity of its citizens under constant surveillance. While the insidiously pervasive controls described in *1984* generally represent the types of sensory invasions into individual privacy which concern many people today, computer technology has added profound new dimensions which threaten personal autonomy. For even in the ultimate totalitarian state which Orwell foresaw, Big Brother was not equipped with the massive, interconnectable, electronic data banks now in common usage by both governments and the private business sector.

II.   THE NATURE OF THE CONCERN

As early as 1972 computer technology existed that could maintain an on-line file containing the equivalent of 20 single-spaced typed pages of information about the personal history and selected activities of every man, woman and child in the United States.[2] It would have been possible to retrieve this information on any given individual within 30 seconds. Since 1972 the capacities and efficiencies of the computer-based files have vastly increased. Although a single giant data bank storing all this information does not exist at this time, separate computer systems can be networked, or othewise connected, to share such data. In effect the network of computers can create such an all-encompassing data bank.[3]

Prior to the evolution of computerized record-keeping, most business decisions concerning such benefits as credit, insurance and medical care were based upon personal knowledge of the individuals involved and upon the limited types of information which could be obtained from friends, associates and decentralized, uncoordinated public records. The very inefficiency of these sources and methods of information collection operated to preserve a measure of individual privacy.[4] In the past, large quantities of information about individuals were not available; information that was available was relatively superficial and maintained in manual, fragmented files with inefficient access. People in a mobile society were difficult to keep track of, and it was difficult to interpret and infer revealing information from the available data.[5]

However, present day business and government social planning requirements have generated increased demands for broad-based, easily accessible record keeping. Major innovations in information processing techniques over the past thirty years have made such record keeping possible. The increasingly pervasive role that government plays in our daily life, from taxation to welfare, from crime control to medical care would be thwarted without easy access to prodigious stores of demographic data amassed from seemingly innocuous lists of personal information.[6]

Alexander Solzhenitsyn observed that "as every man goes through life he fills in a number of forms for the record, each containing a number of questions . . . There are thus hundreds of little threads radiating from every man." Computer technology efficiently collects, combines, and analyzes these threads.[7] The most important organizational and governmental decisions in modern day society are based upon interpretations derived from that data. However, the social and economic benefits of this increasingly sophisticated technology have been achieved through substantial loss of individual privacy.[8]

As the erosion of personal privacy by computer technology has accelerated, the individual's ability to gain access to the information gathered or to control its use has diminished. Individuals are often unaware that personal data has even been gathered, much less combined with other bits of personal information from other data banks to formulate a new electronic "record image" that can affect their lives in many critical ways. Extensive dossiers are easily maintained on individuals who apply for credit, insurance, medical care or employment benefits.[9] Government, too, at all levels maintains extensive electronic files containing sensitive information about individuals who have sought government benefits or who have been subject to any form of criminal investigation. Sharing and combining this data among government agencies, among private organizations and between the government and private sectors is not uncommon and is actually facilitated by the nature of the technology itself.[10]

Aside from the intimidating and inhibiting effect created by the realization that one's "record image" is being formed from a compliation of information from several sources, there is the more chilling prospect that the data used as the basis for the profile may be outdated, inaccurate or both. The need to translate information into machine readable language before it can be stored in computer files increases the possibility of inaccuracies. This fact when combined with the terse, summary, unqualified form which information stored in computer systems often takes, further exacerbates the chances for errors. "The real threat to privacy, therefore, may not be the fact that computers can collect and store facts about individuals, but rather that inaccurate or dated information can be repeatedly used to evaluate the character, reputation, employability, or credit worthiness of an individual [and] that person may never know what information was used in the evaluation or from where the information was derived."[11] Additionally "[i]t has become apparent that as the technology of record keeping accelerates from the locked file drawer to time-shared, interconnected comuter networks systems, legislative and administrative bodies must prescribe the rules and procedures to limit invasions of privacy."[12]

III. DEVELOPMENT OF THE RIGHT TO PRIVACY

A. THE COMMON LAW

The earliest recognition of a legal right to privacy in the United States is attributed to the Michigan Supreme

Court in 1881. That court in the case of *DeMay v. Roberts*,[13] decided that the plaintiff, who had been observed while giving birth by the defendant masquerading as a physician's assistant, was allowed recovery on the basis of an unwarranted intrusion upon her personal privacy.[14] This right was not distinctly articulated until 1890 when Samuel Warren and Louis Brandeis published their treatise, "The Right to Privacy" in the Harvard Law Review.[15] By tracing previous cases, the recovery theories of which rested upon doctrines of defamation, property rights, breach of confidence and contract, the authorities concluded that it was really a central right to privacy that the courts had been protecting. They argued that it would be appropriate and efficient for courts to recognize this new independent right to personal autonomy as a basis for setting claims regarding a disclosure of information.

Once the acceptance of this right became more universal within the United States, protection of privacy was divided into four basic areas: 1) intrusion upon seclusion or solitude, or into the private affairs, of an individual; 2) public disclosure of embarrassing private facts regarding an individual; 3) publicity which placed an individual in a false light; and 4) appropriation of an individual's name or likeness (e.g. photograph) for monetary advantage.[16] At first the protection against intrusion was only applied to cases in which physical invasion or physical searches of an individual's property had occurred. To a great extent the privacy doctrine overlapped with the tort principles of trespass. Protection was then extended to cover certain kinds of sensory intrusions such as peering at individuals through windows and eavesdropping on private conversations with microphones or wiretaps.

The intrusion doctrine has also been extended to the area of personal records. The Third Circuit Court held in *Zimmer v. Wilson* , that an unauthorized prying into the plaintiff's bank records was a tortious invasion of the plaintiff's privacy.[17] Protection in this particular area has not been recognized to a significant extent.[18]

Protection against public disclosure of embarrassing private facts developed more slowly. The defendant in the case of *Brents v. Morgan*, had posted a sign in the window of his garage proclaiming that the plaintiff owed him a sum of money.[19] The court determined that this public disclosure had invaded the plaintiff's privacy. In 1931 the California Court of Appeals allowed recovery in *Melvin v. Reid,* for the defendant's acts of publicizing the plaintiff's past immoral ways.[20] This type of protection has been applied to such past facts as investigation about a robbery, indebtedness, medical history, personal conduct,[21] sentimental associations and the contents of personal letters.[22] The common law recognition of tortious invasions most nearly envision the kind of threat that computer based data banks pose to an individual's "information privacy."

The usual form of relief granted by the courts for these invasions is an award of substantial damages. Specific damage need not be alleged or proven since the nature of the wrong is emotional stress and not monetary loss. In addition, punitive damages may be indicated if malice on the part of the defendant can be established. Because invasion of privacy is generally regarded as a personal right and not a property right, courts of equity rarely grant injunctive relief.[23] A form of action for the tort of invasion of privacy is available in some form in practically all jurisdictions.[24]

B. THE CONSTITUTIONAL PROTECTION OF PRIVACY

The right to privacy is not specifically mentioned in the United States Constitution, yet the Supreme Court has repeatedly recognized such a right in its efforts to preserve the individual's control over personal image projected in the world.[25] This concept of individual autonomy involves a wide variety of interests which an individual might seek to have protected by claims asserted against government intrusions into his private life. The Supreme Court in protecting these interests has found a right of privacy implicit in the guarantees of the First[26] and Fourth Amendments[27] of the U.S. Constitution. In addition the Court has used the Ninth and Fourteenth Amendments and the "prenumbral concept"[28] to create a "zone of privacy" in which the individual is guaranteed a degree of liberty in making personal choices and decisions without fear of government intervention.[29]

For the most part, however, the Supreme Court has only ruled against the public disclosure of information stored in data bases when that disclosure would infringe upon a specific constitutional guarantee. For example, in *N.A.A.C.P. v. Alabama* the Court emphasized that government access to an organization's membership lists could constitute a restraint on the members' right of free association.

The latest Supreme Court decision dealing directly with the question of information privacy occurred in 1977. In that case, *Whalen v. Roe* ,[30] the invasion of privacy claim arose out of New York State's plan to formulate a computerized list of individuals who use certain prescription drugs. While generally denying that such a computer scheme violated a protected sphere of privacy, the Supreme Court indicated it might find otherwise if this sensitive information were not protected by appropriate safeguards. In *Whalen* the computer's security system included a locked wire fence, an alarm system, and off-line reading of the data files and tapes so that no outside computer could read or record the information. Justice Stevens, writing for the majority, stated that the right to collect personal information is typically accompanied "by a duty to avoid disclosure, and that the proper concern and duty were shown in this case." In his concurring opinion Justice Brennan indicated his growing concern with the possible abuses stemming from computer technology: "The central storage and easy accessibility of computerized data vastly increase the potential for abuse of that information, and I am not prepared to say that futher developments will not demonstrate the necessity of some curb on such technology."[31]

Although a number of privacy and computer related cases have arisen since Whalen, none have gone beyond the federal court of appeals level. Consequently, the Supreme Court has yet to specifically address the issues raised by Justice Brennan.

C. THE FEDERAL LEGISLATIVE RESPONSE

As a result of growing concern about perceived abuses of privacy through computerized data banks and in response to the Supreme Court's apparent reluctance to find constitutional violations of privacy in such areas as personal credit information, the U.S. Congress has enacted several statutes dealing with privacy.

Fair Credit Reporting Act of 1970

The main provisions of the Act protect individuals from inaccurate reports and to prevent invasion of privacy.[32] The applicability of the Act is limited to report for credit, employment, insurance and related benefits.[33] To guard against inaccuracies, the Act gives the individual the right to access and to challenge data that a credit reporting agency may have in its files.[34] The statute also mandates specific procedures for imposing civil penalties on credit reporting agencies if they fail to correct inaccurate information.[35]

The Act also requires that agencies follow reasonable procedures to assure the accuracy and proper use of credit information.[36] If an agency is negligent in this area, a person who is harmed may recover actual damages, costs, and attorney's fees.[37] If the agency's action is willful, punitive damages may be awarded.[38] Criminal penalties, imposing fines up to $5,000 or imprisonment for up to one year or both, may be rendered for the willful misappropriation,[39] or unauthorized disclosure[40] of credit information. The federal courts have jurisdiction over violations without regard to the amount in controversy.[41]

Proper uses of credit information include determining eligibility for additional credit and disclosure pursuant to a court order.[42] Limitations are imposed on the length of time certain derogatory information may be retained. For example, bankruptcy information can be kept on file for only 14 years. Arrest records, indictments and convictions can be retained for only seven years.[43]

Privacy Act of 1974

This Act[44] prohibits federal government offices from disclosing personal information about an individual without his written consent, unless it falls within one of the following exceptions: 1) to officers and employers of the agency in the performance of their duties; 2) when required by statute; 3) for routine use; 4) to the Census Bureau; 5) for statistical research; 6) to the National Archives; 7) for a criminal or civil law proceeding; 8) to protect an individual's health or safety; 9) to Congress; 10) to the Comptroller General; and 11) pursuant to a court order.[45] Restrictions and disclosures include not only hard copy but also display and telephone transmissions. The Act requires federal agencies to reveal their data collection activities on individuals, to make their justifications for the collection and use of such data public, and to give indivicuals a right to access to the collected information.

The right to access permits individuals to inspect their records in the presence of any companion and allows a request for corrections to be made. If this request is denied, the individual may file a statement of disagreement, and the agency holding the data has ten days to respond to the subject's assertions. Upon the agency's refusal to amend, the individual has 30 days in which to request a review of the refusal. If the reviewing procedure supports the agency's contentions, the private party has the right to judicial review. Once an agency agrees to amend the file, it must notify all those to whom the record has been transferred. This may be impractical, however, as agencies are not required to maintain records of the entities to which disclosures have been made.[46]

Individuals who believe their rights have been violated and who have been denied relief from the offending agency may sue in federal court for injunctive relief and civil damages. Damages for willful violations of the act are limited to $1,000 plus attorney's fees. Criminal misdemeanor charges and fines of up to $5,000 can be imposed on agency employees for willful disclosure.[47]

Family Educational Rights and Privacy Act

This statute[48] permits federal funds to be terminated to any institution of higher education that denies parents the right to inspect the educational records of their children. The Act provides that funds will be withheld from an institution that releases personal information about a student to persons other than school officials with a "need to know," state or federal education officials, research organizations, or persons with a lawful subpoena.[49]

Freedom of Information Act

This Act, which was supplemented by the Privacy Act, was intended to compel federal agencies to divulge various records, procedures and statements of policy to those requesting such information. The Act requires that each agency publish in the Federal Register a description of the place and manner in which the public may obtain such information. Persons who are refused inspection of federal records may sue to enjoin the agency from withholding the information and recover costs and attorney's fees.[50]

Right to Financial Privacy Act of 1978

This Act[51] provides further protection for the individual by limiting governmental access to the customer records of financial institutions.[52] Congress imposed this duty of confidentiality on financial institutions in apparent response to the Supreme Court decision in *United States v. Miller* which held that an individual had no expectation of privacy regarding his voluntarily submitted banking records.[53]

The federal government may be permitted access to such records by securing the written consent of the individual or by obtaining a subpoena, a court order or a search warrant. Whenever the federal government seeks access to financial records, the individual must be notified. In every instance except when a search warrant is obtained, governmental access may be challenged and civil monetary damages sought against the government or financial institution. The defendant can be finded up to

$100 per violation plus held liable for actual damages, court costs, and attorney's fees. Punitive damages may also be assessed if the violation is willful.[54]

Fair Credit Billing Act

The passage of this act in 1976 further strengthened the protection that an individual has from inaccuracies in credit data. The Act requires an obligor to identify his or her account, register the alleged error and state the reasons for believing that an error exists. The creditor has 30 days in which to respond and may not during that time issue an adverse credit report concerning the obligor's file.[55]

D.   STATE PRIVACY LEGISLATION

The Supreme Court policy has been generally to allow individual states to define privacy rights. In *Katz   v. United States* the Court held that "[p]rotection of a person's general right to privacy - his right to be let alone by other people - is, like the protection of his property and his very life, left largely to the law of the individual State."[56]

At the state level, legal protection afforded to privacy remains limited and inconsistent. Only ten states have provisions in their constitutions which expressly protect privacy.[57] Florida, for example, extends protection only against the unreasonable interception for private communications by any means."[58]

While the notion of privacy is a relatively new area

for the United States Supreme Court, it is even newer
to the states. With the exception of Arizona and Washington, the right of privacy has been included in state
constitutions only since 1968. A Maryland statute prohibits
an employer from asking an applicant questions related
to physical, psychiatric or psychological illness, dis-
ability or handicap, unless such information bears directly
upon the applicant's capacity to perform a particular
job.[59]

Rather than taking this fragmented approach to privacy
protection, one authority suggests that states adopt a
"package of privacy meansures." Such a package should
have three essential elements. The first element is a
provision relating to the physical interception of communication. The second is a freestanding right of privacy
that protects against governmental intrusions. Finally,
appropriate language should be included to assure that
the courts and legislature have a mandate to fashion
remedies against intrustions by the private sector.[60]
Such legislation would help protect an individual's privacy
across the spectrum of possible invasion, especially including that of computer data banks. Most states unfortunately, have not been very active in the privacy
area.

IV. THE JUDICIAL RESPONSE TO INFORMATION PRIVACY IN THE
    COMPUTER AGE.

Even if the Supreme Court expands the right to privacy
to the level of a specific independent doctrine covering
personal information, several problems would remain in
applying it to data collecting activities in the private

sector. First, in any application of a constitutional
principle to a non-governmental entity, the court must
find state action.[61] Arguably, such state action might
be found in information sharing between private and governmental organizations.[62] However, predicating relief for
loss of personal privacy upon a finding of state action
will undoubtedly afford too little protection from the intrusive information practices of private business, since,
in many cases, such a finding will be difficult to support.[63] Specifically, and as will be discussed later
in the chapter, an invasion of privacy can result in an
unauthorized release of personal credit information.
Such releases are not subjected to regulation requiring
the recording of record recipients, thus making any updates,
correction or proof of unauthorized disclosure effectively
impossible. The principle of state action requires a
"pervasive interdependence" between government and private
actors, as when a government function is performed privately
or some delegation of governmental decision-making power
has taken place.[64]

Furthermore, individuals may fail to pursue this
type of relief due to the time, cost and additional exposure
of possibly embarrassing personal information involved
in bringing a court action, or due to a total unawareness
of the information intrustion.[65] Even when individuals
pursue a judicial remedy, the imprecision and fragementation
of a case-by-case approach may make exclusive reliance
on a constitutional principle an inefficient and incomplete
approach to privacy protection.[66] Courts limit their

decisions to the facts before them, and it is not likely that such an approach will result in a comprehensive set of guidelines which will operate to inform the individual of his rights and to inform business of its obligations. To remedy the loss from an omission of personal privacy by resorting to a scheme of monetary damages or after-the-fact injunctive relief raises the same conceptual problems that face courts in dealing with compensation for mental and emotional injuries.[67] Although in some cases, a denial of credit, for example, may present a concrete loss, a precise computation of monetary damages will prove unattainable, since it is difficult to quantify in dollar terms a loss from an invasion of privacy. In addition, injunctive relief following a privacy invasion may do little to repair the individual's situation. A court could, for example, order correction of a personal credit report, but if erroneous reports have already been sent and there are no records of the recipients, equitable relief of this nature alone, will not repair the past injuries. The limits of the judicial approach are apparent, since courts are not inclined to grant such relief unless it is clear that irreparable harm has occurred or could result.[68]

The common law tort approach to privacy applies only to disclosure through a public medium, such as newspaper, television or radio.[69] Most disclosures of personal information by business organizations, however, are not communicated to the public at large. The inconsistent approaches adopted by the different states and the failure of some states to recognize the tort cause of action in

this form diminishes the protection afforded in the individual.[70] Finally, lack of judicial awareness of the
intricacies of computer technology may result in the imposition of undue burdens on business without providing a
correspondingly high degree of protection for the individual.[71]

V. EVALUATION OF THE EXISTING LEGISLATIVE FRAMEWORK AND POSSIBLE FUTURE MODELS TO RECONCILE THE COMPETING IN-DIVIDUAL PRIVACY VERSUS ORGANIZATIONAL NEED FOR INFOR-MATION.

State and federal statute regulating information
activities provide the only significant protection for
the individual's right of information privacy. This
statutory approach seeks to restore a balance between
an organization's legitimate need for personal data and
the individual's desire to be free from unwarranted intrusions into his private life. Both state and federal
legislative controls over the information practices of
governmental and private orgaizations have focused, in
varying degrees, upon the collection, accuracy and confidentiality aspects of information privacy. However,
this statutory response to the threat posed by an infor-
mation-oriented society and its increasing reliance on
computer technology has been limited in scope. The strong-
est emphasis of most such laws has been on limiting the
information practices of the government. Regultion of
private business practices has been much more cautious,
limited to the control of only certain intrusive practices,
particularly in the area of credit ad investigatory reporting, and to the protection of the confidentiality
of very sensitive information.[72] Lack of legislative

or judicial definition of information privacy as well as lack of knowledge of the probable impact of specific regulations have warranted caution in regulating the activities of the private sector.[73]

The Privacy Protection Study Commission[74] has recommended federal legislation aimed at consumer credit agencies, financial institutions and investigative agencies. Generally, such proposed statutes have required only voluntary compliance. However, recommendations that rely on voluntary compliance fail to recognize the importance of the rights involved and the existence of profit motives of business. Leaving protection of individual privacy rights to the discretion of business would create too strong a motivation to ignore or limit protection of these rights. If the right to privacy is a fundamental one, the legal system should provide a basis for its enforcement.[75]

Lauretta E. Murdock in her 1980, Albany Law Review Article, "The Use and Abuse of Computerized Information," proposes a solution which balances competing interests and provides a framework for resolving the conflicts. The proposal includes three recommendations: 1) that the framework for regulation of the information activities of private organizations be nationally conceived; 2) that this national policy formulate standards for fair information practices which can be applied to information activities generally, regardless of the type of organization involved; and 3) that a federal administrative agency vested with adjudicatory, rulemaking and investigatory powers have the responsibility for implementation of this broad policy in order to provide the needed flexibility.[76]

Murdock contends that a national policy promotes uniformity. If regulation is left to the states, great potential exists for the enactment of inconsistent or conflicting legislation, possibly resulting in the imposition of undue burdens on a business operating in more than one jurisdiction.[77] Another advantage of such a national policy lies in the provision of a single regulatory scheme through which an individual may seek relief.

Further, applying the statutory plan for privacy protection to all industry results in fair and equal treatment. Broad standards should be formulated for data collection, dispute resolution, and dissemination of records and personal practices and should be applied to all information activities of private organizations. The particular advantage of broad-based regulation of the collectors and users of information lies in the ability of computer technology to provide the hardware and software packages and management techniques necessary to comply.[78]

The Supreme Court indicates that the question of the constitutionality of such broad delegation of powers to a single administrative agency no longer presents serious difficulty.[79] The main requirement is that the power delegated must be accompanied by strict standards defining the limits of that power. The effectiveness of such a plan involving a single federal agency is further supported by the likely advantage it would have over the present, patchwork legal framework-1) the agency would possess the flexibility necessary to balance the competing interests of individual privacy and technological development; 2) the agency could accommodate varying concepts of fairness in information practices based on the nature of the industry and its information activity as well as on the sensitivity of the information being handled; and 3) as the possibility for self-regulation of a particular industry arose, the agency approach would allow such an industry to formulate its own more detained guidelines.[80]

With regrd to other legislation dealing with the potential for violations of individual privacy, the *Fair Credit Reporting Act* offers the most comprehensive and far reaching domestic legislation to date. Contrasting legislation is provided by the Council of Europe in its *Convention for the Protection of Individuals with Regard to Automatic Processing of Personal Data* which more specifically addresses the privacy issues raised by computers. Two alternatives are therefore presented to control the privacy implications inherent when computers talk to computers.

VI. A DOMESTIC MODEL - THE FAIR CREDIT REPORTING ACT

A. THE NEED FOR ACCURATE CONSUMER REPORTS

The American lifestyle entails a high degree of mobility, which creates a need for instant credit approval, whether it be for the ability to make travel reservations all over the world, a credit purchase 3,000 miles from home, or to finance a house in a community where the person seeking the mortgage might have no credit history. Due to the pace of modern commercial life, lenders and retail merchants must make such credit decisions promptly.[81] The credit decision is ideally based upon a record that is accurate, complete, and up to date, usually supplied by a credit reporting agency.[82]

The record or consumer report, as defined here, is an accounting of an individual's credit history, produced with the aid of a computer.[83] The computer in consumer credit reporting serves as the cataloging and library system where consumer information is stored.[84] With an increasingly sophisticated data processing technology, credit reporting agencies are able to gather, store, re-trieve, copy and disseminate large amounts of information.[85] The enormous amount of information processing that goes on in our society, however, raises the possibility for inaccurate data entering consumer records. When this happens, major problems can arise for the consumer and the credit grantor.[86]

An incomplete consumer record, for example, prevents the credit grantor from making an informed decision as to whether to extend credit to the consumer. The problem is compounded when the inaccurate or incomplete information influences decisions that hinder a consumer's access to certain benefits of society.[87] The figures involved illustrate the magnitude of the problem. In the United States there are about 2,000 credit bureaus, the five largest of which concurrently maintain more than 150.million records on individuals. If 99 percent of the consumer reports are accurate, the one percent of inaccurate ones represent one and one half million people.[88]

Today mistakes in records can be propagated rapidly throughout the world. In many instances, even if individuals manage to identify the original error and its source, they are helpless to stop the damage. More often than not, victims are unaware that their plight is the result of an inaccuracy in their credit record.

A survey conducted at the University of Illinois points out that when most institutions discover incorrect information, they do not attempt to notify the recipients of the errors. As a result, errors are likely to compound and proliferate.[89]

B.   COMMON LAW BEFORE THE FAIR CREDIT REPORTING ACT

Before the Fair Credit Reporting Act the primary remedies at common law for violation of private information and erroneous reporting were actions for defamation and invasion of privacy. In order to bring an action for libel or slander, the consumer had to prove the information used was false[90] or activated by ill will.[91] Most states allow consumer reporting agencies a "conditional privilege based on the theory that there is a common interest in the information and that consumer reporting agencies are entitled to special treatment in collecting and disseminating information needed by credit grantors . . . in the course of their business dealings with consumers."[92]

This conditional privilege presumes good faith on the part of the consumer reporting agency in the collection and dissemination of information. The consumer has the burden of overcoming this presumption by proving malice. In order to destroy this conditional privilege the consumer has to show a wanton and reckless disregard for the rights of another.[93]

When a consumer-reporting agency makes a report to a subscriber, the conditional privilege exists[94] as long as the report is made without malice to one who has an interest in the information.[95] This requirement of malice has the practical effect of giving consumer reporting agencies near absolute immunity in libel suits.[96]

The common law right to privacy, or "the right to be let alone,"[97] was first described in an 1890 law review article written by Charles Warren and Louis D. Brandeis.[98] Before that time no relief was granted for an invasion of privacy.[99] Although the courts, in retrospect, appeared to be recognizing such a right as privacy, such cases afforded relief on the basis of some property right or breach of implied contract.[100] Warren and Brandeis concluded that the cases were in reality based upon a broader principle which was entitled to a separate recognition.[101] Subsequent to the appearance of the article, the courts granted relief based on an invasion of privacy as a recognizable tort.

As briefly discussed earlier in this chapter, a cause of action based on an invasion of an individual's privacy must be classified as one of four types: (1) intrusion upon physical solitude or seclusion,[102] (2) publicity given to objectionable private information,[103] (3) placement of a person in a false, although not necessarily defamatory, position in the public light,[104] or (4) appropriation of a person's name or likeness for commercial use.[105]

The second and fourth theories are inapposite to the area of personal information records. Intrusion may be used as a cause of action in a situation in which an investigator interferes with a person's seclusion. The consumer must show a blatant and shocking disregard for his or her rights which resulted in serious mental or physical injury or humiliation. The conduct must outrage one of ordinary sensibilities; the hypersensitive cannot recover for actions which are rude or inconsiderate.[106]

Public disclosure of private information is another cause of action under which a consumer might recover for an abuse of personal computer information, but it is an unlikely approach. Public disclosure means communication to the public at large and not to an individual credit grantor or data collection service.[107] In order to make an informed business judgement, the decision maker often must have information which normally would be considered private. The decision maker may use this information only for legitimate purposes. The public interest provides the decision maker with protections, similar in principle to a qualified privilege in libel.[108] The right to privacy is not an absolute right.[109] In practice, the common law provides no effective remedy for the victims of false reports or overly intrusive investigations.[110]

C.   LEGISLATIVE OVERVIEW

In the early 1960's, before the Fair Credit Reporting Act was passed, the House of Representatives was investigating the creation of a federal computerized data bank. During the investigation a representative of the credit bureau industry testified that such a network of data banks already existed in the United States among credit bureaus. [111] As a result of this testimony, the House Subcommittee on Invasion of Privacy conducted hearings on credit bureau practices. [112] The purpose of the hearings was to investigate the possible invasion of privacy of individuals who had applied for a home loan. Congressman Cornelius Gallagher proposed that the credit industry develop guidelines for self-regulation. [113] In response, the Associated Credit Bureaus of America coordinated the development of reforms for the industry which were to be followed on a voluntary basis. [114] The industry's display of willingness to regulate itself was a wise move, for some form of regulation was inevitable. However, as one authority observed, "[b]eneath this 'good industry facade' was the more subtle benefit--self-regulation would impose no legal duties. [115]

This suspicion prompted Senator William Proxmire to submit a bill of his own--S.823, The Fair Credit Reporting Bill--at the same time the self-regulating guidelines went before the House. In response to Proxmire's actions, members of the credit industry decided not to oppose the Fair Credit Reporting Act but to help create a piece of of legislation the industry could live with.

Senator Proxmire held his hearings on S. 823 from May 19 through May 23, 1969.[116] In October the bill was passed by a voice vote of the Senate and was sent to the House of Representatives, where it was stalled.[117]

In the House, Congresswoman Leonore Sullivan was holding her own hearings on H.R. 16340, the Good Name Protection Bill.[118] This bill provided more protection for the consumer and more stringent controls on the credit reporting agencies than S. 823.[119] The Good Name Protection Bill, however, was never reported out of committee.[120]

At the same time, the House Committee on Banking and Currency reported out H.R. 15073, a bill to stop the secret depositing of funds in Swiss banks. On May 25, 1970, the House passed H.R. 15073 and sent it to the Senate. Senator Proxmire then tacked S. 823 to H.B. 15073 as a non-germane amendment. In September, the Senate passed H.R. 15073 as amended and sent it to the Conference Committee.[121] Just days before the Congressional recess, the bill was passed by a voice vote in both the Senate and the House. On October 26, 1970, H.R. 15073 was signed by the President and became law.[122]

D.   PURPOSE OF THE FAIR CREDIT REPORTING ACT

Before the enactment of the Fair Credit Reporting Act, the consumer reporting industry was largely unregulated.[123] The Congress, in passing the Act, found that the banking system depends upon accurate credit reports to bolster its efficiency and maintain public confidence.[124] It also found that an elaborate mechanism

had been developed for investigation and evaluating the
credit worthiness, character, and general reputation of
consumers and that consumer reporting agencies play a
vital role in assembling and evaluation information on
consumers.[125] The Congress sought to prevent consumers
from being unjustly damaged because of inaccurate or ar-
bitrary information in a credit report and to prevent
undue invasion of the individual's right of privacy in
the collection and dissemination of credit information.[126]

The stated purpose of the Act is to require consumer
reporting agencies to adopt reasonable procedures to provide
information that is accurate, relevant and fair to the
consumer, and to use this information with proper regard
for confidentiality.[127] The statute prohibits reporting
adverse information older than 7 years, or 14 years in
the case of bankruptcy.[128] At the request of the consumer
the reporting agency is required to disclose the nature
and substance of all information in the consumer's file.[129]
If a consumer challenges the completeness or accuracy
of any of the information, and the challenge is neither
frivolous nor irrelevant, the agency must reinvestigate
and delete any unverifiable information.[130]

When a consumer is rejected for credit, insurance
or employment, or the charge for the credit or insurance
is increased because of information in a consumer report,
the user of the report shall advise the consumer and supply
the name and address of the reporting agency.[131] Consumer
reporting agencies cannot report adverse items of public
record information for employment purposes unless they
maintain strict procedures to keep the information up
to date.[132]

Any person who orders an investigative report must disclose to the consumer that an investigative report may be made and may involve information on the consumer's character, general reputation, personal characteristics, and mode of living, and that the consumer has the right to request a complete and accurate disclosure of the investigation. This provision also applies if the report is for employment purposes and the consumer has specifically applied for that employment.[133] Adverse information contained in an investigative report which is more than three months old cannot be reported again unless it is reverified.[134]

The statute requires reporting agencies to use reasonable procedures to assure accuracy and proper use of the credit report.[135] A consumer who has been harmed by the failure of a reporting agency to adhere to these requirements may bring a civil action for negligent non-compliance and collect actual damages plus attorney's fees. For willful non-compliance, the consumer may collect punitive damages as well as actual damages and attorney's fees.[136] Criminal charges of imprisonment for not more than one year or a fine of not more than $5,000 can be brought against any person who knowingly, willfully, and under false pretenses obtains information on a consumer from a consumer reporting agency.[137] No consumer may bring any action for defamation or invasion of privacy unless false information was furnished with malice or willful intent to injure the consumer.[138] Federal and state courts have jurisdiction,[139] and the Federal Trade Commission has enforcement powers over consumer reporting agencies and users of reports who are not regulated by another agency.[140]

E. THE BALANCING TEST - INFORMATION v. PRIVACY

Industry's Need for Information

Consumer demand for credit requires the gathering
of personal information in order to meet consumer needs.[141]
The information involved in making credit decisions generally comes from two sources--the credit application
completed by the consumer and a credit report. The consumer
has total control over the completeness and accuracy of
the data contained in the application since it is the
consumer who provides it. The credit report, provided
by the credit reporting agency, is used to verify parts
of the application as well as to provide payment history
about the consumer.[142]

Credit grantors such as retailers, banks, oil companies, finance companies and mortgage lenders, report
to the credit reporting agencies the terms of their credit
agreements with customers and the status of their accounts.
Credit reporting agencies also obtain information from
debt collectors, employers, landlords, hospitals, and
other persons having a financial relationship with the
individual concerned. Such agencies may also consult
public records for information about arrests and convictions, bankruptcies, tax liens, divorces, lawsuits,
and property disputes to add to their file on each consumer.
Some of the more sophisticated credit bureaus will actually
monitor the credit files of individuals and notify creditors
when certain status changes occur that could require the
creditor to reassess the account. Such changes might include bankruptcy, divorce, loss of employment or over-
extension of other accounts.[143]

Credit reporting agencies store credit payment information in computers that can be instantaneously accessed.[144] Demand for this information continues to grow with the boom in the public's use of installment credit. The chart below illustrates the explosive growth of consumer installment credit. It covers the amount of credit extended for the ten-year period between 1969 and 1979.[145] (All the figures have been adjusted for inlation and GNP)

	1969 (Dollars)	1979 (Dollars)
CONSUMER INSTALLMENT CREDIT EXTENDED Federal Reserve Bulletin (does not include credit card charges paid within 30 days)	109.4 billion	322.7 billion
IMPLICIT PRICE DE- FLATOR FOR PERSONAL CONSUMPTION EXPEN- DITURES Bureau of Economic Analysis	88.5	1972 100 163.3
EXTENSIONS IN CON- STANT 1972 DOLLARS	123.6 billion	197.6 billion
GNP (Current Values) Federal Reserve Bul- letin	935.5 billion	2,369.4 billion
GNP IN CONSTANT 1972 DOLLARS	1,078.8 billion	1,431.7 billion
CONSTANT DOLLAR CREDIT EXTENSION AS A % OF CONSTANT DOLLAR GNP	11.5%	13.8%

The following chart further illustrates the consumer demand for credit by listing the types of plastic cards estimated to be in circulation in 1980.[146]

	MILLIONS
BANK CREDIT CARDS	219
OIL COMPANY CARDS	143
RETAIL CARDS (National Chains)	100
CHECK CASHING CARDS	50
AIRLINE CARDS	50
AUTO RENTAL	50
CASH DISCOUNT CARDS	25
COMMUNICATIONS CARDS (Telephone)	25
TRAVEL AND ENTERTAINMENT CARDS	15
MISCELLANEOUS (Includes bank debit/ asset/cash cards, local retail, restaurant and hotel).	60
TOTAL	734

Individual's Right to Informational Privacy

Congress has attempted to protect informational privacy by passing a number of statutes.[147] Of these laws, the Fair Credit Reporting Act is the federal government's only significant attempt to impose privacy regulations on information collected and transferred between private entities.[148] The United States Constitution does not explicitly recognize the right to privacy, as before stated. The Supreme Court, in 1965, recognized that privacy is within the legal penumbra of the Bill of Rights, particularly in the First, Fourth, and Fourteenth Amendments.[149] The Court ruled that, except in the most intimate of family matters, there is no basis in the law for a generalized right to privacy.[150]

The Supreme Court in *Whalen v. Roe* stated its cognizance of the potential threats to privacy posed by the collection of personal data in computers but did not attempt to define a precedent.[151] Specifically, Justice Stevens in the majority opinion wrote:

> We are not unaware of the threat to privacy implicit in the accumulation of vast amounts of personal information in computerized data banks...We therefore need not, and do not, decide any questions which might be presented by the unwarranted disclosure of accummulated private data. 152

Even if the Supreme Court did recognize a right of privacy for computerized personal information under the Constitution, it may have little effect on the private sector. Most constitutional guarantees of individual rights operate only against government interference, either federal or state, which must be present before an individual can successfully invoke his constitutional rights.[153]

Though there is no explicit constitutional guarantee of personal privacy, a Louis Harris poll on privacy conducted in 1978 showed that American people are deeply concerned about the erosion of their privacy; many people believe we are approaching the Orwellian "Big Brother" society.[154]

The poll revealed that many Americans feel they are surrendering their privacy when they apply for credit, and that too much sensitive information is being asked, such as when an applicant for credit is routinely expected to fill out a credit questionnaire that may contain a considerable amount of sensitive information.[155] Many times the questions, such as those relating to marital status, age and sex, are not relevant to the purpose of the credit. The applicant knows that refusal to supply the information may be viewed upon with disfavor by the credit grantor.[156]

Because this information is given voluntarily, the applicant has consented to the use of the information by the credit grantor and credit reporting agency, and the information may be passed on to others for use that does not invade the applicant's privacy. Consent, whether it is express, implied or inferred, is one of the major defenses for an invasion of privacy. It is not a simple matter, however, to ascertain the extent to which a person has consented to the invasion,[157] or if the consent given also applies to the use of the sensitive information by a person[158] other than the one to whom it was given.

A classic illustration fo the growing computer age conflict between the right of an individual to keep financial affairs private and the right of business to exchange credit information occurs when a consumer receives an unsolicited invitation for a credit card, for which no formal application is necessary.[159] Credit grantors use a credit reporting technique known as prescreening, a common practice in the credit reporting industry. The use of prescreening has grown with the automated nature of the credit industry[160] and is used by a company to narrow its target audience for a direct mail campaign when it is marketing a product.[161] The consumer reporting agencies use computers to audit extensive lists of consumers in an effort to find the consumers who match a certain low-risk profile established by the credit industry as the hit list, which is the preferred marketing target.

The prescreening criteria used by the submitter to determine the hit list is considered proprietary and is not usually disclosed even upon the specific request of a prescreened consumer.[162] People who would appear on the prescreened list would be those who have: a specific minimum file history of credit transactions for two years, a zip code in a particular geographic area, at least three satisfactory bank or retail credit accounts, or no history of dealing with consumer finance companies.[163] A lender might also seek out vulnerable consumers for high rate loans by editing lists that contain recent bankruptcies.[164]

The real issue is whether there is an invasion of privacy when the credit bureau's files are examined without either the knowledge or consent of the people on the list. When Congress was originally considering passage of the Fair Credit Reporting Act, it asked the Federal Trade Commission for an interpretation of the practice of pre-screening.[165] The Federal Trade Commission said it felt the Act banned prescreening in all direct-mail solicit-ation. But a year later the Federal Trade Commission changed its mind. It legitimized prescreening in an opinion that stated:

> The Commission recognizes that the legislative history of the Fair Credit Reporting Act reveals a concern for the consumer's privacy and the accuracy of information stored at credit bureaus and demon-strates a sensitivity as to the balance between the free flow of credit information for legitimate business purposes and the right of the consumer to keep his affairs private. However, the practice of prescreening results in no significant harm to consumers and the practice is not inconsistent with the basic purpose of the Act. 166

The Privacy Protection Study Commission addressed the issue of whether prescreening constitutes an invasion of privacy and recommended that there be a governmental mechanism to hear consumer complaints and to deal with overly intrusive practices. The Reagan Administration rejected this as out of keeping with its policy of inter-posing as little government control as possible on credit information practices. Instead the Administration's ap-proach has been to open those practices to public scrutiny and allow the public and market forces to decide whether the practices are unduly intrusive.[167]

One consumer in particular, thought that prescreening was intrusive when he received an unsolicited form invitation to become a BankAmericard holder from the Bank of America. Bruce Steinberg resolved to find out how a bank with which he had never done business knew he was a good credit risk. This resolve turned into a court suit challenging the credit system. Mr. Steinberg challenged TRW credit reporting agency to defend its practice of using prescreening by suing TRW Credit Data for $3 million, alleging among other things, invasion of privacy. Steinberg asserted that the prescreenng of him for Bank of America violated the Fair Credit Reporting Act. TRW Credit Data eventually settled out of court. TRW admitted no liability on any of Mr. Steinberg's charges, but it agreed to pay him $20,000 and $15,195 for lawyer's fees.[168] This challenge has changed the way that all credit reporting agencies approach prescreening.[169]

F. PURPOSES FOR WHICH A CONSUMER REPORT MAY BE USED

The Fair Credit Reporting Act recognizes that the credit reporting industry produces two kinds of reports--the consumer report and the investigative consumer report.[170] The Act defines the first type as any information, whether oral or written, bearing on a consumer's credit worthiness, character, reuptation, personal characteristics or mode of living, used or expected to be used or collected for the purpose of serving as a factor in establishing the consumer's eligibility for credit,

insurance, employment, or other business transaction between a business and the consumer.[171] This type of report
is confined mainly to financial information and is used
by merchants who wish to know if extending credit to a
consumer is a sound decision.[172]

The Act defines the second type of report as any
information on a consumer's character and general reputation as well as personal interviews with neighbors,
friends, or associates of the consumer reported on.[173]
Insurance companies investigating applicants, employers
considering prospective employees, and landlords determining
the suitability of prospective tenants are the primary
users of the investigative report. Information obtained
from both types of investigations is kept on file by the
reporting bureaus.[174]

Most of the relevant litigation concerns the permitted
uses of these consumer and investigative reports and the
procedures necessary to ensure accurate reporting.[175]

Section 1681b of the Fair Credit Reporting Act limits
the furnishing of a consumer report to those purposes
involving the obtaining of credit, insurance, employment,
or a government license, or to other legitimate business
needs. Any broader use of the report requires a court
order or the consumer's written permission. The meaning
of the first four uses is straight-forward. However,
the use for 'legitimate business needs' is vague. The
Act does not define what a legitimate business need is.

A New York District Court, in *Boothe* *v.* *TRW &*
Fidelifacts concluded that a 'legitimate business
need' does not include using a consumer credit report
to aid a private investigation of a suspected counter-
feiter.[176] Phillip Boothe was being investigated by
Fidelifacts, for a third party, to determine whether
the whiskey Boothe was offering for sale was contraband
or counterfeit. To aid in the investigation, Fidelifacts
sought a credit report on Boothe. The report, which
TRW made available to Fidelifacts, included personal
and credit information about Boothe and his wife. The
report was listed under Boothe's name rather than his
business name.

Fidlifacts, as a subscriber of TRW's services,
had entered into an agreement which stipulated that
the subscriber "certifies and agrees that it will request
and use credit data received from TRW solely in connection
with a credit transaction involving the consumer as
to whom a credit profile is sought."[177] Fidelifacts
certified to TRW that it would request reports for only
legitimate credit purposes as required in section 1681b
of the Fair Credit Reporting Act.

Contrary to this agreement, the main purpose that
Fidelifacts had in acquiring this report was to aid
in an investigation which attempted to stop a suspected
illicit seller of a third party distiller's goods.
There was no intention on the part of Fidelifacts to
use Boothe's report for the purpose of credit, licnsing,
employment or insurance.

The District Court held that TRW was not liable for releasing information to a private investigative agency that used the information improperly. Although Fidelifacts was held liable, the court found it would be impractical to require TRW to verify the purpose for each credit report.[178]

In not holding TRW liable, the court based part of its decision on the high volume of credit requests that TRW must respond to each day, and the importance of a speedy response to its subscribers. The court stated "by requiring its subscribers to certify the purpose for reports in advance, TRW reasonably strikes a balance between the conflicting goals of protecting the privacy right of consumers and promoting an efficient economy."[179]

The District Court determined that a legitimate business need refers only to those transactions in which there is a 'consumer relationship' between the requesting party and the subject of the report or where the subject was seeking some benefit mentioned in the statute, (credit, insurance, employment, license) from the requesting party. The court held that the release of the credit report violated Boothe's right to privacy, one of the principal rights the Fair Credit Reporting act was enacted to protect.

G.   STANDARD OF REASONABLE CARE IN THE PREPARATION OF A CONSUMER REPORT

Congress, in passing the Fair Credit Reporting Act, has set up a reasonable procedure standard for preparing credit reports. The Act states that "whenever a consumer reporting agency prepares a consumer report it shall follow reasonable procedure to assure maximum possible accuracy in the information concerning the individual about whom the report relates."[180]

The accuracy issue in consumer credit reports was examined by the courts in *Lowry v. Credit Bureau, Inc. of Georgia*.[181] James Francis Lowry of Solana Beach, California, was seeking a home mortgage from the Decatur Federal Savings and Loan Association. As part of its loan processing, Decatur Federal usually orders credit reports on individuals seeking loans.

The inquiry by the Decatur Federal operator resulted in the supplying of information on a James Frank Lowry of San Francisco, California, whose file showed 50 points of information that corresponded with ('points of correspondence') the application records of plaintiff. The Decatur operator made the decision to have the Credit Bureau computer supply its information on James Frank Lowry despite the fact that only the minimum point of correspondence had been indicated. The computer disclosed that James Frank Lowry of San Francisco, California, had been adjudicated bankrupt in 1967.

Decatur Federal informed Mr. Lowry that problems existed concerning the issuance of credit to him, and that a resolution of the difficulty must come from the Credit Bureau, Inc., of Georgia. He notified the Credit Bureau of the denial of his loan application and demanded a correction of his credit report. The inaccuracy in Lowry's credit report was the presence of his, James Francis Lowry's, social security number in the file of the bankrupt James Frank Lowry.

Four months after the initial application was made, the Credit Bureau corrected its mistake and included no allegation of bankruptcy. Mr. Lowry was then offered a loan commitment for the purchase of his home.

The court, in *dicta*, made a distinction between the Credit Bureau's obligation to insure maximum accuracy in the preparation of a report and the potential for confusion of reports inherent in the Credit Bureau's computer. The court examined the compliance section of the Fair Credit Reporting Act, which requires a consumer reporting agency to follow reasonable procedures, and found that this section imposes an obligation to insure maximum accuracy only in the preparation of a report.[182]

A second issue with which the court dealt was whether there was a breach of duty by the Credit Bureau to investigate the accuracy of the information in his 'file' as disputed by James F. Lowry. The court held that a person's file must include all information, including conflicting information, provided by computer reports. All such information is therefore the required subject matter of any necessary investigation. The court further held that a consumer reporting agency is obligated to reinvestigate the accuracy of information in a person's file when it has become the subject of an inquiry. The agency's obligations are not terminated simply by the accuracy of the credit report information alone, when that information, as presented, does not relate to or accurately describe the credit history of the particular individual in question.[183]

The court in *San Antonio Retail Merchants Association* [184] went one step further in setting the standard of duty of resonable care in the preparation of a credit report. Basing its reasoning on *Lowry* , the *Thompson* court stated that, because the preparation of a consumer report must be viewed as a continuing process, the reporting agency's duty extends to updating procedures. The reporting agency must ensure accuracy with every addition of information. [185]

The San Antonio Retail Merchants Association provided a computerized credit reporting service to local business subscribers. This service depends heavily upon credit history information fed into San Antonio Retail Merchants Association's files by subscribers. To update its files, the San Antonio Merchants Association uses a mechanism called computerized automatic capture. A subscriber must feed certain identifying information on a consumer from its own computer terminal to San Antonio Retail Merchants Association's central computer in order to gain access to that consumer's credit history. When the central computer receives this identifying information, it searches its records for the credit history file that most nearly matches the identifying information. This file then appears on the subscriber's computer screen. The decision whether to accept a given file as the correct one is left completely to the terminal operator. When a subscriber does accept this file, the computer automatically captures into its file any information input from the subscriber's terminal that the central file did not already have.

The disadvantage of an automatic capturing feature is that it may accept erroneous information fed in by subscribers. The only way to prevent this is to have special auditing components built into the system that can check the accuracy of such items as social security numbers. In this case San Antonio Retail Merchants Association failed to check the accuracy of a social security number obtained by its automatic capturing feature. As a result, the computer erroneously began to report the bad credit history of William Daniel Thompson, Jr. to subscribers inquiring about William Douglas Thompson, III. To judge the adequacy of the credit reporting agency's procedures, the court imposed a duty of reasonable care. The credit reporting agency must use as the standard of conduct that which a reasonably prudent person would do under the circumstances.

In applying the reasonably prudent person standard, the court found two acts of negligence in San Antonio Retail Merchants Association's updating procedure. First, San Antonio Retail Merchants Association failed to exercise reasonable care in programming its computer to automatically capture information in a file without requiring any minimum number of points of correspondence between the consumer and the file or having an adequate auditing procedure to ensure accuracy. Second, San Antonio Retail Merchants Association failed to employ reasonable procedures designed to highlight the disparity in social security numbers for the Thompsons.

The court awarded actual damages based on humiliation and mental distress to Thompson. Even when there are no out-of-pocket expenses, damages for humiliation and mental distress are recoverable under the Fair Credit Reporting Act.[186] The court also allowed an award of attorney's fees.

The increasing reliance on computers in the credit reporting industry has forced courts to scrutinize the procedures used by the credit bureaus. As a result, the emphasis on accuracy has changed. The credit reporting agencies now have a greater responsibility to report accurate information rather than simply having a duty to report accurately the information that they might have.[187]

VII A FOREIGN MODEL-THE CONVENTION FOR THE PROTECTION OF INDIVIDUALS WITH REGARD TO AUTOMATIC PROCESSING OF PERSONAL DATA

A. THE EUROPEAN APPROACH TO INFORMATIONAL PRIVACY

The countries of Western Europe have recognized the right to privacy as an important fundamental right worthy of protection and preservation. Concern for protecting this right has led to the drafting of an international agreement to protect personal privacy within the west European countries. This agreement is the proposed *Convention for the Protection of Individuals with Regard to Automatic Processing of Personal Data*. The proposed agreement is sponsored by the Council of Europe, which was founded in 1949 and is open to any European state willing to accept the rule of law and ensure the enjoyment of human rights and fundamental freedoms.[188] If the agreement is accepted by the member states of the Council, its influence will be felt not only within Europe but throughout the rest of the computerized world.

The proposed Convention is in many ways an outgrowth of the European Convention on Human Rights and Fundamental Freedoms that was formulated by the Council in 1950. That Convention recognized a right of privacy and provided that it be afforded a basic level of protection. The European Human Rights Convention put in force in 1958, is a regional agreement designed to guarantee a limited but clearly defined standard of individual freedoms. The basis for these freedoms are the constitutional and legal traditions of the member states themselves. The provisions are similar to the common law of many of the contracting parties to the convention.[189]

The purpose of the Human Rights Convention is to secure the recognition of specifically catalogued fundamental rights. Article 1 of the Convention expresses the aim that the "High Contracting Parties shall secure to everyone within their jurisdiction" the rights and freedoms defined in the first section of the Convention.[190] Among those guarantees is the right to privacy.

Computers, with their prodigious capacity to quickly compile, store, process and transfer information, have created potential threats to the privacy and security of individuals throughout the world. Creating a computer profile of a person is now a relatively simple task. Telecommunications, digital networks, and satellite relays

have made this a global capability. Recognizing this,
the new European Convention provides more specific safeguards for the privacy of the citizens of countries which
accept the convention. As an international legal agreement, the convention will affect not only the countries
which accede to it but also countries with which its members have commercial, social, and political relations.
The flow of data across national borders within Europe
or emanating from Europe to the world will become subject
in some measure to the jurisdiction of this international
agreement.

The regulation of data collection, data processing
and data transfer is a social response to technological
change. A scheme of regulation must maintain a proper
balance between the objectives of progress and the acceptance of societies in order to take advantage of changes
in technology.[191] Data protection laws reflect a
traditional conflict between competing groups such as
citizens and their government, consumers and providers,
and employees and employers. In the case of data protection, the conflict is a dispute over the access and
distribution of information. The methods and means by
which information is gathered and distributed has become
increasingly complex. This increase in the complexity
of information exchanges has made it more difficult to
monitor and regulate the uses of electronically processed
data for the purpose of ensuring individual privacy.

Some European nations have already made efforts to
safeguard personal privacy through the use of data pro-

tection laws. The effect of these attempts has often reached further than simply protecting human rights. It often results in a conflict between privacy protection and a more than nominal restriction on the free flow of information.[192]

The Council of Europe perspective on data protection is that there must be legal provisions for the protection of individuals subjected to the automated processing of personal information. Although the established legal systems of the member states are not without their own regulations, uniform principles for privacy protection which are applicable throughout the member states provide a legal safety net for individuals and help to resolve international conflicts.[193]

The Council of Europe is concerned about the extent to which the national legislation of member states afford adequate privacy protection to individuals. There is a special concern about the movement of information in the form of transborder data flow. Transborder data flow involves transmission, storage and computation of data. It consists of digitally encoded units of information in which the transfer, storage and processing occurs in more than one nation. The information can be transmitted or transported by a number of methods. Computers that are combined with telecommunication links open the prospect for data processing on an international scale.[194] Privacy protection becomes more difficult because the speed, volume, and method of transmission do not easily lend themselves to regulation.[195]

Data processing and storage facilities which are located in one country and whose data is passed to another country falls outside the jurisdiction of that country's laws.[196] This creates problems for organizations involved in transborder data flow. National legislative restrictions regulating data protection and personal privacy can prohibit effective, low-cost use of data networks. Countries within a network often have difficulties in complying with the variety of national regulations.[197]

There is concern that data users might take advantage of a weakness in a particular nation's data protection laws by basing their operations either in whole or in part in "data havens." These are countries which would allow the compilation and manipulation of data files in ways not allowed by states with more stringent regulations and enforcement. Overly restrictive domestic laws, however, tend to interfere with the free international flow of information. The goal of the Council of Europe's new convention is to devise a legal formula which will ensure data protection and maintain the principle of international free flow of information. Further, the Council considers it important to create mechanisms at the international level that allow different states to inform and consult with each other on data protection matters. In the past, European data protection laws have developed primarily wihtin a national legal context with some guiding principles being suggested by the Council in the forms of resolutions. Yet even with the adoption of the Convention and its goal of harmonization, there may be some detrimental effect on international business interests, caused by remaining unequal national legislation.[198]

B.   DOMESTIC EUROPEAN DATA PROTECTION

Some European countries enacted laws to regulate data use before and after the advisory resolutions on the subject were advanced by the Council of Europe. In some countries, data protection has been elevated to the level of constitutional priority.[199] In both Spain and Portugal the texts of new constitutions incorporate data protection as a fundamental right. The national legislatures in the Netherlands and Switzerland intend to incorporate data protection as a fundamental right in future consitutional revisions.[200]

Privacy plays a central though not exclusive role in the composition of the various European laws regulating data use. In European legal theory of data protection and privacy much more is made of the citizen's ability to know and control the use of personal information than of the right to be left alone.[201] Emphasis is placed on requiring those who hold, process, transfer and disseminate information in a way that would prove harmful or injurious to the indvidual to be accountable for their actions.

The European data protection laws often include provisions that require data processors or users to give either general or specific information to the individual. This disclosure is accomplished through a variety of means which depend upon the particular national jurisdiction. The location of the data storage facility must usually be revealed. The source of the information, where it will be sent, and for what purpose it will be used must also be disclosed. Generally, personal data can be processed only if the individual data subject has given an informed consent. Implied consent is often construed if the subject would have reason to know or expect such processing to take place.[202]

These European data protection laws have a tripartite structure. They impose obligations on data users, confer rights upon data subjects, and place the duty for supervision upon the government.[203] In many cases protection has been extended to legal persons, as defined by the particular national laws, along with natural persons. Laws often stipulate in detail the regulations that parties must implement to police themselves. Under these types of legal schemes, there must be a registration of identity with the proper authorities. There is a published index from which the public can determine whom should be contacted to discover the content and use of data files. This somewhat passive approach places the responsibility for protection on the data subject. The affected individual must be the one to instigate any inquiries into possible abuses involving the use of information.[204]

A second European approach promotes external control over the data users. In this model, the public data protection authority is more actively involved in the regulation of data collection, processing and transfer.

The regulation can consist of licensing, inspections, consultations and advising the legislatures and executives as to the needs for new laws or enforcement procedures.[205] Often, these data protection agencies combine policy planning with policy making, decision making, and control.[206]

The various domestic laws often restrict transborder data flow.[207] The proposed Convention establishes a binding legal arrangement that supplements the domestic laws and eases the integration of the various legal provisions into a comprehensive body of laws for data protection and transborder data flow.

C. DEVELOPMENT OF EUROPEAN INTERNATIONAL DATA PROTECTION LAW

In 1968, an international conference on human rights was convened in Teheran, Iran, to mark the 20th anniversary of the Universal Declaration of Human Rights. The issues of the use of electronic media and its effect on the rights of individuals were raised at this conference. The conference focused in part on limiting the use of electronic media equipment.

Following the conference, the Council of Europe looked at the issue more closely. The Council's Parliamentary Assembly recommended that the organization's Committee of Ministers study the possible dangers to human rights and freedoms which the Council wanted to protect. The Council's European Convention on Human Rights, which had been adopted almost two decades earlier, had not anticipated the startling changes in technology that had occurred since then. Ironically, computers were at first not considered as grave a danger as other devices then employed for electronic surveillance. However, by 1970, it had become apparent to those conducting the study that the machines did indeed pose a potential for serious abuses of fundamental human rights. In light of advances in technology, the study group found the Convention on Human Rights lacked the specificity and qualifications needed for adequate legal protection of human rights. For one thing, the Human Rights Convention applied to relations between individuals and public authorities but lacked jurisdiction over disputes between private parties. Secondly, a conflict between the Convention's guarantee for the right of privacy in Article 8 and the right to free access to information in Article 10 needed to be resolved. Finally, the jurisdictional provisions of the Convention could not adequately cope with the multiple problems which might be generated by the misuse or abuse of automatic data processing systems.

The Committee of Minsters elected to forego the drafting of a supplement to the Convention and opted to formulate new rules by intergovernmental committee. Out of this process came two resolutions--Council of Europe Resolutions (73) 22 and (74) 29.

D. THE COUNCIL OF EUROPE'S FIRST EFFORTS AT DATA PROTECTION LAW

Council of Europe Resolution (73) 22, adopted by the Committee of Ministers on September 26, 1973, at the 224th meeting of the Ministers' Deputies, and provided the foundation of legal principles on which the present Convention is based.[208]   In this early stage, the scope of the Resolution was limited to the protection of the individual vis-a-vis electronic data banks in the private sector.

The Committee of Ministers recognized that the use of electronic data processing equipment for the keeping of records about individuals had already become widespread and that it was constantly increasing. Resolution 83(22) expressed the Council's concern that in order to prevent abuses in the storing, processing and distribution of te personal information through the use of electronic devices, some immediate legislative measures were needed. While some member states had already enacted domestic legislation, others contemplated establishing their own laws.   In order to prevent further divergence between the laws of the member states, the resolution recommended some data protection principles.   The Council hoped the member states would take all the steps necessary to put these principles into effect.   The Council also expected the secretary general of the Council of Europe to be in-formed about any actions that were taken.   It was thought that the adoption of these common principles would promote a notion of a "European public order".[209]   At the time of the resolution, the Council's preference was for the member states to regard the principles as suggested guide-lines when drafting their own laws.   A formal international agreement would be concluded later.

However states were given latitude in enacting
domestic legislation that would provide protection for
an individual's right of privacy. As a result, there
were likely to be different approaches to applying the
principles. Certain aspects of the privacy protection
problem, such as the transmission of data between and
among the member states through inter-connected computers,
could only be effectively managed by concerted intergovernmental action.

The principles contained within this first resolution
apply only to natural persons. While the Council
recognized that abuses of electronic data processing might
also prove harmful to legal persons, the problem was considered less acute and not within the scope of the resolution.[210] This omission was not intended to discourage
efforts by member states to provide protection for legal
persons in their domestic laws. The resolution also did
not cover those electronic data banks used soley for personnel administration and not for information distribution.
Should those data banks begin to disseminate data, the
principles of the resolution would be applied. In all
cases, the size of a data collection was immaterial.
Both the authorities empowered to regulate data banks
and the data users themselves were to make themselves
aware of the principles and definitions addressed by the
resolution. Since the regulation of data banks was to
be organized by a variety of national methods, the recommended principles were supposed to be regarded as both
a guideline for enforcement authorities and a professional
code of conduct for individual users.[211]

Several definitions are included in the resolution to provide a common terminology among the member states of the Council. To *"handle"* data by the definition of the resolution is to either process it or store it. *"Dissemination"* means the transfer of information by a user to any third party. The gathering of information prior to its recording is not considered part of actual data bank processing.[212]

The first principle advanced in the resolution covers the quality of the information that can be stored. Any information that was to be collected and stored in data banks and that could be used for discriminatory or embarassing purposes is considered outside the acceptable scope of the principle. Special situations in which such information might be used for some remedial effect is allowed, but distribution of the information to curious third parties is prohibited.

The second principle of the resolution promotes the idea that computerized information should be gathered, processed and stored for only a particular purpose. Although this resolution does not specify what those purposes should be, its intent is that automatic data processing files not be established for general, indiscriminate collection of information about individuals. The quantity and quality of the information being collected is also considered. Recognizing the interest of data bank users and operators to fully use the storage and processing capabilities of their machines, this portion of the resolution advises member states "to adopt a rule which would halt the unbridled hoarding of data".[213]

The third principle states that data should not be obtained by fraudulent or unfair means. This safeguard is reaffirmed by other principles within the resolution. The intent in specifying the method by which data should be collected is to avoid improper or abusive collection methods from coming into favor. The rule is simply stated and does not define the term "unfair means."

The fourth principle requires that rules specify the length of time particular categories of information can be maintained. These rules may be the product of either statute or the data bank user. The principle suggests that some form of programmed, automatic erasure procedures be included as part of the process.[214] Exceptions are made for less sensitive types of data such as names, birth dates, academic degrees and the like.[215] Though no requirement for a formal "right to oblivion" is included in the resolution, it is clear that unreasonably long retention of information is to be avoided.[216]

Prompted by the fear that data bank users or operators might try to peddle the information stored in the machines in order to defray costs or enlarge profits, the committee stated in the fifth principle of the resolution that, without authorization, information should be used for only those purposes for which it had been stored.[217] Also, the data should not be communicated to third parties without consent. The precise form of the authorization and who should give it is not specified. This authorization could be the consent of the persons about whom the data is relevant or the appropriate legal authorities.[218] The definition of the term "third party" was left to the national states.

Principle six states that, as a general rule, an individual about whom data has been collected and stored should have the right to know what information has been stored, the purpose of such storage, and the particular purpose for any release of that information.[219] This principle was intended to establish a balance between the interest and rights of the individuals and the interests of the users of data banks.[220] The Committee declined to require any mandatory rules for those who operate the data bank to inform data subjects of the data collection or the content of files. The expectation was that many data subjects would usually be unconcerned about such stored information. Moreover, informing these individuals-which would usually be done by mail--would in itself present a risk to personal privacy, if this printed information were intercepted by an unauthorized person, and supplying data print-outs could create an unreasonable burden on data users.[221]

Maintaining accurate information and protecting against abuses are the objects of principles seven and eight.[222] As a corollary to principles one, three, and four, principle seven is addressed to users of electronic data banks in the private sector. These data banks would have a commercial interest in providing accurate information, but the principle of accuracy is nevertheless emphasized to ensure observance and to encourage a data bank user to keep the files current. The principle also requires that care be taken to expunge obsolete data and to avoid storing data that is out of date.[223]

The eighth principle of the resolution suggests that precautions be taken against the abuse or misuse of information.[224] This principle is to be applied through the use of technical security requirements for the computers and through the methods by which the data banks are organized. It is expected that electronic data systems be equipped with security systems that prevent unauthorized access to them. The principle also suggests that data banks have some means of detecting unauthorized use. The principle places responsibility for the security of information and the protection of the data system squarely upon those who manufacture and operate the systems. Since the final control over system configuration and operation rests with these parties, the imposition of a security principle upon them was considered necessary and fundamental to effective data protection.[225]

Limitations on access to stored information is the ninth principle of the resolution. Only those persons who have a valid reason to know the stored information can be allowed access. As a result, those who operate the data systems must do so in a responsible manner which does not violate the rules of professional secrecy and conduct. The principles of professional secrecy extend not only to those who actually operate the machines but include the machine users and their clients.[226] A code of professional ethics for data bank personnel is a main objective of this principle though no particular uniform code is suggested. The development of professional standards was left to individual countries. Injuries resulting from actions taken by personnel working in the environment of the data bank but not directly related to its operation are to be covered by the ordinary laws.

Lastly, the tenth principle states that statistical data about individuals should be released only in aggregate form and in such a way as to make it impossible for anyone to link the information to particular persons.[227]

The second resolution--Resolution 74(29)--was published in 1974 and recommended principles for data protection in the public sector. These principles were similar in content and purpose to those published in the 1973 resolution. As a general rule, the public was to be regularly informed about the creation, operation, and refinement of electronic data banks in the public sector. The information stored in the data banks had to be obtained by lawful and fair means, be accurate and current, and appropriate and relevant to the purpose for which it had been stored.[228]

For those situations in which automatic data processing involved information relating to the intimate private lives of data subjects or consisted of information that might be used for discriminatory actions, the second resolution advances several rules.[229] First, the existence of such data banks must be provided for by law or made public so that potential data subjects have notice of their existence. Second, the law or regulation which establishes the data bank must clearly state the purpose of the storage and use of the information. These laws must also state the conditions under which that information might be distributed within either the public administrative agencies or to the private sector. Third, unless explicitly excepted by law or permitted by a competent authority, the stored data can not be used for any purpose other than that for which the data bank had been established.

A suggestion for establishing time limits during which information can be kept is also included in the new resolution.[230] Exceptions to the principle of required time limitations are allowed if necessary for statistical, scientific or historical purposes. In those cases, system operators are to develop and institute special provisions for ensuring privacy during the extended period of storage and use.

The right of individuals to have access to their data files is another principle retained from the previous resolution.[231] Any limitations of this principle are to be strictly regulated. As in Resolution 73(22), rules for safeguarding against the misuse and abuse of information are to be developed. The second resolution expects member states to enact laws governing the use of security systems and the conduct of those who operate automatic data processing systems. Only authorized personnel are to be allowed access to information, and no statistical data can be released in any manner that make it possible to link the information to a particular individual.

E.   THE NEXT STAGE: THE EUROPEAN CONVENTION

When the Council of Europe resolutions were being prepared, it had been expected that the next step would be the reinforcement of that legislation by a binding international agreement. Two models for such an agreement were considered. The first model was based on reciprocity. Under the terms of this model a country would not allow data processing operations in its territory about resident aliens if the type of operation being conducted would be illegal in the mother country. The model would function through the application of national data laws standards. This model was discarded because it resulted in legal complications among domestic legislations and did not provide the same basic rights to all persons.[232]

A second model based on common data protection principles applicable to all parties to a formal agreement was chosen instead. The Committee of Ministers directed a committee of experts to prepare a convention covering international and transfrontier data processing. The committee of experts was instructed to cooperate with the *Organization for Co-operation and Economic Development (OCED)* on any venture which that organization might have been undertaking to develop an international agreement.[233] Close contact was maintained between the two organizations by corresponding committees and at the secretariat level. The OCED, Australia, Canada, Japan and the United States were represented by their own official observers to the Council of Europe's committee of experts. Representatives for Finland, the Hague Con-

ference on Private International Law and the European
Communities also participated. The European Economic
Community, which was concerned about the harmonization
of national legislation covering transborder data flow,
data security, and possible distrotions in competition,
maintained close contact with the Council of Europe.
The committee of experts held four meetings between
November 1976 and May 1979. A working party of experts
from Austria, Belgium, France, the Federal Republic of
Germany, Italy, the Netherlands, Spain, Sweden, Switzerland and the United Kingdom met between committee sessions
to attend to details.

The resulting proposed *Convention for the Protection
of Individuals with Regard to Automatic Processing of
Personal Data* has a preamble and seven chapters.[234]
The title of the instrument does not contain a reference
to it being a European convention. This was purposely
omitted to promote accession to the Convention by nations
other than the European states. The document covers
three basic areas--provisions for substantive law in
the form of basic principles for data protection, special
rules for transborder data flow, and mechanisms for mutual
assistance and consultation among the parties to the
Convention. The preamble states that the aim of the
Council is to achieve greater unity between members based
on respect for the rule of law and fundamental human
rights and freedoms. While reaffirming a commitment
to the free flow of information, the Council states that
it desires to extend safeguards for individual rights
and especially that of privacy.[235] Implicitly recognizing

the right of freedom of information, the Council also
acknowledges that under certain conditions that exercise
of this right might adversely affect other important
rights.[236] It is for the purposes of safeguarding those
other protected rights that the contracting parties to
the Convention accepted it.

The first chapter of the convention contains general
provisions and consists of three articles describing
object and purpose (Article 1), definitions (Article
2) and scope (Article 3). The state object and purpose
of the document is the secuing in the territory of each
party to the Convention respect for rights and fundamental freedoms, especially the right of privacy with
regard to automatic processing of personal data. Since
this is a new international legal concept, the Council
deemed it necessary to explain clearly the reason for
the document. The guarantees in the Convention are to
be extended to all individuals within a state acceding
to it regardless of nationality or residence. Any attempt
by a contracting party to restrict protection to only
its own nationals or legally resident aliens is to be
considered contrary to the Convention.[237]

Article 2 contains definitions of terms or concepts
used in the legislation of the national states that participated in the Convention. They are much the same
as those used in the earlier resolutions advanced by
the Council. Some changes were made in order to account
for subsequent national legislation and problems that
result regulating transborder data flow. For the purposes of the Convention, "personal data" means any in-

formation relating to an identified or identifiable individual (data subject). " *subject* " is a term of art and was chosen in order to convey a sense of subjectivity about the individual. An *identifiable person*" is one who is easily identified without sophisticated or extraordinary means. *"Automated data file"* is defined as any set of data undergoing automatic processing. In turn, " *automatic data processing*" includes the storage of data, the carrying out of logical or arithemetic operations on the data, and the alteration, erasure, retrival, and dissemination of data carried out in whole or in part by automated means. This definition covers not only data files in a particular location but also files distributed geographically and linked by a communications network for processing. The term *"electronic data bank"*, which had been used in Resolution 73(22) and Resolution 74(29) and in some national legislation, was replaced by *"automated data file"*. The collection of information is not considered part of "processing". *"Dissemination"* includes the disclosure of data to third parties and allowing third parties access to data. A *" controller of the file "* is a natural or legal person, public authority, agency or other body that is authorized according to national law to create a file. The authorized agency can decide the purpose for the automated data files, the categories of data to be used, and the type of processing to be done.

Article 3 covers the scope of the Convention. In this article contracting parties agree to apply the Convention to automated data files and automated processing. The Convention applies to both the public and the private sector even though most international data flow occurs in the private sector. The Convention also has an impact on the public sector because Article 3 forces the member States to employ data protection principles when processing public files within their national borders. Further, the Convention provides a vehicle for individuals to exercise their right to be informed when their records are being kept by a public authority in a foreign country.

Exceptions to any of the provisions of the Convention are to be filed with the secretary general of the Council of Europe. These exceptions must be clearly specified in order to avoid problems of interpretation by other parties. Any state may notify the secretary general that it will not apply the Convention to specific categories of automated personal data files. Conversely, a nation may decide to apply the rules of the Convention to data files not usually subject to automatic data processing. If a nation chooses to extend the application of the Convention principles, it may limit that extension to specific categories of data files. In any of these cases, a list of the files in question must be deposited with the secretary general, but this list may not include any files which would be regulated by a member state's own domestic data protection law. As any new categories of data become subject to the national laws, the deposited list must be amended. A nation may notify the secretary general that it wishes to extend the application of the Convention to include information relevant to groups of persons, associations, foundations, companies, corporations or other bodies consisting of individuals whether or not those bodies are legal entities.

Parties which have expressly excluded categories may not try to apply the rules of the Convention to such categories against a party tht has not excluded them. If a country has not extended the Convention to cover a category, it may not claim the application of the Convention for that category against a party which has extended coverage. Declarations by any party-state to the Convention take effect upon that party's entry into the Convention if the party-state has made these declaations at the time of signature or deposit of its instrument of ratification. Otherwise, there will be a three-month wait after deposit with the secretary-general before the declarations become effective. Declarations may be partially or totally withdrawn subject to notification of the secretary general and a three-month waiting period.

Chapter 2 is the central part of the Convention. The basic principles for data protection are established in this chapter. It is expected that each county upon its entry into the Convention, will take the steps necessary to effectuate the fundamental principles in their domestic legislation. The principles, intended as guidelines for legislation, supplement those contained in Resolution (73)22 and (74)29. The method of implementation of the principles is for the the member states to decide. The intent of the Convention is that these principles be applied in a way that would harmonize with the laws of the countries acceding to the Convention. This in turn should reduce conflicts of law and facilitate transborder data flow.[238]

Article 5, contained within Chapter 2, states that personal data undergoing automatic data processing must be obtained lawfully, stored for specified and legitimate purposes, and used in ways that are consistent with those purposes. The data must be accurate and current, and it must be stored in a manner which permits individual identification for no longer than is necessary. Special protected categories of data which reveal racial origin, political inclinations, religious or other beliefs are the subject of Article 6. These protected categories also include information about the sexual life and the health records of individuals.[239] These records may not be processed unless there are particular provisions for safeguards within the national data protection legislation. The list was not meant to be a complete statement of the types of information to be protected. Countries bound by the Convention are free to include other categories of sensitive data in their domestic law. The importance attached to types of sensitive information is to be determined by the member nations.

Article 7 states that security measures must be implemented to protect personal data stored in data files against accidental or unauthorized access, alteration, dissemination, loss or destruction. It is expected that the security methods employed will keep pace with the technology available in the field of data processing. The security measures must be tailored to the type of system that is to be protected.

Article 8 provides for additional safeguards for the data subject. Any person may determine the existence of an automated personal data file and its purpose. Also open to discovery is the identity and the habitual residence or principal place of business of the controller of the file. In countries with a public index of such groups, the requirement is already satisfied. In nations without that provision, the laws must provide that the name of a controller be supplied upon request. Anyone may also obtain, at reasonable intervals and without delay or expense, a confirmation as to whether information on that individual is stored and a copy of that data intelligible form.[240] Depending on the national law, this information can be supplied either directly from the processor or through an intermediate supervisory authority.

The opportuity for correction or erasure of data as been provided if the information has been processed contrary to the domestic law or the principles of Articles 5 and 6. If a request for correction or erasure is not honored, the aggrieved party is to be given a legal remedy or right of action against the offending party.

No exception to the provisions of Articles 5, 6 and 8 are allowed unless within limits defined by Article 9. Derogation from those articles will be allowed when they are necessary to protect state security, public safety, the monetary interest of the state or the suppression of criminal offenses.[241] Derogation may also be allowed in order to protect the data subject or the rights of others. These exceptions are limited to steps clearly necessary for the protection of the fundamental values of the democratic society. The decisions of the Court of Human Rights indicated to those drafting the Convention that "necessary measures" could not be con- cretely established, but should be construed in light of particular set circumstances.[242]

The exercise of individual privacy rights under the Convention regarding data files used for statistical or scientific research purposes will be more restricted if there is no risk for infringement upon the privacy of the data subjects.[243] Such a risk-free situation would be the presentation of data in aggregate form and without any identifying qualities.

Article 10 is a provision for establishing sanctions in order to guarantee effective data protection. The parties to the convention agree to establish appropriate sanctions and remedies for violations of their domestic laws implementing the basic principles of data protection. Since the Convention is of a non-self-executing character, the nature of the civil, administrative, and criminal sanctions is left for the individual states to decide.[244]

Article 11 states that a contracting party may choose to extend a wider protection to data subjects. This article is modeled after Article 60 of the European Human Rights Convention. The principles contained within the present Convention are intended to establish a min- imum level of protection. They are not to be perceived as a limitation upon member states for enlarging the scope of data protection laws.

Transborder data flow is regulated by Article 12. A major purpose of the Convention is to harmonize data protection with the principle of the free flow of information stated in Article 10 of the European Human Rights Convention. The new legal relations governing the quality and content of information that may be transmitted and received by the acceding parties will affect the general international data flow. Article 12 applies to personal data either undergoing automatic processing or collected for that purpose and transferred across national borders. The wording of the Convention is structured to accunt for the variety of ways in which data can be transferred. The transfer of information to another party must not be refused solely on the grounds of personal privacy. Since all contracting parties have subscribed to the common principles of the Convention, it is reasoned that the same type of protection should be available throughout the different nations. This helps to protect the free international flow of information. Countries may, however, choose to derogate from the provisions.

The Convention additionally allows states to derogate their national legislation including specific regulations for certain categories of data and the regulations of other parties which are equivalent. A Convention member may refuse to allow certain information to be transmitted through its borders if the final destination of the information is a state which has not subscribed to the Convention. In such cases the information must be intended to simply pass through the member country without any further processing steps to be taken, as the processing of data will subject the member country to responsibility for the data merely the presumption or expectation that the information might eventually pass to a non-member third party is not sufficient grounds to invoke derogation. Hidden restrictions based on purposes other than for data protection will not be allowed. General business or economic concerns are not sufficient to interfere with the free flow of information between the state acceding to the Convention. It is expected that those parties which are European Economic Community members are bound by the tenets of the Treaty of Rome in regard to principles of fair trade and competition.

The subject of Chapter 4 of the Convention is mutual assistance. The Chapter is comprised of Articles 13, 14, 15 and 16, which contain provisions based on other European conventions regulating mutual assistance in administrative matters.[245] Specific provisions for mutual assistance were included in the present Convention in order to attract a greater number of countries. In addition, the special nature of data protection makes it desirable that the administration of mutual assistance be entrusted to the specially designated data authorities.

Article 13 covers the form of cooperation between the countries. The agreement to render mutual assistance to enforce the Convention is to be implemented through the designated national authorities. The secretary-

general of the Council of Europe is to be notified of
the competency and powers of these authorities. These
agencies are required to transfer upon request, information on the law and administrative practice used within
their jurisdictions for data protection.[246] The agencies
are also bound to take all appropriate measures that
are provided for under the member states domestic laws
when furnishing information on the data processing within
their respective states. Multilateral as well as bi-
lateral exchange of legal information is considered permissible under the formulation of the mutual assistance
principles.

Article 14 deals with providing assistance to data
subjects resident abroad. It ensures that individuals
living abroad in a member or in a non-member state will
be able to exercise their right of data protection in
the country of origin. The members are bound to honor
the Convention for the purpose of protecting their own
nationals or the nationals of other contracting parties.
When the data subject resides in the territory of another
party to the Convention, the individual is given the
option of pursuing his rights either directly in the
country where the information is to be processed, or
through the intermediary national authority designated
to handle such affairs in the country of residence.
The request for such assistance must be made in a fairly
specific manner. The name, address and other particulars
identifying the person making the request must be supplied as well as the nature of the material requested
and the group or person to whom the request should be

directed. This level of specificity is intended to ex-
pedite the procedure and to avoid abuses.[247]

Provisions concerning how assistance is to be rendered by the designated authorities are in Article 15.
The article demands that data protection authorities exercise discretion and confidentiality. An authority which
has received information when acting upon a request for
assistance may not use that information for any purpose
other than the subject of the request. Any persons in
the service of a data protection authority are bound by
restrictions of secrecy. Requests for assistance must
originate from an individual and not from an authority.[248]

Pursuant to Article 16, a designated authority can
only refuse requests for assistance in particular, designated situations. It may refuse if the request is for an
action outside the jurisdiction of the authority or if
the request doesn't comply with the provisions of the Convention. A party can also refuse if compliance with the
request would be offensive to the national sovereignty,
security, public policy or fundamental rights of persons
within that nation.[249]

Provisions covering the procedure to be used for
assistance rendered by an authority and the payment of
costs are dealt with in Article 17. The cost of the use
of experts and interpreters needed in giving the assistance are charged to the party whose authority requested
the assistance. The particular procedures, forms, and
other details for mutual assistance can be agreed upon
by the parties.[250]

The establishment of a consultative committee is provided for in Chapter 5, Articles 18 through 20.[251] The ultimate purpose of the Consultative Committee is to ensure the smooth operation of the Convention and to make modifications or adjustments as they are deemed necessary.[252] Each party is charged with appointing a representative and a deputy representative to the Committee. Member states in the Council of Europe which are not parties to the Convention may also be represented by an observer. By unanimous decision the Consultative Committee may invite non-members of the Council also not party to the Convention to enjoy observer status. The Consultative Committee will render advice for the resolution of problems. It will make proposals for improvements in the Convention and propose amendments. The Committee must also offer opinions on proposed amendments and, upon requests, on controversial issues. The Committee is to be convened by the secretary-general of the Council of Europe. The first meeting being within 12 months of the Convention's entry into force. Regular meetings are to be held thereafter at least every two years or when at least one-third of the representatives from member states of the Convention requests a meeting. A majority of the representatives shall constitute a quorum, and the Committee is required to submit regular reports on its work and the functioning of the Convention to the Ministers of the Council of Europe. All other procedural rules have been left to the design of the Committee itself.[253]

Amendments to the Convention may be proposed by

a member state, the Committee of Ministers of the Council of Europe, or the Consultative Committee. The proposal for an amendment must be communicated to the secretary-general of the Council of Europe and to the member states individually. All non-member states which have acceded or have been invited to accede must also be notified. After the Consultative Committee has rendered an opinion on the proposed amendments, the Committee of Ministers must consider the proposal and Consultative Committee's opinion. If approved, the text of the amendment is forwarded to the individual members for acceptance. Thirty days after acceptance by the parties, the amendment comes into force.

Chapter 7 contains final clauses in Articles 22 through 27. The Convention is open to signature by the member states of the Council of Europe. Instruments of ratification are to be deposited with the secretary general of the Council, and the Convention entering into force three months after the date on which five members of the Council of Europe have deposited their instruments of ratification. Any members acceding thereafter become subject to the Convention three months after deposit of their own instrument of ratification. States may specify particular territories to which the Convention will apply, and they are able to further extend protection to more territories upon notification to the secretary general and a three-month wait. Retraction of this protection is possible but only upon notification to the secretary general and a six-month waiting period. No reservations with respect to the provisions of the Convention are to be allowed. It is possible, however, for a party at any time to denounce the Convention, and by notifying the secretary general of the Council, this denunciation becomes effective six months after receipt of notification. In turn, the secretary general of the Council is bound to notify members to the Convention of this international agreement.

F.   IMPLICATIONS OF THE EUROPEAN CONVENTION FOR U.S. DATA PROCESSING

The fundamental data protection principles in the Convention have been established by the Convention for some time. The principles have been incorporated into the domestic data protection laws of members in the Council of Europe. With this common point of departure, the individual states have developed their own laws to suit their specific legal, political and social needs.

Unlike the Council of Europe, the United States has been reluctant to become involved in comprehensive agreements to control the use and flow of data.[254] However, it seems that the United States could very well find its business subject to the controls placed upon data protection by the countries in Europe. With the acceptance of the Convention, the coordination of legal enforcement mechanisms which regulate the international flow of data could very likely impede the transmission of information from Europe to the United States or other states not party to the Convention. The types of information that can be gathered or processed by American companies doing business in Europe may now fall under a stricter scrutiny. In addition, the legal roadblocks to the transmission of data might inhibit the develoment of business providing processing services. The lack of reciprocal legislation limits the United States' ability to receive information even if it should choose to alter its present policy and accede to the Convention.[255]

United States policy on data protection and data flow is now entering a period of transition.[256] Understanding the dimensions of the conflict that will develop when the Convention is finally adopted requires careful study of the basic principles of European data protection at the national and international levels. In order for the United States to maintain access to information originating outside its borders and to continue its data processing operations, lawyers and lawmakers must understand the parameters of European data regulations. Having considered the scope of such regulation, it may then be necessary to either adjust the organizational basis of American business intersts to comply with the international regulation or to formulate laws which allow for a more direct integration of alternate data protection principles into United States law.

VIII.   CONCLUSION

Since the advent of computerized personal information files, the erosion of individual privacy has accelerated. At the same time, the individual's ability to gain access to the information collected and to control its use has diminished. The magnitude of this information processing as well as the mechanics involved in entering the information into a computer have greatly increased the possibilities for errors in the files. Indeed, many who have been involved in the formulation of privacy is not so much the existence of the files as it is the potential for inaccurate data being repeatedly processed without the individual knowing about it.

The authors of the United States Constitution, however, did not anticipate the computer revolution and its impact on individual rights. The Constitution does not specifically grant a right to privacy. Congress has attempted to rectify this lack of foresight with five major pieces of legislation:

1) the Fair Credit Reporting Act, whose purpose is to prevent abuses by credit reporting agencies in collecting, storing and disseminating financial information on individuals;

2) the Family Educational Rights and Privacy Act, which guarantees parents access to their children's records in any educational institution receiving federal funds;

3) the Freedom of Information Act, which allows individuals access to records the government has on them;

4) the Right to Financial Privacy Act, which limits government access to consumer records in financial institutions; and

5) the Fair Credit Billing Act, which helps protect individuals from inaccuracies in credit data.

Legislation on the state level to safeguard individual privacy is piecemeal and inconsistent. Only ten states have privacy protection provisions in their constitutions.

The Fair Credit Reporting Act is the only significant federal legislation to impose privacy regulations on information gathered and transferred among non-governmental entities. The Act requires consumer reporting agencies to adopt procedures for ensuring that the information they provide is accurate, relevant and fair and that it be used with proper regard for confidentiality. Both consumer reports, which evaluate an individual's character as a prospective employee or tenant, come under the purview of this Act. The passage of this legislation and the resulting court scrutiny of credit reporting agency procedures have engendered a greater sense of responsibility among reporting agencies to process accurate information.

Yet, for all the privacy protection the Fair Credit Reporting act affords, it does not cover the reporting of non-financial data, such as an individual's medical history. The Act's scope is limited to consumer reports for credit, insurance, employment, government license and other "legitimate busines needs." The Act does not define this phrase. While civil penalties are imposed on reporting agencies that are negligent in complying with the Act, consumers cannot bring action for defamation or invasion of privacy unless they can prove the agency supplied erroneous information with malice or willful intent to harm.

A more comprehensive scheme than what is available in the United States for regulating the collection and flow of personal information has been drafted by the member nations of the Council of Europe. The aim of this proposed *Convention for the Protection of Individuals with Regard to Automatic Processing of Personal Data* is to create a consistency of national privacy protection legislation that harmonizes data protection with the need for free flow of information across national borders. This document covers any kind of information processing that could pose a threat to individual privacy.

However, as encompassing as the Convention is, in terms of providing real protection from invasion of privacy, it is weak. While one of the principles of the Convention requires that data files be established for only particular purposes, the allowable purposes are not specified. Another principle stipulates that information cannot be fraudulently or unfairly obtained, but unfairness is not defined. The Convention gives individuals the right to know what information is stored on them and for what purposes but also states that transfer of information cannot be stopped for reasons of personal privacy alone. Becoming a party to the Convention is voluntary, and each party is allowed to devise its own methods for implementing the Convention principles.

Thus, despite the lofty tone of the Convention's title and stated purpose, it reflects a higher concern for the consistency of restrictions placed on transborder data flow than for the preservation of individual privacy.

In the United States, with its tradition of individual
independence, there is greater likelihood for legislation
that would provide broader privacy protection. Before this
can happen, however, public awareness of the ramifications
of computerized personal information files will have to
increase to the point that there is a demand for such
protection.

IX.   FOOTNOTES

1. *"1984"*,George Orwell, Harcourt Brace Janovich, Inc.,
    (1949).

2. A. Westin & M. Baker, *Databanks in a Free Society*,
    337-406 (1976).

3. *Id.*at 321-30.

4. Miller, *Personal Privacy in the Computer Age; The
    Challenge of a New Technology in an Information-
    Oriented Society*, 67 Mich. L. Rev. 1091, 1108-09
    (1969).

5. Miller, *Computers Data Banks and Individual Privacy;
    An Overview.*

6. D. Sanders, *Computers and Management in a Changing
    Society*, 49-91 (2d ed. 1974).

7. Bazelon, *Probing Privacy*, 12 Gonz.L.Rev. 587 (1977).

8. Linowes, *Must Personal Privacy Die In the Com-
    puter Age* (1973).

9. Murdock, *The Use and Abuse of Computerized Infor-
    mation*, 44 ALB.L.Rev. 589-619 (1980).

10. Privacy Protection Study Commission, *Personal Privacy
    in an Information Society*, 3-4 (1977) [hereinafter
    cited as Privacy Report].

11. Reubhausen & Brim, *Privacy and Behavioral Research*,
    65 Colum. L. Rev. 1184, 1205 (1965).

12. Miller, *Data Banks and Privacy*, *In Computers & the
    Law* 157, 159 (R. Bigelow ed., 2d. ed. 1969).

13. 46 Mich. 160, 9 N.W. 146 (1881).

14. Meldman, *Centralized Information System and the
    Legal Right to Privacy*, Marquette Law Rev. 1969.

15. Warren & Brandeis, *The Right to Privacy*, 4 Harv. L. Rev. (1890).

16. Prosser, *Privacy*, 48 Cal. L. Rev. 383, 389 (1960).

17. 81 F.2d 847 (3rd Cir. 1936).

18. Meldman, *supra* note 14, at 27.

19. 211 K.Y. 765, 299 S.W. 967 (1927).

20. Soma & Wehmhoefer, *A Legal and Technical Assessment of the Effect of Computers on Privacy*, 60:30 Den. L.J. 440 (1983).

21. Prosser, *supra* note 16, at 393.

22. F. Harper & F. James, *Torts* §9.6, at 682 (1956).

23. Soma & Wehmhoefer, *supra* note 20, at 461.

24. W. Prosser, *Handbook of the Law of Torts*, 49-62 (4th Ed. 1971).

25. L. Tribe, *American Constitutional Law*,

26. *N.A.A.C.P. v. Alabama* 357 U.S. 347 (1967).

27. *Katz v. United States*, 389 U.S. 347 (1967).

28. *Griswold v. Connecticut*, 381 U.S. 479, 484 (1965).

29. *Eisenstadt v. Baird*, 405 U.S. 438, 453 (1973).

30. 429 U.S. 589 (1977).

31. 41 Am. Jur. *Privacy* §34-45 (1968).

32. 15 U.S.C. §1681-1681T (1976).

33. Organization for Economic Cooperation and Development Policy Issues in Data Protection and Privacy 148 (1976).

34. 15 U.S.C. §1681 i (1976).

35. *Id.* §1681 n .

36. *Id.* §1681 e.

37. *Id.* §1681 o.

38. *Id.* §1681 n.

39. *Id.* §1681 q.

40. *Id.* §1681 r.

41. *Id.* §1681 p.

42. *Id.* §1681 b.

43. *Id.* §1681 c.

44. 15 U.S.C. §522 (1976 & Supp. IV 1980).

45. See exceptions under 5 U.S.C. §552a(B) (1976).

46. *Id.* §552a(e).

47. *Id.*

48. 20 U.S.C. §1232 *et. seq.*(1976).

49. 20 U.S.C. §1232g(B) (1976 & Supp. IV 1980).

50. 5 U.S.C. 552 (1976 & Supp. IV 1980).

51. 12 U.S.C. §§3401-3422 (1976 & Supp. IV 1980).

52. The statute overrules the holding in *U.S.
     Miller* 425 U.S. 435 (1976).

53. 425 U.S. 435 (1976).

54. H.R. Rep. No. 1383, 95th Cong., 2d Sess. 7.

55.   15 U.S.C. §1666 (1976).

56.   389 U.S. 347 (1967).

57.   Ala. Const. Art. I, §22; Ariz. Const. Art. II, §8;
        Cal. Const. Art. §12; Fla Const. Art. I, §12; Haw.
        Const. Art. I §5; Ill. Const. Art. I §§6, 12; La.
        Const. Art. I, §5; Mont. Const. Art. II, §10; S.C.
        Const. Art. I, §10; Wash. Const. Art. I §7.

58.   Fla. Const. Art. I, §12.

59.   Md. Ann. Code, Art., 100, §95A (1979).

60.   Karst, *The Files: Legal Controls Over the Accuracy
            Accessibility of Stored Personal Data* 31 Law
        & Contemp. Prob. 342, 347 (1966).

61.   Tribe, *supra* note 25, at 889.

62.   Comment, *Commercial Credit Bureaus: The Right to
        Privacy and State Action*, 24 Am. U.L. Rev. 421,
        470-84 (1975).

63.   *Toward A Right of Privacy As A Matter Of
        State Constitutional Law*, 5 Fla. St. U. Rev.
        631, 740-42 (1977).

64.   *Evans* v. *Newton*, 382 U.S. 296 (1966).

65.   Comment, *The Computer Data Bank - Privacy Contro-
        versy Revisited: An Analysis And An Administrative
        Proposal*, 22 Cath. U.L. Rev. 628, 631-32 (1973).

66.   Miller, *supra* note 4, at 1222-23.

67.   Prosser, *supra* note 16, at 50-51.

68.   Miller, *The Assault on Privacy* 189 (1971).

69.   *Sam and Esteban* v. *Goodyear Tire & Rubber Co.*, 306 F. 2d 9 (5th Cir. 1962).

70.   For example, New York rejects common-law doctrine, *Roberson* v., *Rochester Folding Box Co.*, 171 N.Y. 538, 64 N.E. 442 (1902).

71.   Miller, *supra* note 4, at 1222-25.

72.   Privacy Protection Study Commission, *Privacy Law in the States*, 2-7 (1977).

73.   Murdock, *supra* note 9, at 608.

74.   Privacy Report, *supra* note 10, at 75-87.

75.   Miller, *supra* note 4, at 1170.

76.   Murdock, *supra* note 9, at 610.

77.   Note, *Let Industry Beware; A Survey of Privacy Legislation And Its Potential Impact on Business*, 11 Tulsa L.J. 68 (1975).

78.   Federal Information Systems and Plans, Hearings Before The Subcomm. on Foreign Operations & Govt. Info of The House, 93d Cong. 2d Sess. 819 (1974).

79.   *Schechter Poultry Corp.* v. *U.S.*, 295 U.S. 495 (1935).

80.   Grenier, *Computer and Privacy; A Proposal For Self Regulation*, 170 Duke L.J. 495.

81.   Arthur R. Miller, *The Assault on Privacy* (1971).

82.   15 U.S.C. §1681a(f)(1970) defines "consumer reporting agency" to mean any person which, for monetary fees, dues, or on a cooperative nonprofit basis, regularly engages in whole or in part in the practice of assembling or evaluating consumer credit information

or other information on consumers for the purposes
of furnishing consumer reports to third parties,
and which use any means of facility of interstate
commerce for the purpose of preparing or furnishing
consumer reports.

83.   15 U.S.C. §1681a (d) (1970) defines "consumer report"
as any written, oral, or other communication of any
information by a consumer reporting agency bearing on
     consumer's credit worthiness, credit standing,
credit capacity, character, general reputation,
personal characteristics, or mode of living which is
used or expected to be used or collected in whole
or in part for the purpose of serving as a factor
in establishing the consumer's eligibility for (1)
credit or insurance to be used primarily for personal, family, or household purposes, or, (2) employment purposes, or (3) other purposes authorized
under 15 U.S.C. §1681b. The term does not include
(A) any report containing information solely as to
transactions or experiences between the consumer
and the person making the report; (B) any authorization or approval of a specific extension of credit
directly or indirectly by the issuer of a credit
card or similar device; or (C) any report in which
a person who has been requested by a third party
to make a specific extension of credit directly or
indirectly to a consumer conveys his decision with
respect to such request, if the third party advises
the consumer of the name and address of the person
to whom the request was made and such person makes
the disclosures to the consumer required under 15
U.S.C. §1681m.

84.   The Fair Financial Information Practice Act: Hearings on S. 1928 Before the Subcomm. on Consumer
Affairs of the Senate Comm. on Banking, Housing,
and Urban Affairs of the 96th Cong., 2nd Sess. (1980)
(statement of Michael Monroney, V.P., Gov. Relations,
TRW, Inc.) [hereinafter cited as Hearings on S.
1928].

85.   Id., (testimony of David Linowes, prof. of political
economy and public policy, U. of-Ill.).

86. 15 U.S.C. §1681a (c) (1970) defines "consumer" to mean an individual.

87. Rights to Privacy Proposals of the Privacy Protection Study Commission: Hearings on H.R. 10076 Before Subcomm. of the Comm. on Gov. Operations House of Representatives 95th Cong., 2nd Sess. (1978) (statement of John H.F. Shattuck, Dir., ACLU Washington, D.C.).

88. Feldman and Gordin, *Privacy and Personal Information Reporting: The Legislative Boom,* 35 Bus. Law 1259, at 1260.

89. Hearings on S. 1928, *supra* note 84 (statement of David F. Linowes).

90. Mortimer, Brandel and Geltzer, *Consumer Credit* 1983, P.L.I. (1983).

91. *A.B.C. Needlecraft Co.* v. *Dun & Bradstreet,* 245 F.2d 775 (1957).

92. Mortimer, Brandel and Geltzer, *supra* note 90, at 369.

93. *A.B.C. Needlecraft supra* note 91.

94. *Barker* v. *Retail Credit Co.,* 8 Wis. 2d 664 (1960).

95. *Stationer's Corp.* v. *Dun & Bradstreet,* 398 P.2d 785.

96. *Judicial Construction of the Fair Credit Reporting Act: Scope and Civil Liability,* 76 Colum L. Rev. 458 (1976).

97. Judge Cooley coined the phrase "the right to be let alone" Cooley, *Torts* 29 (1888).

98. Warren and Brandeis, *supra* note 15, at 193.

99. W. Prosser, *The Law of Torts* 2d, (1941).

100. *Id.* at 635.

101. Warren & Brandeis, *supra* note 15, at 194.

102. Prosser, *supra* note 99, at 637.

103. *Id.* at 638.

104. *Id.*

105. *Id.* at 639.

106. *Shorter v. Retail Credit Co.* 251 F. Supp. 329 (D.C.S.C., (1966).

107. Spear, *Computers in the Private Sector; Right to Informational Privacy for the Consumer*, 22 Washburn L.J. at 476 (1983).

108. *Tureen v. Equifax, Inc.*, 571 F.2d 411 (8th Cir. (1978).

109. *Shorter, supra* note 106.

110. *Judicial Construction, supra* note 96, at 461.

111. Debt Collection Act of 1980: Hearings on S. 3160 Before the Comm. on Gov. Affairs, 96th Cong., 2nd Sess. 56 (1980) (statement of John L. Spafford, Pres. of Associated Credit Bureaus, Inc.) [hereinafter cited as Hearings on S. 3160].

112. Hearings on Commercial Credit Bureaus Before Subcomm. on Invasion of Privacy of the House Comm. on Government Operations, 90th Cong., 2nd Sess. (1968).

113. McNamara, *The Fair Credit Reporting Act: A Legislative Overview*, 66 Journal of Public Law at 75 (1973).

114. Denney, *Federal Fair Credit Reporting Act*, 88 The Banking L.J. at 581 (1971).

115. MaNamara, *supra* note 113, at 76.

116. Senate Committee on Banking and Currency, Fair Credit

Reporting, S.R. No. 823, 91st Cong., 1st Sess. (1969) reprinted in Fair Credit Reporting Manual at B-18 (1977) [hereinafter cited as Fair Credit Reporting Manual].

117. McNamara, *supra* note 113, at 97.

118. Denney, *supra* note 114, at 585.

119. McNamara, *supra* note 113, at 97.

120. Denny, *supra* note 114, at 585.

121. McNamara, *supra* note 113, at 98.

122. Denney, *supra* note 114, at 586.

123. Mortimer, Brandel and Geltzer, *supra* note 90, at 369.

124. §1681(a)(1).

125. §1681(a)(2)(3).

126. Fair Credit Reporting Manual, *supra* note 116, at B-3.

127. 15 U.S.C. §1681(b).

128. 15 U.S.C. §1681(c).

129. 15 U.S.C. §1681(g).

130. 15 U.S.C. §1681(i).

131. 15 U.S.C. §1681(m).

132.   15 U.S.C. §1681(k).

133.   15 U.S.C. §1681(d).

134.   15 U.S.C. §1681(l).

135.   15 U.S.C. §1681(e).

136.   15 U.S.C. §1681(o).

137.   15 U.S.C. §1681(n).

138.   15 U.S.C. §1681(q).

139.   15 U.S.C. §1681(p).

140.   15 U.S.C. §1681(s).

141.   Spear, *supra* note 107, at 448.

142.   Hearings on S. 1928, *supra* note 84, (statement of Michael Monroney, V.P., Gov. Relations, TRW, Inc.).

143.   *Id.*, (statement of Henry Geller, Ast. Sec. of Communications and Information).

144.   R.W. Day, the Role of Credit Reporting in the 1980's, speech before the Credit Research Center of Perdue University (March 1980) [hereinafter cited as R.W. Day].

145.   Hearings on S. 1928, *supra* note 84, at 6. (Information requested of Henry Geller, Asst. Sec. of Communications and Information, by Sen. Paul F. Tsongas, Chairman Subcomm. on Consumer Affairs, at hearings before that Subcomm. on Titles I and II).

146.   *Id.* at 551 (These figures are extrapolated from estimates that appeared in the Nilson Report as well

as internal estimates from American Express as given by Aldo Papone in response to a request for information from Sen. Paul Tsongas).

147. Congress passed the Privacy act of 1974 which provides informational privacy protection for material collected by government agencies. The Right to Financial Privacy Act gives protection against government agencies obtaining access to financial files collected and kept in the private sector.

148. Spear, *supra* note 107, at 482.

149. *Griswold* v. *Connecticut*, 381 U.S. 479 (1965).

150. *Roe* v. *Wade*, 410 U.S. 113, (1973).

151. 429 U.S. 589 (1977).

152. *Id.* at 605, 606.

153. Spear, *supra* note 107, at 478.

154. Louis Harris Poll on Privacy (1978), see also *1984*, *supra* note 1.

155. *Id.*

156. J.A. Meldman, *Centralized Information Systems and the Legal Right to Privacy*, 4 Computer L. Serv. §5-2 Article 2 (1979).

157. *Id.* at 19.

158. 15 U.S.C. §1681 defines the term "person" to mean any individual, partnership, corporation, trust, estate, cooperative, association, government or governmental subdivision or agency, or other entity.

159. Wall Street Journal, at 1, col 4.

160. Hearings on S. 1928, *supra* note 84, at 1007 (statement of Lewis H. Goldfarb, Asst. Dir. for Credit Practices, FTC).

161. Wall Street Journal, *supra* note 159.

162. Hearings on S. 1928, *supra* note 84, at 290-291.

163. *Id.* at 863 (statement of John L. Spafford, pres. Associated Credit Bureaus, Inc.).

164. *Id.* at 1007.

165. Compliance is enforced by the FTC with respect to consumer reporting agencies and users of reports who are regulated by another federal agency. The views of the FTC are not binding, but they are authoritative.

166. FTC interpretation at 16 CFR §600.5.

167. Hearings on S. 1928, *supra* note 84, at 123 (answers to questions asked by Senator Paul Tsongas on February 27, 1980, in his letter to Asst. Sec. of Commerce Henry Geller).

168. Wall Street Journal, *supra* note 159.

169. Telephone interview with Kark Breyer, Senior Counsel, American Express Travel Related Services Co., Inc. (February 17, 1984).

170. *Notes, Protecting Privacy in Credit Reporting*, 24 Stanford L. Rev. at 551 (1972) [hereinafter cited as Notes].

171. 15 U.S.C. §1681(a)(e).

172. Notes, *supra* note 170 at 552.

173. 15 U.S.C. §1681(a)(e).

174. Notes *supra* note 170, at 553.

175. Kaswell and Sullivan, *Credit Reporting and Collection Practices*, 38 Bus. Law. 1372 (1983).

176. 557 F. Supp. 66 (1982).

177. *Id.* at 71.

178. *Id.*

179. *Id.* at 69.

180. 15 U.S.C. §1681e(b).

181. 444 F. Supp. 541 N.D. Ga. (1978).

182. 444 F. Supp. at 544.

183. *Id.*

184. 682 F. 2d 509 (1982).

185. *Id.* at 513.

186. §1681o - if the consumer can show a grossly negligent violation, he can collect actual damages plus attorney's fees.

187. Kaswell and Sullivan, *supra* note 175, at 1374.

188. Council of Europe, *Convention For the Protection of Human Rights and Fundamental Freedoms*, November 4, 1950 213 U.N.T.S. 222 reprinted in R. Lillich & F. Newman, *International Human Rights: Problems of Law and Policy* (1st ed. 1979) p. 963 [hereinafter cited as Human Rights Convention].

189.   Lillich & Newman, *id.* at 552.

190.   Human Rights Convention, *supra* note 188, Article 1.

191   Burkert, *Institutions of Data Protection-An Attempt At A Functional Explanation of European National Data Protection Laws* 3 Comp. L.J. 167, 170 (1981).

192.   McGuire, *The Informational Age: An Introduction to Transborder Data Flow* Jurismetrics J. 1,3 (1979).

193.   Council of Europe, *Draft Explanatory Report on the Convention For the Protection of Individual with Regard to Automatic Processing of Personal Data* C.O.E. Doc cj-cd (30) [hereinafter cited as Draft Explanatory Report].

194.   *Id.* at 301.

195.   Bigelow, *Transborder Data Flow Barriers* Jurimetrics J 8, 10 (1978).

196.   Novotny, *Transborder Data Flow Regulation: Technical Issues of Legal Concern* 3 Comp. L.J. 105, 106 (1981).

197.   *Id.* at 113.

198.   Draft Explanatory Rept. *supra* note 6 at 302.

199.   *Transborder Data Flows:International Privacy Protection and the Free Flow of Information* 6 B.X. Int. & Comp L.R. 591, 622 (1983).

200   Hondius, *Data Law Europe* 16 Stan. J. Int. L. 87, 94 (1980).

201.   *Id.* at 95.

202. Burkert, *supra* note 191, at 173.

203. Hondius, *supra* note 200, at 93.

204. *Id.* at 101.

205. *Id.* at 101, 102.

206. Burkert, *supra* note 191, at 185.

207. Novotny, *supra* note 196, at 113.

208. Council of Europe, *Resolution (73)22 and Annex* reprinted in 9 C.L.S.A. App. 9-5.2b [hereinafter cited as Resolution (73)22].

209. Council of Europe, *Resolution (73) 22-Explanatory Report* §4 reprinted in 9 C.L.S.A. App 9 p.5 [hereinafter cited as Resolution (73)22 Report].

210. *Id.* at §12.

211. *Id.* at §15.

212. *Id.* at §§16,17.

213. *Id.* at §21.

214. *Id.* at §23.

215. *Id.*

216. *Id.* at §24.

217. *Id.* at §26.

218. *Id.* at §27.

219.   Resolution   (73)22 *supra*   note   208, at Principle 6.

220.   Resolution (73)22-Report, *supra* note 209, at §26.

221   *Id.* at §31.

222.   Resolution   (73)22, *supra*   note   208 at   Principles
7 & 8.

223.   *Id.* at §33.

224.   *Id.* at Principle 8.

225.   Resolution   73(22)-Report, *supra*   note 209, at §35.

226.   *Id.* at §36.

227.   Resolution 73(22) *supra*   note 208, at Principle 10.

228.   Council of Europe, Resolution (74)29, §2 reprinted
in 9 C.L.S.A. App. 9-5.2b 16.

229.   *Id.* at §3.

230.   *Id.* at §4.

231.   *Id.* at §5.

232.   Draft Explanatory Report, *supra* note 193, at §12.

233.   *Id.* at §14.

234.   Council of Europe, *Convention   for   the   Protection
of Individuals With Regard to Automatic Processing
of Personal Data*, Jan. 28, 1981 Europ. T.S. No. 108,
reprinted in 20 I.L.M. 317 (1981) [hereinafter, Con-
vention].

235. *Id.* at Preamble.

236. Draft Explanatory Report, *supra* note 193, at §25.

237. *Id.* at §27.

238. *Id.* at §9.

239. Convention, *supra* note 234, at Article 6.

240. *Id.* at Article 8(b).

241. *Id.* at Article 8(b).

242. Draft Explanatory Report, *supra* note 193, at §49.

243. *Id.* at §52, See also Convention, *supra* note 234, at Article 9 §3.

244. Convention, *supra* note 234, at Article 10, See also Draft Explanatory Report, *supra* note 193, at §53.

245. Draft Explanatory Report, *supra* note 193, at §60.

246. Convention, *supra* note 234, at Article 13 §3.

247. *Id.* at Article 14.

248. *Id.* at Article 15 §3.

249. Draft Explanatory Report, *supra* note 193, at §§67, 68.

250. *Id.* at §72.

251. Convention, *supra* note 234, at Article 20 §4.

252. Draft Explanatory Report, *supra* note 193, at §72.

253.   Convention, *supra* note 234, at Article 20 §4.

254.   Bigelow, *supra* note 195, at p. 11.

255.   McGuire, *supra* note 192, at p. 5.

256.   Bigelow, *supra* note 195, at p. 16.

Original research and preliminary writings by:

Arlene C. Halliday, B.A. Political Science, Merrimack College, J.D. Franklin Pierce Law Center, has been an independent businesswoman and is presently in private practice.

John P. Murphy, B.S. Political Science, Fordham University, J.D. Franklin Pierce Law Center, has been an independent businessman and is presently in private practice.

Joseph Nicastro, B.A. Political Science and Philosophy, Boston College, M.A. International Relations, University of Massachusetts, J.D. Franklin Pierce Law Center, has been an independent businessman and is presently in private practice.

CHAPTER 6 - COMPUTER CRIME

I.   INTRODUCTION

In the beginning man created computers. And they were fruitful and multiplied. Computer presence in homes and businesses continues to surpass past predictions of anticipated usage. There are more than 9.1 million personal computers being used in the United States. It is also estimated that more than 55,000 multipurpose computers are used by the private sector and upwards of 16,000 large computers are used by the federal government.[1]

The characteristics of a computer that contributed to its meteoric rise in usage - its storage capacity, speed and ability to gain access to organized data - are the same characteristics that make computers targets for crime. Behind the news stories of teenages accessing for fun the data bases of government agencies and large hospitals are the questions of whether these incidents represent anomalies or widespread practices.[2] The traditional legal framework has been severely tested in its ability to cope with these new forms of abuses. Underlying the difficulties present in legislating and enforcing effective criminal statutes is the uncertainty as to the definition and scope of what a computer is and therefore what constitutes a computer crime.

II.   A WORKABLE DEFINITION

Because computer crime is usually committed by people who do not fit the stereotypical image of a criminal (i.e. poor, uneducated, addicted to drugs, a member of a minority group) the crime is classified in the 'amorphous category of white collar crime.'[3] White collar crimes include forms of burglary and larceny. The distinguishing factors of white collar crime are the types of people involved, and the covert nature of the acts.

Among researchers who study computer crime there is disagreement over its definition. A central point of agreement is that the use of a computer in any way in the commission of a crime constitutes computer crime. Beyond this broad definition there is little agreement as to what computer crime actually is. The courts have offered little guidance in determining a definition and case law is sparse. In *United States v. Jones*, the Maryland court used the term 'computer abuse' without defining it.[4] In this case the defendant had received foreign checks in the United States. These checks had been issued by a computer which had been programmed to issue them to a non-existent account. The lower court had dismissed the indictment which was based on two federal statutes prohibiting the interstate transportation and receipt of stolen, converted, or fraudulently obtained securities.[5] On appeal, the Fourth Circuit Court of Appeals reversed the lower court by delineating the distinction between fraud and forgery.[6] The court decided that alteration of supporting documents to produce a *bona fide* instrument is actionable as the crime of false pretenses, which is fraud.[7] Here the computer was used as an instrumentality that the court coined as 'computer abuse.'

Donn B. Parker, senior management systems consultant at SRI International, and author of many journal articles based on his computer research, uses the term 'computer abuse' as any intentional act associated in any way with computers where a victim suffered, or could have suffered a loss, and a perpetrator made, or could have made, a gain."[8]

John Taber, a computer systems programmer and author of many computer crime articles, considers Parker's terminology to be unnecessarily confusing to laymen, who tend to interpret the terms 'abuse' and 'crime' synonymously. Taber notes that efforts to devise legislation directly aimed at computer crime are hampered by the lack of sufficient empirical data showing the existence of such crimes. He faults the media for contributing to this deficiency through its sensational coverage of certain crimes involving a computer. This type of coverage, he theorizes, adds to the distorted view of the problem. Accordingly, the difficulty with defining computer crime is that the term is an abstraction rather than a specifically proscribed action. Therefore, in order to define the crime one must look to the substantive action and not solely to the means used to achieve that action.[9] While not extensive, some empirical data is available dealing with the scope of computer crime.

In a study commissioned by the U.S. Government, the General Accounting Office (GAO) investigated the extent of computer crime in the federal government. The GAO used the term 'computer-related crime' and defined it as "acts of intentionally caused losses to the Government or personal gains to individuals related to the design, use, or operation of the systems in which they are committed." The report further notes that "[c]omputer-related crimes may result from preparing false input to systems and misuse of output as well as more technically sophisticated crimes, such as altering computer programs."[10]

In June, 1984, the Criminal Justice section of the American Bar Association issued the results of its task force survey entitled "Report on Computer Crime." The task force adopted broad definition of computer crime, which included criminal activities directed against computers and criminal activities in which computers were used as the instruments to perpetrate the crime. The task force viewed computer crime as a phenomenon rather than a specific action. The group purposely adopted a broad definition so that it would not be subjected to 'semantic hairsplitting' but would provide a constructive basis for distinctions and comparisons with existing laws.[11]

The American Bar Asociation's broad utilitarian definition of computer crime is most practical because it divides the concept into two parts: one in which computers are the facilitators of the offense (in theft, fraud, or embezzlement), and one in which computers are the victims of the offense (in sabotage and vandalism). Likewise the main parts of a computer also lend themselves to different types of protection. The hardware of a computer is tangible. Its protection under traditional criminal statutes for larceny, burglary, or vandalism is therefore not unduly problematic. Alternatively, the software is both intangible and effenescent. Because of these attributes, the protection of software is less definite under traditional theories of criminal and property law.

III.   SOFTWARE AS PROPERTY

Classifying computer crime as a white collar crime
places it in a general category of crimes which includes
types of burglaries and larcenies. The definition of
any crime always includes two basic components which must
be proven to exist in order to sustain a cause of action.
They are the *res*, the activity which is done, and the
mens rea, the requisite intent.[12] The courts have had
difficulty identifying and defining the *res* element in
crimes involving computers. The concept of property,
and specifically the differences between tangible and
intangible property, has been the area of greatest confusion for the courts.

In the traditional notion of property, tangibility
was integral to the definition of property. However,
the concept of tangibility is no longer as necessary
to the definition of property as it once was, as can be
seen in the application of the federal statute 18 U.S.C.
§ 641. The statute prohibits the theft, sale, disposition,
embezzlement, or unauthorized conversion of federal property, whether it be from government agencies or corporations,
in which the federal government has a proprietary interest.
The statute also prohibits the unauthorized sale of any
records or 'thing of value'. Prosecution under this
statute has required judges to interpret property and
'thing of value'.

The Second Circuit Court of Appeals in *United States
v. Girard*, specifically defined 'thing of value' to include
intangibles such as computer programs.[13] The court noted
various jurisdictions which had considered a variety

of intangibles which had been construed as a 'thing of value.'[14] The United States District Court for the District of Columbia in *United States v. Hubbard* concluded that tangible copies of computer information were considered property under the statute.[15] However the court declined to consider the issue of whether the copying of the date without translating it into tangible form would be covered by the statute. The different circuits have not been uniform in their interpretation of 'thing of value'.[16] To date, the United States Supreme Court has not considered this question.

In a civil matter concerned with the tax consequences of hardware and software purchases,[17] the Circuit Court for the District of Columbia held that because of the intangible nature of software, it was not included in the statute's definition of property.[18] In reaching its decision, the court relied on the Internal Revenue Code's ruling regarding the basis for computer hardware and software depreciation.[19] The appellate courts have yet to decide whether software is a commodity under federal antitrust law.[20]

Intangible property has been defined to include patents, trademarks, trade secrets, and copyright. Of these subject areas, only trade secret law and copyright law include criminal sanctions for proscribed actions. Copyright criminal sanctions are governed by federal statute.[21] However, there is neither federal statutory nor constitutional provision for trade secret protection. Such protection can be found only under applicable state statutes.

Criminal trade secret protection can be classified into three types: 1) general theft statutes which have been construed to include trade secret thefts; 2) statutes in effect in approximately half of the states, that specifically proscribe theft or misappropriation of trade secrets;[22] and 3) state statutes that directly proscribe computer crime and may be applied to the misappropriation of trade secrets embodied in software.

Case law based on the first type of protection includes *Hancock v. State*,[23] *United States v. Lambert* [24] and *United States v. Girard*. [25]Of these cases, *Hancock v. State* best illustrates the difficulty in applying this kind of statute when what is taken is a trade secret, and nothing of tangible evidence is also taken. Courts are often reluctant to assign value to an intangible. *Hancock v. State*involved the theft of numerous computer programs by an employee of Texas Instruments Corporation (TI) and an employee of an insurance company.[26] The pair attempted to sell a listing of these programs to a competitor of TI, who reported this offer to TI management. The attempted sale price was $5 million. The issue raised here was whether the programs were worth their intrinsic value when used, or the cost of the paper on which they were printed (tangibility). Expert testimony indicated that the programs were conservatively worth $2.5 million. This estimation was based on what the information stored would allow its user to create. The court held that the programs were worth their intrinsic value. The great difference in value between the printed program paper itself and the value of the program when actuated may have greatly influenced the court in reaching its decision in this case. This holding, regarding the value issue, has not been cited further.

The second type of protection is exemplified by *Ward v. Superior Court*,[27] which was prosecuted under the California trade secret statute.[28] *Ward* involved the unauthorized transfer of a computer program from one terminal to another.[29] Prosecution was brought under the state's general grand theft and criminal trade secret statutes.[30] The victim was a time-sharing service bureau which operated a computer, access to which was only allowed through approved customers. Access to the computer was via the telephone and the bureau's unlisted telephone number. The defendant claimed that the computer's electronic impulses were not considered tangible property as defined by the trade secret statute. Applying the principles of *ejusdem generis* the court agreed with this argument.[31] However, the court further reasoned that because these impulses had been transcribed onto a printout sheet, the data was clearly tangible property and would be within the parameters of the trade secret statute. The court also indicated that whenever particular property is accorded trade secret status under this statute, proof of value or intent to permanently deprive the owner of his property is not relevant to the proceedings. All that need be shown is that the owner took precautionary measures to ensure the confidentiality of the secret.[32] The holding in this case strongly suggests that if the electronic impulses had not been translated onto the computer printout, there would not have been tangible evidence of the misappropriation, and prosecution under the trade secret statute would not have been possible.

There are good reasons for using criminal trade secret sanctions for the protection of computer software. One reason is the wide applicability of trade secret protection to many kinds of subjects. Another reason is the broad scope of protection. Trade secret law protects the idea as well as its expression from unauthorized disclosure or use. The immediacy of protection is another reason for seeking trade secret sanctions. Unlike patent law, under which protection may take upwards of two years to secure, copyright and trade secret protection is in force upon creation. Copyright protection, however, requires that the idea be expressed in tangible form before protection is accorded. A final reason for using trade secret protection is the duration of that protection. A trade secret may be "protected" forever, so long as there is no unauthorized use or disclosure. Unfortunately once either of those situations occurs, the protection is lost.[33]

To ensure the maintenance of secrecy of a trade secret, an owner must take certain precautions. Such precautions include confidentiality agreements between the trade secret owner and interested others. To allow for commercialization of a trade secret, the trade secret owners require customers to enter into exclusive licensing agreements which incorporate this confidentiality clause. A breach of any part of these agreements constitutes grounds for criminal and civil sanctions.

There are difficulties with using criminal trade secret sanctions against computer crime. One immediate difficulty is the inherent secrecy basis of any trade secret. If computers are divided into their two basic parts--hardware and software--each component has its unique protection needs which may or may not be met under the scope of trade secret protection.

There is less need for trade secret protection for hardware because the design of the hardware is more adequately protected by patent law. It is the software, in its binary stored form and in its printout form, which requires protection for the value of its information. Any commodity which is widely distributed may not be well suited for trade secret protection. As proliferation of use of the secret increases, so does the risk of disclosure, both deliberate or by chance. Such disclosure consequently means loss of protection. Another problem with the use of trade secret protection for software is the nature of that which is secreted. There may be inherent in the definition of trade secret the idea that what is being protected must not be generally known by the owner's competitors. According to the Restatement of Torts, "[a] trade secret may consist of any formula, device, or compliation of information which is used in one's business and which gives him an opportunity to obtain an advantage over competitors who do not know or use it."[34]

Another factor to be considered in weighing the appropriateness of criminal trade secret protection for computer software is the type of information stored. For example, a computer company may store its master service code in its computer system. Access to that code would allow the user to be privy to information about the methods used to operate the system as well as the actual information stored. This type of information should easily be covered under the definition of trade secret noted above. However, general businesses, such as hospitals and retail outlets, store general business records in their computers. Such information, although probably confidential, would not be considered trade secrets because disclosure of such information may not affect competition. Thus, although trade secret protection may be appropriate for protecting some software information, it may not be appropriate for all.

The risk of disclosure, with its concommitant need for extensive surveillance, would be the greatest factor in deciding that criminal trade secret protection would not alone be an adequate means of protecting computer software. There is also the possibility that trade secret protection may be preempted by section 301(a) of the Copyright Act of 1976.[35]

IV   THEFT OF SOFTWARE

Theft has traditionally meant the dispossession of a tangible item belonging to another with the intent of retaining it.[36] This thinking pre-supposed that possession by one person precluded the possession by any other person. Such is usually not the case in computer crime. Typically the storage medium containing the information is rarely stolen. Such theft of a physical storage device falls within the scope of traditional larceny statutes. What usually occurs in computer software theft is that the perpetrator copies the software either by electronic transfer or by computer printout. There is usually never dispossession, and often there is little indication that any damage or loss occurred. The loss suffered therefore is not one of dispossession, but rather

one of diminution in value of the owner's property. In
order for theft statutes to adequately protect computer
crime, they must also address this concept of deprivation
of value.

A case which illustrates the difficulties the
judicial system has faced in prosecuting such crimes
is *United States v. Siedlitz.*[37] The defendant was indicted
for interstate transportation of stolen property,[38] and
two counts of fraud by wire.[39] He was convicted of the
latter two offenses. These convictions were affirmed
by the Fourth Circuit Court of Appeals. The case involved
Siedlitz's use of the telephone to access and transmit,
without authority, computer software information from
a main computer terminal in Maryland to his terminal in
Virginia. Successful prosecution was not possible under
the interstate theft statute because of the court's
hesitancy in defining the computer's electronic impulses
as property within the meaning of the statute, or in defining the unauthorized transmission of these impulses
from one terminal to another as the taking of property
within the meaning of the statute.[40]

In addition to depriving the owner of the value
of the information contained within the computer, computer
crime in the form of unauthorized use of the computer,
also presents the circumstances of depriving the owner
of the time or sevices of the computer. The use of the
computer machine has costs. The question raised, therefore,
is whether a user can be prosecuted under traditional
larceny statutes for the unauthorized use of a computer,
including the improper use by an authorized computer user.

The Virginia Supreme Court answered negatively, in *Lund v. Commonwealth*, finding no property interest in the use of a computer.[41] In *Lund* a graduate student used the school's computer to type his dissertation. Unknown to him, his faculty advisor had neglected to secure permission for him to do this. Permission would have been granted had it been requested. The defendant was convicted under the state's grand larceny statute.[42] Evidence presented indicated that the computer printouts were considered as mere worthless 'scrap paper', but the value of the unauthorized time used was appraised at between $5,000 and $26,000. On appeal, the state Supreme Court held that labor and services were not to be construed as being covered under the larceny statute, unless specifically mandated by the legislature. Since this was not the issue here, and at common law, theft of labor and services were also not subject to a cause of action in larceny, the court would not extend the interpretation and reversed the conviction. The court also held that the computer printouts had no ascertainable monetary value and, therefore, could not be the basis for a larceny conviction.

The New York courts addressed this same issue of theft of comuter time and services in *People v. Weg.*[43] However, here prosecution was brought under that state's Theft of Services Act.[44] The defendant was a New York

Board of Education employee who used his work computer to tabulate horsebreeding data (non-work related). The court dismissed the indictment The policy reason for the dismissal was the court's belief tht the legislature had not intended to punish every governmental employee who used the computer for an unauthorized use. The technical basis for the dismissal was a narrow interpretation of the word 'business' in the statute. The court stated that the Board of Education did not conduct a business, and, therefore, its activities were not governed by the statute.[45]

Nothwithstanding, the District Court for the Northern District of California in *United States v. Sampson* [46] held to the contrary that "the uses of the computer and the product of such uses would appear to the court to be a 'thing of value,'[47] In *Sampson*, defendants were prosecuted under 18 U.S.C.§ 641 for unlawfully accessing and using a NASA time-sharing computer. The court emphasized that the use of computer time was inseparable from the physical identity of the computer itself.[48]

V.   CURRENT LEGISLATION

Although some authorities in computer law consider that traditional legislation is sufficient to successfully prosecute any type of computer crimes,[49] to date 31 states have enacted legislation specifically aimed at computer crime.[50] In other states the definition of larceny has been expanded to encompass electronic media.[51] The states which have amended older legislation to include computer crime have only confronted the concept of property and its application to deprivation of value, instead of its traditional application to dispossession of property. Successful prosecution of computer crimes under these statutes will be hindered if the statutes continue to retain the concept that theft requires dispossession. Requirements of strict construction and due process in the interpretation of criminal statutes will deter courts from liberally interpreting larceny statutes to include the methodology usually employed in computer crime.[52]

Florida was the first state to enact a state statute specifically proscribing computer crime. This was done in 1978.[53] In the six years since then, although 30 more states have passed similar legislation, there have been no appellate cases interpreting any of these computer crime statutes in any enacting jurisdiction, as yet.

Ideally a computer crime statute should be general and flexible enough to be applicable to the rapidly changing computer technology, yet narrow enough to exclude calculators, digital watches and automatic traffic signals. The statute should address special considerations that computers raise without unnecessarily infringing on areas already covered by existing law. Such a statute should also specify exactly what acts are prohibited and what are not.[54]

Congress has, on three occasions, considered bills aimed at creating a federal computer crime law, but none of those bills has been enacted.[55] The most discussed of these rejected bills was the "Federal Computer Systems Protection Act of 1979" (S.240). Introduced in the 96th Congress, the bill was defeated because it was overbroad and difficult to apply to intangible property, as well as providing only a blanket penalty for any infraction regardless of magnitude.[56] However, this bill may have served as a model for many of the present state computer crime statutes.

On October 12, 1984, Congress enacted into law the Counterfeit Access Device and Computer Fraud and Abuse Act.[57] The law amends Chapter 47 of Title 18 of the United States Code by adding at the end of it the following: "1030 Fraud and related activity in connection with computers."[58] This is the first and only federal legislation specifically proscribing unlawful behavior by a person using a computer to accomplish the crime. House testimony given during the bill's debate indicated[59] that most federal prosecution of crimes involving unauthorized access to a computer to obtain valuable information had been brought under federal laws proscribing wire fraud,[60] mail fraud,[61] or interstate transportation of stolen goods.[62] These prosecutions have not always been successful ostensibly because of the lack of specificity of the statute in relation to the offense prosecuted.

The legislative history of the statute indicates that defining the term 'computer' has been a problem for Congress since 1979.[63] The House Committee on the Judiciary decided to define the term as specifically as possible in order to avoid future attacks on the statute for vagueness. The definition is a combination of that suggested by the Justice Department, and the Federal Computer Systems Protection Act of 1983 (H.R.1092)[64] The new statute defines the term 'computer' as,

"...an electronic, magnetic, optical, electro-
chemical, or other high speed data processing
device performing logical, arithmetic, or storage
functions, and includes any data storage facility
or communications facility directly related to
or operating in conjunction with such device, but
such term does not include an automated typewriter
or typesetter, a portable hand held calculator,
or other similar device."65

The main provisions of the new computer crime law
primarily address unauthorized access to computers. The
statute disallows unauthorized access, as well as authorized
access for 'other purposes' for which the authority does
not extend. An exception to this other purpose prohibition
is the use of a computer without accessing the files of
others, as when an authorized person uses the computer
to play games, or balance a personal checkbook. Congress
did not intend to legislate theft of computer time.66

A major flaw in this statute, at least in terms
of its application, is the narrowness of its scope. The
only types of computers which cannot be illegaly accessed,
according to this statute, are those operated for or on
behalf of the Government of the United States and such
conduct affects such operations."67 The statute also
prohibits the accessing of certain types of information-
-that having to do with national defense, foreign relations
or restricted data and that having to do with financial
records of a financial institution, or contained in a
file of a consumer reporting agency on a consumer.68
In the House bill that spawned this statute (H.R. 5616)
the scope of the protection was intended to include foreign

and interstate commerce.[69] This scope, however, did not become a part of the statute.

The statute includes the element of requisite intent[70] and a section providing sanctions against conspiracy to use unauthorized access.[71] The statute further provides a gradation of penalties dependent on the type of information accessed, the value of that information, and the number of previous convictions sustained under this statute.[72] The United States Secret Service is granted concurrent power with the Justice Department to investigate crimes under the statute, and the United States Attorney General is required to submit to Congress an annual report for the next three years enumerating the prosecutions made under this statute.[73] The House Committee on the Judiciary's purpose for requiring these reports is to ascertain just how significant the statute will be in deterring computer crime.[74]

The implementation of any legislation to combat computer crime can be as problematic as the creation of that legislation. State and federal constitutional safeguards against unreasonable search and seizure require probable cause to effect an arrest.[75] Procurring a sufficiently specific search warrant is *prima facie* evidence of reasonableness.[76] This specificity requirement mandates that a warrant include information regarding the objects to be seized, the place to be searched, and the purpose of the search. Ideally all persons involved in the warrant process, judges, prosecutors, defense attorneys, and law enforcement officers, should become educated in the rudiments of computer usage.

The search warrant used in *Ward v. Superior Court* is a good example of the technical specificity that should appear in computer crime search warrants. The *Ward* warrant specified the "computer memory bank or other data storage devices, magnetically imprinted with Information Systems Design (ISD) remote plotting computer programs."[77] In addition to the difficulty in determining what to request in the search warrant, there is the uncertainty of the form of the requested items to be seized. This is a problem for the drafter as well as the executor of the warrant. A requested computer program may be found in the form of punch cards, printout sheets, or still in intangible form within the computer.[78] Certain state[79] and federal jurisdictions[80] allow police officers to use civilian assistance in conducting warranted searches. The experts are considered special police agents, so their actions are protected by the laws of agency.[81] Until police become more adept at conducting such searches, the practice of having computer experts accompany police on these search and seizure forays appeas to be worthwhile.

VI.   EVIDENTIARY PROBLEMS

The presence of computers has created additional complexities and definitional problems within the accepted rules of evidentiary procedure. Such difficulties are inherent whether the prosecution is for a computer crime or a more traditional offense. The basis for seeking admission of computer evidence in litigation is under the business records exceptions to the hearsay rule. Like any other conforming document, computer-generated evidence which meets the specifications of the appropriate statute or common law rule will qualify as a 'business record.'

Until computer-generated documents are generally accepted, photocopy statutes can be used as a basis for admision of computer evidence. Photocopy statutes allow admission of reproductions made in the regular course of business, thereby allowing the reproductions to be considered equal to the originals. However, authorities consider computer outprint microfilm to be the production of originals and not copies of information.[82] There is usually the requirement that the reproductions be made on a durable medium. There are also federal[83] and state[84] photocopy statutes. Most of the state statutes are modeled after the Federal Uniform Photographic Copies of Business and Public Records as Evidence Act,[85] which has been adopted by 39 states.[86]

There are a number of specific business records rules which allow for the admission of computer evidence. These rules are basically similar, and courts of various jurisdictions have frequently cited cases concerned with admissibility, from jurisdictions following differing evidentiary rules. These rules are:

1) the Federal Rules of Evidence, Rule 803[87], especially subsectioned (6)[88], (7)[89], and (8);[90]

2) the former Federal Business Records Act,[91] which was repealed and replaced in 1975 by the present Federal Rule of Evidence 803(6);

3) the Uniform Business Records as Evidence Act (UBREA).[92] As of 1977 26 states had adopted his rule;[93]

4) common law rules in effect in Mississippi and Illinois;[94] and

5) specific state statutes governing the admissibility of computer evidence, as in Massachusetts,[95] New Jersey,[96] North Carolina,[97] and Arkansas.[98]

Some of these rules are sufficiently similar in construction, as the Federal Rules of Evidence and the Former Federal Business Records Act, that some courts have readily applied the interpretations of the old statute to cases founded on the newer rule.[99] In general all these rules require that the offering of evidence be made in good faith in the regular course of business, prior to the current judicial proceeding, and that it was in the regular course of the business to make such a record at the time of the transaction, or within a reasonable time thereafter. There usually is also a requirement that a witness present information indicating the accuracy and reliability of the computer system that generated the evidence. In some statutes the courts have the discretion to also require that the original data be made available.[100]

Under The Best Evidence Rule, when the terms of a writing are the basis of a question in litigation, the original writing must be produced unless it is unavailable for some reason other than the fault of the producer.[101] This rule does not apply to the question of the existence of a writing. The focus of the best evidence rule is just that - securing the best available evidence. The rule is not aimed at excluding evidence. Once a satisfactory explanation is given for the absence of an original writing, secondary evidence is admissible.

The scope of the federal best evidence rule is equivalent to the same common law rule.[102] Computer art is specifically included in the definition section of the federal rule.[103] Generally, admissions allowed under one of the recent business records exceptions are exempt from the Federal best evidence rule.[104] Also courts have allowed the admission of a computer printout (deemed a copy) made specifically for litigation because the stored information was constructed during the normal business routine, and the printout was just a manifestation of that information.[105]

One of the first appellate computer evidence cases was *Transport Idemnity Co. v. Seib.*[106] The issue was the admissibility of the computer printout. The suit involved payment on a contract for sales commissions. A computer printout indicating accounting payments was admitted into evidence over the objection that there was a lack of proper foundation for its admission. This was later the basis of appeal. The trial record indicatd that the defendant produced a witness who testified as to the computer procedures, their accuracy, and the general business procedure of putting accounting records into the computer. The court held that it was the intent of the UBREA statute to permit the admission of systematically entered records. Because a foundation indicating this had been shown, the decision was affirmed.

In a widely cited case, *United States v. De Georgia,* the court admitted a computer printout into evidence as corroborative proof that the car the defendant had been charged with stealing had in fact been stolen.[107] The printout indicated no evidence that the car had been properly rented. The only foundation laid for admission of this printout was testimony that it was the company's procedure to enter all of its business records immediately into the computer terminal. Therefore there was no tangible listing of this information other than the computer printout. Although this case is frequently noted for the holding that computer printouts are admissable evidence, the court in its opinion noted that it had not ruled on the adequacy of the foundation for the admission because at trial the defendant did not raise any objection to that issue.[108]

In Mississippi, a state that does not have any business record statute, a good example of common law interpretation of the admissibility of computer evidence occurred in the case of *King v. State ex rel. Murdock Acceptance Corp.*[109] The court here relied on *Transport Indemnity v. Seib*[110] in ruling that no particular form of record was required, so long as the best form of evidence was secured. The court indicated that the law must take notice of commercially sanctioned means of business. Additionally, the court required that the computer equipment be identified as to its accuracy and procedure, that the policy of entering information into the computer was a matter of business routine, and that the equipment used was considered standard in the business. The court did not require that witnesses be present to testify as to the time and place of information entry into the computer.

VII   PREVENTION AND SECURITY

Breaching the security of computer data can take many forms. Unauthorized access to a program allows data to be destroyed, copied, or modified. Data transmission lines can be tapped. Of greater importance is the potential for the modification of the system's programmed security processes. In order to implement the laws enacted to prosecute computer crime, security measures must be devised to detect the law breaker.

Case law reflects that the detection of most of the perpetrators of computer crime is by accident and not by any deliberate security measure. In *United States v. Siedlitz*, the crime was accidentally detected by a programmer of the accessed system who noticed that an obsolete password was being used in the system.[111] The criminal action in *Ward v. Superior Court* was detected only because of the accidental dumping of computer punch cards simultaneously with the telephone intrusion into the system.[112]

Detection becomes easier when there is an immediate tangible effect of a breach. This ease parallels the impact that the tangible factor has in the prosecution of computer crime. Law enforcement information indicates that the probability of detection and prosecution of computer crime is 1 in 22,000.[113] Studies reflect that only approximately 15 percent of computer crime is reported.[114]

A recent survey of 283 large state and federal government agencies and private corporations indicated that the average annual individual loss from computer crime ranged from $2 million to more than $10 million.[115] This was a conservative estimate based on 'known and verifiable losses due to computer crime'.[116] The study indicated that the greater percentage of these losses were sustained when the computer was the object of the crime;[117] the greater percentage of the perpetrators of these crimes were people within the organization;[118] the most influential factor motivating these perpetrators was personal financial gain and the second most influential reason was the intellectual challenge of doing it;[119] respondents to the study indicated that they perceived more comprehensive self-protection by the private sector as the most effective means of detecting and preventing computer crime;[120] and finally, that the most prevelant methods that the respondants used to accomplish this goal was limiting access to computer programs and logic, and limiting access to computer operations.[121]

The American Society for Industrial Security (ASIS) has promulgated a listing of specific recommendations for improved computer security. These guideline summaries include:

1) 'separation of knowledge' through division of responsibilities, job rotation, physical isolation, controlled access, logging of stop-pages and interruptions;

2) written programming instructions with threat monitoring and audit trails built in;

3) careful accounting of all input documents;

4) periodic changes in access codes and passwords; and

5) scramblers and cryptographic applications in data transmission. [122]

Large computer companies, such as IBM, have also developed similar recommendations for commercial user security programs.[123]

Equipment security features cannot be the sole method of deterrence. The education of the public regarding the uses and abuses of computers, and the consequences of any actions with and against computers, must accompany any security plan in order for the plan to be successful. In our society today, computer skills are most rapidly being developed for school children. The computer is a very powerful tool. Power is accompanied by corresponding responsibility. Because of the inherent damages in the abuse of that power, society will be derelict in its duties if it teaches only how to use the computer without also explaining the possible consequences.

Deterrence of computer crime can best be achieved by educating the public about the problem, by developing finer equipment security, by enacting specific laws to give notice of proscribed behavior, and by enforcing those laws.

VIII   CONCLUSION

Although individual courts and legislatures have been slow to adopt comprehensive computer crime statutes, the apparent legarthy is due to a deficit in the technical skill necessary to define what constitutes a computer rather than the belief that the existing statutes are sufficient. Primarily the uncertainties in treating software intrusions have provided the greatest concern.

Redefinition of property values to provide violation of rights for diminution of value rather than the traditional loss of possession has provided a basis for a new era of statutes aimed at computer violators. Trade secret protection also provides a measure of protection by providing criminal sanctions for the unauthorized use of another's effenescent, through valuable, computerized data. However, trade secret protection alone provides only a limited range software that can be considered. Current legislation has attempted to use new definitions of computers, property, theft and larceny to give notice of prescribed computer-related behavior; however, this new legislation is largely untried by the courts and lacks inter-jurisdictional consistency.

Evidentiary acceptance of computers has been more easily adopted. Under the Federal Rules of Evidence, and other evidentiary procedure acts, the courts have generally allowed the introduction of computer generated information with only the most common of formalities.

Legislation alone, however, will not protect computers in the modern world. Efficient self-help measures, such as the installation of security devices and educating users as to the possible consequences of unauthorized computer useage will provide the other two cornerstones in the construction of a computer-secure society.

IX. FOOTNOTES

1. Report on Computer Crime, Task Force on Com-
    puter Crime Section of Criminal Justice, American
    Bar Association, June, 1984, p. 39 [hereinafter
    cited as ABA Task Force]

2. See *The 414 Gang Strikes Again*, Time Magazine, Aug-
    ust 29, 1983; *Guilded Youth*, *Jaded Youth*, Forbes, Aug-
    15, 1983; *Lawmakers   Tackle   Computer   Crime*,
    Trial, February, 1984.

3. C. Silberman, *Criminal Violence*, Criminal Justice.
    (1980) pp. 55-62.

4. 414 F. Supp. 964 (D. Md. 1976) rev'd, 553 F. 2d
    351 (4th Cir. 1977), cert. denied, 431 U.S. 968
    (1977).

5. 18 U.S.C. §2314, 18 U.S.C. §2315 (1982).

6. 553 F.2d at 354-356.

7. *Id*. at 355.

8. Parker, *Computer Abuse Research Update*, 2 Computer
    L.J. 329 at 333 (1982).

9. Taber, *On Computer Crime* (Senate Bill 5240) 1 Com-
    puter, L.J. 517 (1979) [hereinafter cited as Taber,
    On Computer Crime].

10. Gen. Accounting Off., Computer-Related Crimes
     in Federal Programs 1 (1976).

11. ABA Task Force *supra* note 1, at 37.

12. 4 W. Blackstone, Commentaries 821.

13. 601 F.2d 69 (2d Cir. 1979), aff'd *United States v.*
     Lambert, 446 F. Supp.

14. E.g. *Giomi v. Chase*, 47 N.M. 22, 132 P.2d 715 (1942);
     Hightower v. State,   156 S.W. 2d 327 (Tex. Civ. App.

359

1942);   *State v. Baitler*,131 Me.   285,   161 A.   671
(1932); *McDonald v. State*,   57 Ala. App. 529, 329
So. 2d 583 (1975), 141 N.E. 19 (1923); (1975),   cert.
denied 429 U.S.   834 (1976); *Scott v. State*, 107 Ohio
St. 475, 141 N.E. 19 (1923); *People ex rel. Dickinson
v. Van De Carr*,   87 App. Div. 386, 84 N.Y.S. 461
(1st Dep't 1963); *People v. Hochberg*, 62 A.D.2d 239,
404 N.Y.S.2d 161 (3d Dep't. 1978); *United States v.
Zouras*, 497 F.2d 1115 (7th Cir. 1974).

15.   474 F. Supp. 64 (D.D.C. 1979).

16.   *Id.* see also *United States v. Girard*, 601 F.2d 69;
United States v. DiGilio, 629   F.2d 908 (4th Cir.
1980); 538 F.2d 972 (3rd Cir. 1976), cert denied
429 U.S. 1038 (1977).

17.   *District of Columbia v. Universal Computer Assoc.,
Inc.*, 465 F.2d 615 (D.C. Cir. 1972).

18.   D.C. Code 47-501 provides: "For the purpose of de-
fraying such expenses...there hereby is levied for
each and every fiscal year, a tax at such rate on
the real and personal property subject to taxation
in the district..."

19.   Rev. Proc. 69-21, 1969-2 Cum. Bull. 303, provides
in pertinent part:

> Sec. 4 Costs of Purchased Software. 0.1 With
> respect to costs of purchased software, the Ser-
> vice will not disturb the taxpayer's treatment
> of such costs if the following practices are
> consistently followed: 1. Where such costs are
> included, without being separately stated, in
> the cost of the hardware (computer) and such
> costs are treated as a part of the cost of the
> hardware that is capitalized and depreciated;
> or 2. Where such costs are separately stated,
> and the software is treated by the taxpayer as
> an intangible asset the cost of which is to be
> recovered by amortization deductions rateably
> over a period of five years or such shorter
> period as can be established by the taxpayer
> as appropriate in any particular case if the

useful life of the software in his hands will
be less than five years. Under the above-quoted
revenue procedure, the Internal Revenue Service
will not require a taxpayer to separate the software from the hardware, but it does consider
the software to be an 'intangible asset' which
can be separated from the hardware if the taxpayer so desires. Whether for IRS purposes,
the original cost must be separately stated is
immaterial to the issue under the D.C. tax law."

20. Reback, *Of Bits, Bytes and Price Discrimination:
The Robinson-Patman Act*, The Computer Lawyer, August, 1984, p.5.

21. 17 U.S.C. §506 (1977 & Supp. 1983).

22. Those states include: Arkansas, California, Colorado, Georgia, Illinois, Indiana, Maine, Massachusetts, Michigan, Minnesota, Nebraska, New Hampshire,
New Jersey, New Mexico, New York, North Carolina,
Oklahoma, Pennsylvania, Tennessee, and Wisconsin.

23. 402 S.W.2d 906 (Tex. Crim. App. 1966) rev'd sub nom.
379 F.2d 552 (5th Cir. 1967).

24. 601 F.2d 69 (2nd Cir. 1979).

25. 446 F. Supp. 890 (D. Conn. 1978).

26. 402 S.W.2d 906.

27. 3 C.S.L.R. 206 (Cal. Super. Ct. 1972).

28. Cal. Penal Code 499c(b) (West 1970 & Supp. 1979).

29. 3 C.S.L.R. 206.

30. Cal. Penal Code 499c(b), Cal Penal Code 487 (West
1970 & Supp. 1979).

31. Cal. Penal Code 499c(b) defines 'article' as any
"...object, material, device or substance or copy
thereof, including any writing, record, recording,
drawing, sample, specimen, prototype, model, photograph, microorganism, blueprint or map."

32.   3 C.S.L.R. at 209.

33.   Bender, *Computer Law: Evidene and Procedure (release 5, 1983),*p.4A-180, [hereinafter cited as Bender, Computer Law].

34.   *Restatement of Torts,* 757, comment b (1939).

35.   17 U.S.C. 301(a) (1977).

36.   LaFave, and Scott, *Criminal Law* (1972).

37.   589 F.2d 152 (4th Cir. 1978), cert, denied, 441 U.S. 922 (1979).

38.   18 U.S.C. §2315 (1976).

39.   18 U.S.C. §1343 (1976).

40.   *Supra* note 37, at 160.

41.   217 Va. 688, 232 S.E.2d 745 (1977).

42.   Va. Code 18.2-95 (1975); Va. Code 18.2-178 (1975).

43.   113 Misc. 2d 1017, 450 N.Y.S.2d 957 (Crim Ct. 1982).

44.   N.Y. Penal Law 165.15(8) (McKinney Supp. 1982-1983).

45.   113 Misc. 2d at 1023, 450 N.Y.S. at 961.

46.   6 C.S.L.R. 879 (N.D.Cal. 1978).

47.   *Id.* at 880.

48.   *Id.*

49.   See, Taber, On Computer Crime, *supra* note 9; see also *A Survey of Computer Crime Studies,* 2 Computer L.J. 275 (1980); Computer Systems Protection Act of 1979, S. 240; Hearing before the Subcomm. on Criminal Justice of the Senate Comm. on the Judiciary, 96th Cong., 2d Sess. 8 (1980) (statement of Hon. J.D. MacFarlane,

Atty. Gen. of Colorado); Conference on Computer-Related Crime: Hearings before the Comm. on Criminal Justice of the House of Representatives of the Commonwealth of Massachusetts, (September 1, 1982), (statement of Roy N. Freed, partner, Powers & Hall).

50. Alaska Stat. 11.46.985 (1983); Ariz. Rev. Stat. Ann. 13-2301 E, 13-2316 (1978); Cal. Penal Code 502 (West 1984); Colo. Rev. Stat. 18-5.5-101, 18-5.5-102 (1984); Conn. Pub. Acts 84-206 (1984); Del. Code Ann. tit. 11, 858 (1982); Fla. Stat. Ann. 815.01 to 815.07 (1983); Ga. Code Ann. 26-9949a to 26-9954a (1983); Idaho Code ch. 24 tit. 18 18-2402 (1983); Ill. Ann. Stat. ch. 38 15-1, 16-9 (Smith-Hurd 1983); Iowa Code Ann. 716A.1 to 716A.16 (West 1984); Mass. Gen Laws Ann. ch. 266, 30 (West 1983); Mich. Comp. Laws Ann. 28,529 (West 1981); Minn. Stat. Ann. 609.87 to 609.89 (West 1984); Mo. Ann. Stat. 569.093 to 569.099 (Vernon 1984); Mont. Code Ann. 45-2-101, 45-6-310, 45-6-311 (1983); Nev. Rev. Stat. 205.473 to 205.477 (1983); N.M. Stat. Ann. 30-16A-1 to 30-16A-4 (1984); N.C. Gen Stat. 14-453 to 14-456 (1981); N.D. Cent. Code 12.1-06.1-01(3), 12.1-06.1-08 (1983); Ohio Rev. Code Ann. 2901.01(J)(1), 2901.01(J)(2), 2913.01(E), 2913.01(F), 2913.01(L) to (Q); Okla. Stat. Ann. tit. 21 1951 to 1956 (West 1984); Pa. Stat. Ann. tit. 18 3933 (Purdon 1983); R.I. Gen. Laws 11-52-1 (1981), 11-52-2 to 11-52-5 (1984); S.D. Codified Laws Ann. 43-43B-1 to 43-43B-8 (1984); Tenn. Code Ann. 39-3-1401 to 39-3-1406 (1983); 152.14 (1984); Wash. Rev. Code Ann. 9A48.100 (1983); Wis. Stat. Ann. 943.70 (West 1984); Wyo. Stat. 6-3-501 to 6-3-505 (1983).

51. Rhode Island, Illinois, Connecticut, Virginia and Florida.

52. Marcellino & Kenfield, *Legislative Developments in Hi-Tech*, 28 B. Bar Journal, 19 (Mar./Apr., 1984).

53. Fla. Stat. Ann. 815.01 to 815.07 (1983), effective August 1, 1978.

54.   Gemignani, *Computer Crime: The Law in '80*,   13 Ind. L. Rev. 681 at 712 (1980).

55.   H.R. Rep. No. 3970, 97th Cong., 1st Sess. 3141 (1981); Federal Computer System Protection Act of 1979, S. 240, 96th Cong., 1st Sess., 125 Cong. Rec. 710 (1979);

56.   See, Comment, *Computer   Crime,   Senate   Bill   S.240,* 10 Mem. St. U.L. Rev. 660 (1980).

57.   Counterfeit Access Device and Computer Fraud and Abuse Act Of 1984, Pub. L. No. 98-473, 98 Stat. 2190 (1984).

58.   *Id.* at 2190.,

59.   H. Rep. No. 98-894, 98th Cong., reprinted in 1984 U.S. Code Cong. & Ad. News 509, [hereinafter cited as 1984 U.S.C.C.A.N. 509].

60.   18 U.S.C. §1341 (1970).

61.   *Id.*

62.   18 U.S.C. §2315 (1970).

63.   1984 U.S.C.C.A.N. 509, *supra* note 59, 529.

64.   *Id.*

65.   98 Stat. 2190, 2191.

66.   1984 U.S.C.C.A.N. 509, *supra* note 63, at 528.

67.   *Supra*   note 65.

68.   *Id.,* at 2190-2191.

69.   1984 U.S.C.C.A.N. 509, *supra* **note** 63, at 526.

70.   *Supra*   note 65.

71.   *Id.,*at 2191-2192.

72.   *Id.,*at 2191-2192.

73.   *Id.,*at 2192.

74.   1984 U.S.C.C.A.N. 509, *supra* note 63, at 530.

75.   U.S. Const. Amend. IV.

76.   *Katz v. United States,* 389 U.S. 347 (1967).

77.   J. Becker, *The Investigation of Computer Crime,* app. 5 (1980).

78.   J. Becker, *The Trial of a Computer Crime,* 2 Computer L.J. 441, 444, (1980).

79.   See, *People v. Boyd,* 123 Misc.2d 634, 474 N.Y.S.2d 661 (Sup. Ct., 1984); *State v. Klosterman,* 317 N.W.2d 796 (N.D.1982); *State v. McColgan,* 631 S.W.2d 151 (Tenn. Cr. App. 1981); *People v. Superior Court,* 25 Cal. 3d 67, 157 Cal. Rptr. 716, 598 P.2d 877 (1979); *Commonwealth v. Farrar,* 271 Pa. Super. 434, 413 A.2d 1094 (1979); *State v. Scigliano,* 120 Ariz. 6, 583 P.2d 893 (1978).

80.   See, 18 U.S.C. §3105 (1969); *United States v. Wright,* 667 F.2d 793 (9th Cir. 1982); *United States v. Clouston,* 623 F.2d 485 (6th Cir. 1980).

81.   See, *People v. Esposito,* 37 N.Y.2d 156, 371 N.Y.S. 2d 681, 332 N.E.2d 863 (1975); *People v. Luciani,* 120 Misc. 2d 826, 466 N.Y.S.2d 638 (1983).

82.   Bender, Computer Law,, *supra* note 33, at 6-19.

83.   18 U.S.C. §1732 (1976).

84.   As of 1980 the following states had enacted state photocopy laws: Alabama, Alaska, Arkansas, Calif-ornia, Colorado, Connecticut, Delaware, Georgia, Hawaii, Idaho, Iowa, Kansas, Kentucky, Maine, Mary-

land, Massachusetts, Michigan, Minnesota, Montana, Nebraska, New Hampshire, New Jersey, New York, North Carolina, North Dakota, Oklahoma, Pennsylvania, Rhode Island, South Carolina, South Dakota, Tennessee, Utah, Vermont, Virgin Islands, Virginia, Washington, West Virginia, Wisconsin, Wyoming.

85.   14 U.L.A. Civ. Proc. and Rem. Laws 145 (Master ed. 1980).

86.   *Supra*   note 84.

87.   Fed. R. Evid. 803.

88.   Fed. R. Evid. 803(6) states:

> A memorandum report, record, or data compilation, in any form, of acts, events, conditions, opinions, diagnoses, made at or near the time by, or from information transmitted by, a person with knowledge, if kept in the course of a regularly conducted business activity, and if it was the regular practice of that business activity to make the memorandum, report, record, or data compilation, all as shown by the testimony of the custodian or other qualified witness, unless the source of the information or the method or circumstances of preparation indicate lack of trustworthiness. The term 'business' as used in this paragraph includes business, institution, association, profession, occupation, and calling of every kind, whether or not conducted for profit.

89.   Fed. R. Evid. 803(7) *Absence of Entry in Records Kept in Accordance with the Provisions of Paragraph (6)* states:

> Evidence that a matter is not included in the memoranda reports, records, or data compilations, in any form, kept in accordance with the pro-

visions of paragraph (6), to prove the nonoccurrence or nonexistence of the matter, if the matter was of a kind of which a memorandum, report, record, or data compilation was regularly made and preserved, unless the sources of information or other circumstances indicate lack of trustworthiness.

90. Fed. R. Evid. 803(8) states:

Records, reports, statements, or data compilations, in any form, of public offices or agencies, setting forth (A) the activities of the office or agency, or (B) matters observed pursuant to duty imposed by law as to which matters there was a duty to report, excluding, however, in criminal cases matters observed by police officers and other law enforcement personnel, or (C) in civil actions and proceedings and against the Government in criminal cases, factual findings resulting from an investigation made pursuant to authority granted by law, unless the sources of information or other circumstances indicate lack of trustworthiness.

91. 28 U.S.C. 1732(a) (1968).

92. 9A Uniform L. Annot. 506 (1965).

93. As of 1977 the following states had adopted UBREA: Arizona, California, Connecticut, Delaware, Georgia, Hawaii, Idaho, Michigan, Minnesota, Missouri, Montana, Nevada, New Hampshire, New Jersey, New York, North Dakota, Ohio, Oregon, Pennsylvania, Rhode Island, South Dakota, Tennessee, Texas, Vermont, Virgin Islands, Washington, and Wyoming.

94. Bender, Computer Law, *supra* note 33, at 6-96, 6-98.

95. Mass. Gen. Laws Ann. ch. 233, 78 (1970).

96. N.J. Stat. Ann. 2A:84, Rules 62(5) and 63(13) (1982).

97. N.C. Gen. Stat. 55-37.1 (1981).

98. U.R.E. 28-1001, Rule 803(6).

99. Bender, Computer Law, *supra* note 33, at 6-46.

100. E.g. Massachusetts.

101. McCormick, *Handbook of the Law of Evidence 229* (2d ed. 1972).

102. Bender, Computer Law *supra* note 33, at 5-54.

103. Fed. R. Evid. 1001 *Definitions* states:

> (1) Writings and Recordings. 'Writings' and 'recordings' consist of letters, words, or numbers, or their equivalent, set down by hand-writing, typewriting, printing, photostating, photographing, magnetic impulse, mechanical or electronic recording, or other form of data compilation....(3) Original. An 'original' of a writing or recording is the writing or recording itself or any counterpart intended to have the same effect by a person executing or issuing it. An original" of a photograph includes the negative or any print therefrom. If data are stored in a computer or similar device, any printout or other output readable by sight, shown to reflect the data accurately, is an 'original'....

104. See, *United States v. Kimmel*, 274 F.2d Cir. 1960); *United States v. Vandersee*,279 F.2d 176 (3d Cir. 1960); *United States v. Anderson*, 447 F.2d 833 (8th Cir. 1971); *United States v. Miller*, 500F.2d 751 (5th Cir. 1974), rev'd on other grounds, 421 U.S. 1010 (1975).

105. *Transport Indemnity Co. v. Seib*, 178 Neb. 253. 260, 132 N.W.2d 871 (1965);*Com. v. Hogan*, 7 Mass.App.236 387 N.E.2d 158, 168 (1979), aff'd., 8 Mass. App. 921, 396 N.E.2d 978 (1979), aff'd., 17 Mass. App. 186, 456 N.E.2d 1162 (1983).

106. 178 Neb. 253, 132 N.W.2d 871 (1965).

107. 420 F.2d 889 (9th Cir. 1969).

108. *Id.*, at 894.

109. 222 So.2d 393 (Miss. Sup. Ct. 1969).

110. 178 Neb. 253.

111. 589 F.2d 152. (4th Cir. 1978).

112. 3 C.S.L.R. 206.

113. Volgyes, *The Investigation, Prosecution, and Prevention of Computer Crime:* A State-of-the-Art Review, *2 Computer L.J. 385, 388.*

114. *Id.* at 388.

115. ABA Task Force, *supra* note 1, at 14-15.

116. *Id.* at 13.

117. *Id.* at 17.

118. *Id.* at 19.

119. *Id.* at 22.

120. *Id.* at 23.

121. *Id.* at 24.

122. Sokolik, *Computer Crime - The Need for Deterrent Legislation,* 2 Computer L.J. 353, 368-369 (1980).

123. *Id.* at 369-370.

Original research and preliminary writings by:

Carla Ottaviano, B.A. Smith College, J.D. Franklin Pierce Law Center, was a Senior Probation Officer for the State of Connecticut Office of Adult Probation, now in private practice.

CHAPTER 7 - ELECTRONIC FUNDS TRANSFER

I.   INTRODUCTION

The computer has revolutionized the way money is moved in the industrialized world. With the computer, direct electronic debit and credit procedures came into being. The general term for this electronic movement of money is Electronic Funds Transfer (EFT). Today almost every adult member of our society is involved in some way with EFT.

Such widespread use of the computer in every-day financial transactions has created many unique legal ramifications which, until recently, were not dealt with directly by existing law. As a result of the problems foreseen in trying to fit into existing legal categories such as the Uniform Commercial Code (UCC)--designed to deal with paper-based transactions such as checks--Congress has enacted legislation to deal with potential EFT problems between consumers and financial institutions. The Electronic Fund Transfer Act (EFTA)[1] and its implementing mechanism, Regulation E[2], are virtually the only forms of federal governance which regulate the consumer/financial institution relationship in EFT. The legislative goal is to protect the consumer while keeping the cost to the financial institutions which bear the initial burden of providing that protection low enough to promote both consumer and industry confidence in EFT and encourage its development.[3]

There are a myriad of law review articles and books which discuss the various aspects of EFT, the EFTA, and Regulation E.

There is, however, very little case law dealing with consumer issues in EFT. Therefore, interpretations of EFT-
related legislation and analyses of its effectiveness in
protecting the consumer are found only in the writings of
a few authorities in the field.

II.   HISTORY AND BACKGROUND OF ELECTRONIC FUNDS TRANSFER

The computer was introduced to the banking industry
in the 1950s, when financial institutions began to shift
their focus from servicing primarily big business towards
servicing smaller businesses and individual consumers.[4]
Coincidentally came public acceptance and increased use
of checks and credit cards as systems for payment as
opposed to cash transactions, which had been the primary
method of payment prior to the 1950s. The use of checks
and credit cards made life safer and easier for the public
since consumers had to carry less cash. Consumers readily
appreciated the ability to reverse payments made by check
and the documentary value of checks and credit slips as
receipts. The use of the check-based system created not
only business for the financial institutions through consumer checking accounts but also costly paper handling
because checks had to be manually counted, categorized,
and processed separately from cash.

Banks first used computers to handle and process
the ever increasing "paper ocean" created by checks. As
computers became more sophisticated and easier to use,
financial institutions began to put them to greater use.

Beginning in the 1950s, Magnetic Ink Character Recognition (MICR) enabled the computer to electronically "read" an encoded check to determine its amount and the account which must be debited. With the additional capability to do check truncation (the stopping of a check and not allowing it to go through the entire processing cycle) and wire transfer, the computer began to make banking faster and easier for the consumer as well as the financial institutions. Increased speed and reduced need for manual handling of checks lowered operation costs for financial institutions, the intent being to pass savings, eventually, on to the consumer.

Through computer-assisted banking, the use of checks grew from an annual volume of approximately five billion in 1950 to thirteen billion in 1960. By 1963 the technology had advanced to allow financial transactions to be completed electronically, using no paper (i.e. checks) whatsoever.[5] The computer automatically debited the account of the payor and simultaneously credited the account of the payee.

The concept of direct electronic movement of funds instituted by the consumer has just left its infancy, becoming prevalent only in the mid-1970s. The delay in EFT use since its original institution in the mid-1960s is said to have been due to poor consumer acceptance and increased reliance on the paper-based system[6]. The financial industry, however, continued throughout this period to promote electronic banking. Since the mid-1970s, consumer acceptance has been growing rapidly. [7]

III.   TYPES OF ELECTRONIC FUNDS TRANSFER

There are eight major types of electronic fund transfers, some of which involve no paper transfer, and some of which stop the handling of the paper somewhere in the system. The eight types, which will be discussed in further detail, are: 1) check truncation, 2) automated clearing houses, 3) check authorization/check guarantee, 4) wire transfers, 5) automatic teller machines, 6) point of sales systems, 7) preauthorized transfers, and 8) telephone bill paying. These eight types can be broken into two general categories--those which are consumer-related and those which are non-consumer-related. The distinction is based upon the role of the consumer in the transaction.

In consumer-related transfers, the consumer is directly involved either as the initiator of the transaction or the direct recipient of transferred funds. In non-consumer transfers, the consumer is either not directly involved or has no control over whether an electronic transaction takes place.

A.   NON-CONSUMER ELECTRONIC FUNDS TRANSFER

The four types of EFT which do not directly involve the consumer are: check truncation, automated clearing houses, check authorization/check guarantee systems, and wire transfers.

Check truncation is one of the most basic forms of EFT and combines the paper-based system (checks) with computer-assisted banking. There are two major types of paper truncation--with the first, the check is held at the payor's bank; with the second, the check is held at the payee's bank. In the first type of paper truncation, the consumer makes a normal payment by check to a creditor[8]. The creditor then deposits the check at its own bank. The creditor's bank credits its customer's account, then forwards the check through banking channels to the payor's bank. The payor's bank debits the payor's account and holds the check. When the bank sends its periodic statement of transactions to the consumer, it does not return the check to the consumer as is the practice followed in traditional check systems. Instead the check is held at the bank, thus saving the time and cost involved in returning the cancelled checks to the consumer. Consumers wishing to see the checks, or a copy of them, may ask the bank for them.

The second type of paper check truncation involves the same procedure as the first up to the point where the creditor deposits the payor's check at its own bank. The creditor's bank, however, keeps the payor's check and sends an electronic code to the payor's bank to debit that account. The check is thus truncated at the creditor's bank. The electronic code identifies the payor's bank account number, the dollar amount of the check, and the holding bank. The check is held for a period of time in case the payor wishes to retrieve it. After the requisite period, the checks are held on microfilm and the paper check is destroyed. This method of check truncation is even more economical to financial institutions due to the savings of time and expense in handling and forwarding the checks through the remainder of the cycle. The intent of such truncation methods is to pass these cost savings eventually on to the consumer. Payors wishing to retrieve a check for any reason, may contact their own bank, which will then request the check from the holding bank.

Automated Clearing Houses

Automated clearing houses (ACH) are "computerized clearing facilities that affect the paperless exchange of funds between banks". ACHs are regionalized facilities which accept funds transfer instructions on magnetic tape or other computer media from financial institutions within the region or from other ACHs in other regions. While ACHs are often involved in consumer direct transfers, and are within the coverage of the Electronic Fund Transfer Act, they are only incidental to consumer-direct EFT since the consumer has no control over whether a transfer of funds, initiated or received, involves an ACH. In addition, ACH-cleared transactions can involve any transfer of funds, not only consumer transactions. In 1979 there were 32 ACHs in the United States, an increase from nine such facilities in late 1975. Banking industry experts believe that ultimately ACHs will be involved in all EFT transactions. [9]

There are two methods by which funds data are transmitted to and from an ACH--carrier delivery of magnetic tape entries and direct electronic wire transfers. In the first, depository institutions record account debit and credit data on magnetic computer tapes which are sent directly to the local ACH. The ACH computer, usually owned by a federal reserve bank, processes the information and sends the net debit and credit information to each involved financial institution. Shipping the tapes, usually by truck, is an inefficient manner of transferring the data. A more efficient way is to transmit the data electronically directly from the depository institution to the ACH. This involves the use of a direct data communication link between the financial institution and the ACH.

Check Authorization/Check Guarantee

Check authorization/check guarantee systems combine electronic transactions with the traditional paper-based systems. In check guarantee systems a financial institution issues to the consumer a computer-readable card, similar to a credit card. The consumer uses the card at local merchant establishments which have computer terminals directly linked to the financial institution. When the consumer presents a check in an establishment which has one of the bank's terminals, the cashier inserts a computer-readable card into the terminal, activating the consumer's account. The cashier then enters the amount of the check into the computer, and if the consumer's account has enough money to cover the account, the cashier accepts the check. Under this system, the financial institution effectively guarantees the check. The financial institution will pay the merchant even if the consumer's account contains insufficient funds by the time the check clears.

The concept of check authorization is similar to
that of check guarantee in that the customer presents
a check and computer-readable card to the merchant. The
difference is that the merchant uses the information
supplied by the card-accessed account as criteria to
determine whether to accept the consumer's check. Common
criteria used for this decision include: whether the
customer has an account with the bank indicated on the
check, whether the customer is regarded by the bank as
a good credit risk, and whether there are sufficient funds
to cover the check at the time of the transaction. The
financial institution, however, does not guarantee that
the check will be honored should there be insufficient
funds in the consumer's account at the time the check
clears.

Check authorization and check guarantee use some
aspects of EFT by electronically determining from a remote location the amount of funds available in a consumer's account. These systems are not true EFT systems,
however, because there is no capability for directly
debiting or crediting the access account. The payment
system still relies upon the transmittal of the· paper
check through the banking system.

Wire Transfers

Wire transfers are probably the oldest and truest
forms of electronic funds transfer. They are included
in this discussion as a form of non-consumer EFT because
they generally involve extremely large sums of money.
In 1978, for example, the average transfer through Fedwire, one of the wire transfer services, was 1.8 million
dollars.[10] Wire transfers usually involve large dollar

transactions between banks, between corporations, or between corporations and banks.

The four major wire transfer systems in the United States are Fedwire, Bank Wire, Clearing House Interbank Payment Systems (CHIPS), and the Society for Worldwide International Financial Telecommunications (S.W.I.F.T.).

Fedwire

Fedwire, operated by the Federal Reserve System, carries electronic messages between federal reserve banks and branches to accomplish transfers of reserve balances between member banks, transfers of federal government and agency securities, and administrative information. Only financial institutions which belong to the Federal Reserve System may transfer funds via Fedwire. Under Fedwire all money transfers involve reserve balances and are therefore credit-transferred.

The procedure operates as follows: A Fedwire member bank instructs the Federal Reserve to transfer funds to another member bank. If both institutions are members of the same federal reserve bank, the account of the transferor is debited and the account of the trans-feree is credited simultaneously. If the involved financial institutions have accounts at different federal reserve banks, the procedure is somewhat different. The federal reserve bank of the transferor first debits the transferor's account and then credits the account of the transferee's federal reserve bank, which will have an account at the transferor's bank. The debit message is electronically sent to the transferee's federal reserve bank, which, in turn, debits the account it holds for the transferor's bank and credits the account of the transferee, which it also holds. Non-member financial institutions, corporations, or individuals who wish to use Fedwire may do so by requesting a member bank to send funds through the system.[11]

Bank Wire

Bank Wire is the private sector counterpart of Fedwire, and allows non-federal reserve banks to send fund transfer messages, miscellaneous reimbursement messages, and administrative messages. In 1980 Bank Wire handled approximately 23,000 messages per day, averaging 1.1 million dollars per transaction. There were 187 member financial institutions at that time. By comparison, Fedwire handled approximately 80,000 messages per day, at 1.8 million dollars per transaction and has almost 6,000 member banks.[12]

Clearinghouse Interbank Payment System

The Clearinghouse Interbank Payment System (CHIPS) is a privately owned, automated facility operated by the New York Clearing House Association, which processes international and domestic funds transfers among its members. It is estimated that CHIPS is responsible for approximately 90 percent of all international inter-bank money transactions.[13] The average volume of United States dollars handled daily is approximately one hundred billion.[14] Chips is operated by 12 member banks, which set the rules of the system and determine which financial institutions may participate. The basic requirements of a participating bank are that it must have an office

in New York City and be subject to New York State regulations. The reason for these requirements is that
CHIPS regulates the rights, responsibilities and
liabilities of its members contractually. Since many
of the participating banks are foreign banks, the requirement assures that each participant is aware of
and agrees to regulation under New York State Law.

CHIPS basically operates by receiving and storing
transaction orders from its participating banks, settling
all accounts on a net debit or credit basis at the end
of each business day. For instance, if a foreign bank
(A) wishes to transfer two million dollars to another
foreign bank (B), Bank A first transfers the money into
a CHIP member bank in New York with which Bank A has
an account. Bank A instructs the member bank to transfer
the funds to Bank B's New York member bank account.
The transfer request is entered into the CHIPS computer
and is held while Bank A's member bank verifies adequate
funds. Once verified, the transaction to Bank B's
member is carried out, and the transferring member bank
is responsible for making the transfer even if Bank
A does not make good to its own member bank. Once the
funds are credited to Bank B's member bank, it, in turn,
credits B's account. CHIPS computes all of the transactions of all participating banks during the day,
arriving at a net debit or credit figure for each participant. These figures are then passed through the
Federal Reserve Bank of New York to the member banks
for payment or receipt at the end of the day.[15]

Society for Worldwide International Financial Telecommunications

The Society for Worldwide International Financial Telecommunications (S.W.I.F.T.) is a non-profit co-operative organization owned by its eight hundred-plus member banks and organized under Belgian law. Operating costs are shared between the users of the system according to the number of terminals connected and the number of messages generated by the participating bank. S.W.I.F.T. reports 1979 average daily message volume of 140,000 transactions.[16]

S.W.I.F.T. is a communications system only, and, unlike CHIPS, has no settlement capability. S.W.I.F.T., however, allows transfers of a variety of currencies while CHIPS deals only in U.S. dollars. Basically S.W.I.F.T. carries transactions and messages from one bank to another, the banks themselves carrying out the debiting and crediting of the involved accounts on a per-transaction basis. For instance, if foreign Bank A wishes to transfer funds to foreign Bank B, with which it does not have an account, it wires a correspondent bank which holds accounts of both A and B. The correspondent bank debits the account of Bank A, and credits the account of Bank B. If Bank A and B do not have a common correspondent bank, Bank A must make the transfer through one of its correspondent bank which, in turn, has a correspondent bank in common with Bank B. The transaction is completed by correspondent A first debiting the account of Bank A. Then the mutual correspondent bank between correspondent A and Bank B debits correspondent A's account and credits the account of Bank B.[17]

B.   CONSUMER-RELATED ELECTRONIC FUNDS TRANSFER

There are four major types of electronic funds transfers in which the consumer is directly involved, either because the consumer actually initiates the transfer directly to or from his own account, or because the consumer's account is directly debited or credited by another party. Included are automated teller machines, point of sales systems, pre-authorized debits and credits, and telephone bill paying.

Automated Teller Machines

The ATM is probably the best known by the average consumer. ATMs are elctronic terminals found at financial institutions and at remote locations such as supermarkets and shopping centers, where consumers can conduct many routine banking transactions. ATMs handle deposits of cash or checks into savings or checking accounts, transfers of funds between accounts, cash withdrawals, and balance inquiries. They can also be used to initiate payments to creditors. ATM transactions are, in large measure, exactly what the federal government sought to regulate in the recent Electronic Fund Transfer Act (EFTA).

A consumer typically uses an ATM as follows: the bank's customer is issued a plastic card, called a debit card, on which his or her name and account number are electronically encoded. The card is very similar to a credit card. The customer is also issued or chooses a number called a personal identification number (PIN), also magnetically coded onto the card. In order to carry out an ATM transaction, the customer inserts the card into the ATM, then punches in the PIN. The account is then accessed so the consumer can carry out banking business[18] via instructions which appear on the ATM video screen. For example, a customer wishing to withdraw $50 from his or her account merely instructs the computer to do so by pushing the proper buttons. The computer automatically debits the customer's account by $50 and issues $50 to the customer.

ATMs benefit both consumers and banks in several ways. First, many ATMs are available 24 hours a day and are located at convenient non-bank locations such as shopping malls, supermarkets, and airports. The impetus for financial institutions to use ATMs includes increased competition, marketing considerations and desire to increase revenues, and cut costs. Time considerations alone are substantial when customers do not have to stand in long lines in order to conduct their banking. Banking industry analysts theorize that increased accessibility will cause more people to put more of their money into the bank, thus increasing usable bank revenues. Cost savings to the bank, include reduced need for tellers, cutbacks on extended weekday and weekend hours, and a decreased paper work. At least one study has shown that the cost of ATMs over time were less than tellers' salaries for the same services performed.[19]

Despite the many benefits to consumers and financial institutions resulting from AMTs, there are risks. Consumer risks include fraudulent use of access cards, robbery, and improper fund distribution due to ATM malfunction. Congress addressed some of these considerations in the Electronic Fund Transfer Act. Financial institution risks include lack of use of AMTs due to consumer dissatisfaction resulting from the consumer risks, poor planning regarding degree of use, retailer resistance, and federal and state legal restrictions.[20]

The public has thus far found that the benefits of ATMs far outweigh the risks. Despite slow acceptance of the concept, from the time of its institution in the mid-1960s to the early 1970s, the number of ATMs has grown from approximately 1700 in 1973 to 12,000 in 1979,[21] to approximately 36,000 in 1983. [22]

Point of Sales

Point of sales (POS) systems are similar to ATMs in that they involve the use of an electronic terminal which is accessed by the consumer's debit card and PIN. The major difference is that POS terminals, found exclusively at merchant locations such as supermarkets and retail stores, require the involvement of both the consumer and the merchant. The usual POS procedure is as follows: a consumer brings goods to the checkout counter where the POS terminal is located. Instead of payment by cash, check, or credit card, the consumer activates his or her bank acount by inserting the debit card and PIN into the computer terminal. The merchant then enters the rest of the required information, such as the merchant's account number and the store location, as well as the transaction amount. The consumer's account is automatically debited, and the merchant's account is credited. Usually a transaction receipt is provided for the consumer's records.

If the customer and the merchant have accounts at the same financial institution, the transaction is called an "on us" entry. The transaction will debit the consumer's account, and credit the merchant's account automatically. If the consumer and merchant do not have accounts at the same financial institution, the transaction, called a "transit item," must be sent to a central processing switch which directs the debit to the consumer's bank. The bank then transmits the transaction authorization back through the switch to the merchant's bank, where the merchant account is credited. The completed transaction information is then forwarded to the terminal.

POS systems necessarily involve the many financial institutions of the consumers and merchants using the system. Though the consumer and the merchant accounts are automatically debited and credited at the time of a POS transaction, the bank themselves must still settle at the end of each day since no money actually changed hands. This account settling can be accomplished by net-debit banks forwarding checks to the net-credit banks at the end of each business day. A second method involves financial institutions settling through accounts held at a federal reserve bank. Finally, in areas where the number of involved financial institutions makes it feasible to do so, the banks may establish accounts with each other, allowing immediate debiting or crediting at the time of the customer-merchant transaction.

Consumer and financial institution risks with POS systems are much the same as with ATMs. Consumers face fraudulent use of stolen or copied debit cards and PINs, but the risk is higher with POS systems due to the comparatively public setting in which they are normally used. There is a significant chance that a cashier or other customers in line behind the user can gain access. At ATMs the individual can usually take more care to ensure that he is alone. In addition, a mistake by the merchant in debiting or crediting the POS accounts or a machine malfunction are always possible. Machine malfunction can be especially problematic or embarrassing to the consumer. If the amount shown in the consumer's account is incorrect, purchases may not be accepted. There is also the risk that the POS machine will not work at all. If the consumer does not have cash or some other payment form on hand at the time, the purchase cannot be made. Most of these risks are allocated or assumed by contract between the users and the involved financial institutions. Most of these risks are also controlled by the Electronic Fund Transfer Act.

Preauthorized Debits and Credits

Preauthorized debits and credits are simply standing orders by the consumer to have his account debited or credited at specific times (i.e. monthly) for payment of recurring bills such as insurance premiums and utility payments,[23] or receipts of recurring payments such as social security or paychecks. To arrange for pre-authorized debits, the consumer must complete and submit a form to his financial institution authorizing a creditor to periodically withdraw funds from the consumer's account. The creditor then initiates each debit by delivering the authorization tapes in machine-readable form, such as on tape, to the consumer's bank. The tape authorizes and initiates the debit on a predetermined schedule for as long as the customer authorization is held. Usually the creditor will have to provide an indemnity agreement to the bank for losses arising from the arrangement, [24] as the bank will have little or no control over the availability of funds in the consumer's account. Preauthorized credits operate in much the same way as preauthorized debits, except the bank will not be concerned over its liabiliies since money is being deposited into the consumer's account instead of being withdrawn from it. Both preauthorized debits and credits are addressed in the Electronic Funds Transfer Act. [25]

Telephone Bill Paying

Telephone bill paying operates by the consumer instructing a financial institution via the telephone to debit his or her account and pay creditors. The consumer may either verbally instruct a bank employee or send electronic impulses to the bank's computer through a touch-tone telephone. While both methods can involve an electronic transfer of funds at some point, only the latter is covered by the Electronic Funds Transfer Act because payments initiated through a conversation with a bank employee are not electronically initiated.[26]

The touch-tone telephone bill paying method
operates by the consumer calling a special number which
directly accesses the financial institution's computer.
Transaction instructions are then entered into the computer via the code frequencies produced by the telephone
push-buttons. The computer debits and instructed amount
from the consumer's account and credits or transfers the
money to the account of the creditors as instructed by
the consumer.

VI. THE ELECTRONIC FUND TRANSFER ACT AND REGULATION. E

A. History and Purpose

Legislative action in response to consumer use of
EFT Systems, which can encompass "an almost infinite
variety of modern payment services,"[27] began with the
establishment of the National Commission on Electronic
Fund Transfers (NCEFT) in 1974.[28] This 26-member panel,
which consisted of mostly bankers and bank regulators,
was formed to conduct a thorough study into consumer use
of EFT, and to recommend appropriate administrative action
and necessary legislation. In its 1977 interim report,
the NCEFT concluded there was a lack of legal standards
governing EFT and recommended measures for protecting
consumer rights. The commission's final report was even
more specific, recommending immediate action. The problems addressed by the NCEFT has evolved from a combination
of the rapidly growing use of EFT and the realization
that existing legislation, specifically the UCC, was not
adequate to deal with some of the unique problems associated with EFT.

The applicable sections of the UCC were developed primarily to deal with the paper-based system of checks, which is precisely what EFT use eliminated. As a result, EFT was not governed by existing law. Liability for EFT losses was unclear at best, with many banks at that time holding the customer fully liable for any unauthorized transfer until notification of loss of theft of the customer's debit card.[29] This meant that if a customer's card was stolen, and the customer did not realize it for a number of days, all money withdrawn from the customer's account was solely the customer's responsibility.

During Congressional consideration of EFT legislation, there were two widely divergent views--the consumer advocates on one side and the banking and retailing groups on the other. The consumer advocates cited a need for legislative consumer protection, especially in the areas of unauthorized use, error correction, and transaction records.[30] Bankers and retailers, on the other hand, did not believe that the proposed EFT legislation was in *anyone's* best interest. They contended that regulatory burdens would impose compliance costs on banks and retailers that would eliminate the impetus for EFT in the first place. This group wanted to adopt a wait-and-see attitude to let time determine whether any initial problems could be worked out as they arose, thus avoiding the need for enacting restrictive legislation. But the consumer groups and the recommendation

of the NCEFT for legislation carried the day. Congress
passed the Electronic Fund Transfer Act (EFTA)[31] in
the final hours of the 95th Congress, in October, 1978.
Two sections became effective on February 8, 1979,[32]
while the remainder became effective on May 10, 1980.

The stated purpose of the EFTA is to provide a
framework establishing the rights, liabilities and responsibilities of participants in Electronic Funds
Transfer Systems.[33] The primary objective of the act,
however, is "the provision of individual consumer rights."
Congress was also concerned that "the uncertainties
that surrounded the change from a paper-based to an
electronic system had slowed electronic systems development."[34] The EFTA, Congress hoped, by defining each
participant's role in the EFT scheme, would promote
financial industry and consumer confidence in EFT and
thereby encourage its development. [35]

Though the EFTA was designed to cover all aspects
of the consumer-financial institution relationship in
EFT, Congress recognized that the Act was just a begin-
ing. EFT had been discussed on the floor of Congress
at least since the establishment of the NCEFT in 1974.
As a result of the nature of the Act and its hasty
passage, Congress wished to allow for changes should
they become necessary. It, therefore, directed the
Federal Reserve Board (FRB) to develop regulations
to implement the EFT, giving the FRB guidelines and
broad authority. The FRB developed Regulation E[36] as
the basic regulatory framework implementing the EFTA.

Regulation E is continually being refined and updated,[37] and includes model disclosures which financial institutions may follow to protect themselves from questions as to whether they are acting to properly protect the consumer. Through Regulation E, the FRB interprets the EFTA, clarifies ambiguities and inconsistencies, and makes other changes where necessary in order to ensure a proper balance between consumer protection and financial institution freedom in supplying EFT services.[38] Congress has recognized that an improper balance on either the side of consumer protection or financial institution freedom will have the result of impeding the development and expected cost savings of electronic fund transfer systems.

B. EFTA or Regulation E

There are some sections of the EFTA which Regulation E has not yet implemented.[39] In addition, in many of the sections which have been implemented, the EFTA requirements have been altered entirely by Regulation E. In some areas the EFTA and Regulation E requirements may even conflict.[40] The practitioner may sometimes wonder whether to follow Regulation E or the EFTA in certain circumstances. Another problem is that many states have passed EFT legislation which may be different from the federal EFTA or Regulation E.

Federal law supercedes state law only when state law is less favorable to the consumer.[41] More restrictive

state law, providing greater protection to the consumer
will be used by the courts as primary legislation since
the Federal acts have not pre-empted the field. As to
whether a practitioner should follow primarily the EFTA
or Regulation E, the act itself provides many of the
answers. For instance, there is no liability for any
person's failure to comply with an EFTA requirement if
the failure was done in good faith and in compliance with
The Federal Reserve Board's rules or interpretations.[42]
Similarly, a financial institution is excused if it fails
to make a necessary disclosure[43] in proper form if the
disclosure followed an FRB model disclosure provided in
Regulation E.[44] The general hierachy of use of the
existing laws as compliance sources are as follows: 1)
Regulation E, 2) EFTA, 3) FRB opinions or official staff
interpretations, 4) judicial decisions in the jurisdiction.[45]

V.   LEGAL ISSUES FACED BY CONSUMERS UNDER EFTA AND REGULATION E

The Electronic Fund Transfer Act is codified at
15 U.S.C. Section 1693 et. seq. (Supp. 1983). The first
section, section 1693, states the Congressional findings
and declarations of purpose. The remaining 18 sections,
1693 a through r, contain the substantive provisions of
the act. Regulation E is codified at 12 C.F.R. Section
205.1 through Section 205.14 (1982). The most recent
update which has not yet been codified is found at 48
FED. REG. 14,800, April 6, 1983.

The EFTA is divided into 18 distinct sections,
remained unchanged since promulgated. By contrast,

Regulation E contains 14 sections, is constantly updated and provides Federal Reserve Board interpretations of the law. Regulation E implements only those sections of the EFTA which it directly addresses. Though the EFTA and Regulation E are relatively detailed, there are a number of issues which have yet to be resolved.

THE ELECTRONIC FUNDS TRANSFER ACT: 15 U.S.C. SECTION 1693 a through SECTION 1693 r

SECTION 1693 a DEFINITIONS

This section sets the tone for the rest of the act by defining key words and phrases which are either unique to EFT or which may have a meaning under the Act which is other than their plain meaning. Since most of the definitions are clear or will be discussed in context under other sections of the act, only a few are discussed here.

The meaning and intent of two sections of EFTA definitions were decided in *Kashanci v. Texas Commerce National Bank*.[46] The plaintiff had, at her financial insitution, an account capable of access via electronic funds transfer. An imposter allegedly initiated a $4,900 withdrawal by calling a bank employee on the telephone and convincing the employee to transfer the money. Apparently the imposter convinced the bank employee that she was the plaintiff account number holder. When the plaintiff received her next bank statement, she notified the bank that the withdrawal was unauthorized. However, the bank refused to recredit her account. The issues

in the case were whether the telephone call which initiated the transfer was an electronic funds transfer
as defined in the Act, and whether the unauthorized
caller was a consumer as defined. The court found that
the transfer in question definitely fell under the general definition of electronic fund transfer under the
EFTA.[47] An electronic fund transfer is defined in
Section 1693 a as "any transfer of funds other than a
transaction originated by check, draft, or similar paper
instrument, which is initiated through an electronic
terminal, *telephone instrument,* or computer or magnetic
tape *so as to order, instruct or authorize a financial
institution to debit or credit an account".* The limiting
clauses of the definition under this sceion of EFTA,
however, exclude any transfer of funds initiated by a
telephone conversation between a *consumer* and a financial
institution, not pursuant to a plan for periodic transfers.[48] Since the transfer in question was initiated via
a telephone conversation with a bank employee and was not
pursuant to a plan for periodic transfers, the question
hinged upon whether the alleged imposter was a "consumer"
under the act. Consumer is defined under the act as "any
natural person".[49] The plaintiff argued that "consumer"
though defined as any natural person, referred only to
an account holder. She relied on an interpretation that
legislative intent was that the entire act referred to
consumers as those who had a contractual relation with
the financial institution in question. The plaintiff
agreed that the transfer in question would not have

fallen under the EFTA had she initiated it, but that since a non-account holder (thus non-consumer) initiated the transfer, the exclusion did not apply. Thus the transaction fell within the general definition of an electronic funds transfer, requiring the financial institution to resolve the error. The court, however, interpreted the legislative history differently, concluding, that the word "consumer" in the exclusion was used purposely because its definition was "any natural person", and did not refer only to an account holder. The bank concluded that the imposter was a consumer; therefore the entire telephonic transfer was not under coverage of the EFTA. While it appears that this would be a case of an account holder suffering a $4,900 loss through no fault of her own merely because the transfer did not fit the specific definition of the electronic funds transfer act the court did point out that the plaintiff may have other legal avenues, such as breach of fiduciary duty, through which to seek reimbursement. The plaintiff's intent in attempting to recover for the loss under electronic funds transfer act rather than using other legal options, was that the plaintiff, if victorious, would have received favorable treatment under the error resolution section of the EFTA.[50] That section, discussed in detail later, outlines the procedures and time constraints under which a financial institution must operate after such a claim by an account holder.

The remainder of the terms defined in this section of the EFTA are relatively clear. Regulation E has, however, added some definitions, in order to make the law

more clear.[51] Regulation E also includes additional exemptions.[52] These refer mainly to transfers which are
electronic in nature, yet are not covered under the EFTA
because they do not meet the general purpose of the act,
to provide for consumer protection.[53] Electronic transactions included in these exemptions are check guarantee and authorization, wire transfers, and certain in-
tra-financial institution transfers.[54] The regulation
also expands the Act's exclusion of coverage for transactions which have as a primary purpose the purchase
of sale of securities or commodities through a broker
or dealer who is registered with or regulated by the
Securities and Exchange Commission.[55] The regulations
delete the broker-dealer requirement because the Federal
Reserve Board concluded that these transfers are adequately regulated by other federal laws whether made
through broker-dealers or not. Still, if the primary
purpose of the electronic fund transfer in question is
some form of payment by the consumer, and securities
or commodities purchase or sale is only incidental to
the payment motive, the EFTA and Regulation E would
apply to the transaction.[56]

SECTION 1693 b REGULATIONS

This section merely authorizes the Federal Reserve
Board to promulgate the regulations (Regulation E) which
implement the act. The FRB, through this section is
given broad discretion in modifying the act and is urged
to issue model disclosures for banks and consumers to
follow. Interpretation of the meanings of specific

parts of the act and regulations are provided in FRB staff intrepretations[57] and in the question and answer section of Regulation E.[58]

SECTION 1693 c TERMS AND CONDITIONS OF TRANSFER

This section, implemented by Regulation E, Section 205.7, specifies that certain initial disclosures must be made by the bank at the time a consumer contracts for any EFT service. Terms that must be disclosed include: 1) the extent of consumer liability for unauthorized transfers, 2) the phone number and address of a person to contract in case of a missing EFT debit card or other problem, 3) the financial institution's normal business days, 4) the kind and frequency of electronic fund transfers allowed, 5) the amount of any charges for use of the financial institution's EFT system, 6) a summary of the consumer's rights to receive documentation of transfers, 7) stop payment rights in the case of regular and preauthorized payment plans, 8) the financial institution's liability for failure to make or stop transfers which were properly requested, and 9) circumstances under which consumer account information will be disclosed to third parties. During the Congressional hearings on EFT this particular section was hotly debated. Opponents argued that such all-inclusive disclosure and corresponding documentation requirements would place substantial compliance burdens upon the banks. This would drive up the cost of providing EFT services, and impede technological development. The relative benefits to the consumer were seen as slight by comparison. As promulgated, the Act and regulations have struck a balance between the needs of the financial institutions and the consumer. The FRB model disclosures, if followed, will relieve the financial institution of any liability for failure to make a proper disclosure. Likewise, the financial institution is protected if it acts, or fails to act, in good faith reliance upon any rule or interpretation made by the FRB or one of its officials. Financial institutions are also protected against subsequent adverse judicial decisions.[59]

The consumer is protected by the disclosed information itself, as well as the requirement that the language of the disclosures be in "easily understandable" language.[60] Because EFT is so wholly different from the familiar paper-based systems, it is important that consumers be provided with a written explanation of their rights, responsibilities and liabilities. The consumer must be able to weigh the financial risks, privacy, and other ramifications against the convenience and benefits of EFT systems, when the consumer is deciding whether to augment or replace a traditional payment system with an EFT system.[61]

Part (b) of this section requires that a financial institution notify a consumer account holder at least 21 days before any terms of disclosure change which will increase fees, or consumer liabilities, or which will restrict consumer use or benefits. Thirty-day notice is required for permanent changes. Regulation E has added to these disclosures, the requirement that error resolution procedures, and the customer's rights under such procedures be disclosed.[62] The regulations also provide a sample disclosure clause.[63] The EFTA and regulations also require that the financial institution provide the error resolution notice to the consumer at least once each year, as well as at the time of contracting. [64]

While this section of the Act and the regulations provide for disclosures of possible consumer liability for unauthorized transfers, disclosure of the extent of consumer liability for delayed reporting or loss or theft of an EFT access device or personal identification number (PIN) is optional.[65] In fact, consumer liability under this section can be increased from $50 to $500 for such delay.[66] The FRB should amend Regulation E to require disclosure of the extent of consumer liability for delay in reporting loss or theft of an EFT access device or PIN, just as it requires disclosure of possible consumer liability for unauthorized transfers. [67] This would be in keeping with the stated purpose of the Electronic Fund Transfer Act to provide a basic framework which establishes the rights, liabilities and responsibilities of participants in the electronic fund transfer system.[68]

SECTION 1693 d DOCUMENTATION OF TRANSFERS

The costs to financial institutions of handling and storing checks is eventually passed on to the consumer. EFT reduces and in many cases stops the need for such costly paper handling. In a pure EFT system, however, the consumer would have no record or proof of the kind, date, and amount of any transfer of money to or from his account. Congress sought to balance consumer protection with the compliance costs when it decided that some form of documentation should be required whenever an EFT transaction is carried out.

The Electronic Fund Transfer Act and Regulation E actually requires documentation which is as detailed or more so than that required in a paper-based transaction.[69] The three types of documentation required of any electronic fund transfer are: 1) a receipt for any transaction initiated by consumer at an electronic terminal, 2) written notice as to whether a regularly scheduled pre-authorized deposit has been credited to a consumer's account, and 3) a monthly descriptive account summary for any consumer account which is capable of performing an EFT function.[70]

For any transaction initiated by a consumer at an electronic terminal, a financial institution must make available to the consumer written documentation which sets forth the amount and date of transfer, type of transfer, identity of the account affected, name of any third party involved, and the location of the terminal at which the transaction was carried out.[71] Originally, the EFTA required that the transaction receipt identify the specific account accessed if the debit card or other access device could access more than one account. But in order to preserve the use of older POS and ATM systems that are incapable of providing that identification,[72] the Federal Reserve Board has exempted them from this requirement. The regulations also grant an exception to the requirement that the name of any involved third party be disclosed on the terminal receipt. If the third party name is provided by the consumer in a form in which the computer is able to duplicate on the receipt, the financial institution is required to list the name of the third party only on the required periodic statement.[73]

The receipt requirement of the Act provided the consumer with the equivalent of a cancelled check. The receipt acts as prima facie evidence that the transaction in question was completed if the receipt represents proof of payment made to another person.[74] Thus ATM cash deposits and receipts are not considered prima facie evidence since they are not transfers to another person. The reason for the distinction between deposits and transfers to a third party is that a cash deposit receipt shows the amount entered by the consumer, regardless of the amount actually deposited. The actual deposit amount will not be known at the time the deposit is made, but only after the deposit has been counted by a financial institution employee. The account credit is thus not completed until the deposit amount is verified. Transfers to third parties, however, create an immediate debit to the account of the consumer, meaning that his receipt should show the exact amount actually withdrawn from the account.

One fault in the documentation requirements of the EFTA and Regulation E is that only consumer-initiated transactions must be documented at the time of the transfer. Transactions initiated by the financial institution do not require a receipt. Thus if the financial institution transfers money from the consumer's account for some reason, the consumer may not be aware of the transfer until receipt of the periodic statement. Since Congress recognizes the need to provide documentation to the consumers whenever they conduct their own transactions, certainly that protection should extend the documentation requirements to cover bank-initiated fund transfers. Otherwise consumers have little or no control over the amount of funds kept in their accounts or whether such transfers by the bank were proper.[75]

Some banking industry advocates have argued that individual receipts are not necessary as long as monthly descriptive statements are sent to each consumer. These advocates point out that the monthly receipt contains the same information as the terminal receipt and can still act as prima facie evidence of a transaction. They also contend that holding and organizing terminal receipts is more burdensome to the consumer than maintaining a check register.[76]

As for saving and organizing terminal receipts, it is certainly no more burdensome than keeping a check balance. However, in a check-based system, the consumer can verify transactions listed on the monthly statement with the actual checks written. For EFT transactions,

if the consumer has no terminal receipt, there will be
no way to verify that the amount of the transaction he
or she actually carried out is the amount the bank
transferred and listed on the periodic statement.

Without terminal receipts, if an unauthorized
user gains access to an account and makes withdrawals,
the owner of the account might not even notice. For
example, suppose a consumer withdraws $100 cash at an
AMT on day one of a monthly statement cycle and receives
no terminal receipt. When the next monthly statement
arrives, it shows that $150 was withdrawn on that date.
Without the transaction receipt, the consumer may have
no evidence to dispute the $150 showing. Even more
likely, the consumer may not have kept track of all the
withdrawals and might not notice the error since the
transaction occurred up to 30 days previously. Also,
without terminal receipts, the consumer has no way of
determining whether the discrepancy is due to unauthorized access to the account, bank error or simply poor
memory. [77]

Though the EFTA and Regulation E do not regard
ATM deposits or withdrawal transactions receipts as
prima facie evidence, it does not mean that such receipts are of no value. In case of a discrepancy, however, the consumer has to prove his position by other
than the transaction receipt alone. In *McEvans v. Citibank N.A.* [78] a consumer claimed he had made a $600
deposit at an ATM. The bank claimed it had not received
such a deposit and was unwilling to credit the con-

sumer's account. The bank was found liable for the
missing money when it was shown that the bank failed
to follow its own procedures for opening accounts and
verifying cash deposits.[79] In *Proctor v. National
Savings and Trust Co.*[80], a pre-EFTA decision, a
different result was reached. The consumer argued that
she had made a $50 deposit at the bank's ATM. When the
bank showed that it had followed its usual standards
for opening accounts and verifying cash deposits, and
that the machine had been working properly on the date
of the alleged deposit, the court concluded that the
bank had never received the deposit. The court took
the view that the consumer had probably inserted the
money into the machine improperly, and failed to notice
that the deposit was rejected. When the consumer left
the area, the bank theorized, the money was left un-
deposited and was probably taken by a subsequent
customer.[81] While the court's version of the events
in *Proctor* may be speculative, a comparison with the
McEvans case shows first that a customer *can* be
victorious in a dispute over an ATM deposit without the
use of transaction receipt as prima facie evidence.
Secondly, the banks occupy a strong position if they
can show that usual procedures for accounting for such
deposits were followed. These cases also point out
that it may be unwise to deposit cash at an ATM. Deposited checks which are lost or misplaced can be
traced or stopped, whereas cash cannot. Consumers
depositing cash should do so via a human teller and get
a transaction receipt.

Consumers should also consider the security aspect of EFT documentation versus that of traditional payment methods such as checks and credit cards. Checks and credit cards provide additional security because both must be completed or reviewed and signed by the consumer, thus creating traceable documentation as a result of the consumer's signature.[82] With EFT access devices, on the other hand, the transaction receipt does not specifically identify a particular consumer. If a consumer debit card and PIN are obtained by an unauthorized user, it is impossible to stop its use. The financial institution cannot know an imposter is using the account until the account holder notifies the institution that the card has been stolen or used without authorization. No signature trace is available as with checks and credit card receipts.

The EFTA requires that preauthorized transfers into a consumer's account as well as consumer-initiated transfers must be documented. Preauthorized transfers, such as automatic payroll and social security deposits, have been in existence since long before the EFTA. Documentation requirements, therefore, created burdens upon financial institutions which had not before existed. The EFTA provides that if a consumer's account is to be credited by a preauthorized transfer from the same payor at least once every 60 days, the consumer must be made aware whether the transfer occurred as scheduled. If the consumer is notified by the payor, the financial institution need not duplicate the effort. The act allows for either "positive" notice, given to the consumer when the payment is made as scheduled, or "negative" notice, when the deposit is not made as scheduled.[83]

Regulation E has provided a third alternative to the positive or negative notification requirement. The financial institution may provide a readily available telephone line which the consumer may use to find out whether a transfer occurred. The financial institution must disclose the telephone number along with the unsual information provided consumers when they open an EFT account. In addition, the telephone number must be included with each periodic statement.[84]

Though receipts are required at the time of an EFT transaction for both consumer-initiated transactions and preauthorized credit, the EFTA and Regulation E also require that the consumer receive periodic statements. Statements must be sent monthly for any month during which an EFT transaction has occurred, or at a minimum of every three months if there has been no EFT activity. Each periodic statement must contain the same information required in the transaction receipts. In addition, the periodic statement must list any charges assessed by the financial institution for transfers or account maintenance, the beginning and ending account balance, and an address and phone number that the consumer can call in the event of any problems or questions.[85]

Initially the EFTA required that transaction receipts and periodic statements indicate the date of the initiation of the transfer.[86] The Federal Reserve Board, through Regulation E, has amended the requirement to list the date of completion of the transaction.[87] The change was effected to provide a greater degree of accuracy in specifying the date when the consumer account was actually debited or credited.

Regulation E also changed the requirement that the terminal location of each transfer be included on the periodic statement. Originally all transactions had to be recorded as to whether they wer ATM or non-ATM. Compliance with the original law would have forced financial institutions to manually separate ATM deposits from other deposits and other ATM transactions in order to record the terminal location.[88] To balance the cost of financial institution compliance with the benefit of the requirement to consumers, the Federal Reserve Board exempted ATM terminal deposits from including the terminal location on the periodic statement. [89]

The EFTA originally required that charges for EFT services be disclosed separately from charges for other account activities.[90] This again created substantial compliance burdens for financial institutions, so the regulations were modified to require listing only the total charges for any account.[91]

The rationale behind requiring banks to provide both transaction receipts and periodic statements to consumers is that with both documents a consumer can adequately account for any and all EFT activity. The periodic statement fills any gaps left through issuance of only the transaction receipts.[92] Consumers can balance EFT statements just as they would a checkbook by comparing the transaction receipts with the periodic statements.

One problem with this system is that EFTA allows other account information besides EFT transactions on the periodic statement.[93] A statement may contain transactions from regular checking ATM deposits and withdrawals, preauthorized debits and credits, and POS transactions.[94] A further complication is that the various types of transactions may be identified by code instead of simply named. Consumers must be willing and able to carefully analyze the entire statement. In order to do so, they must gather all checks, transaction receipts, and ledgers identifying preauthorized debits and credits, and must identify each transaction by its code. They must then shuffle between the checks, transaction receipts and ledgers to verify that each transaction made was for the correct amount and on time. He must also verify that any third party payments were made to the right party.[95]

The point of all this is that, upon opening an account with a full range of EFT and non-EFT functions, many consumers may be unaware of the tedious bookkeeping they face each month. Consumers who were unwilling or unable to keep up with the complicated balancing act run the risk of being unaware of an unauthorized with-drawal from the account or of drawing on insufficient funds.

Some of the burden on the consumer could be avoid-ed by requiring financial institutions to provide notice of the ramifications of opening an account in which numerous types of transactions will be carried out. Another alternative would be to require banks to offer the option of periodic statements with separate sections for the type as well as the chronology of transactions. The account holder could pay the cost of this option, thus minimizing compliance costs to the financial in-stitution.

Whether such record keeping problems will be pre-valent is merely speculative at this point. With the legislation that now exists, the consumers have no legal remedy even if harmed by inability to properly balance a multi-use account. In keeping with the goal of Con-gress to protect the consumer and that of the Federal Reserve Board to promote EFT services, both bodies should address this issue. Consumer distrust in EFT systems could inhibit their growth.

SECTION 1693 e PREAUTHORIZED TRANSFERS

This section of the EFTA, implemented by Regulation E section 205.10 (b), refers to automatic authorized transfer from a consumer's account, such as for the payment of insurance premiums or mortgages. The regulations do not significantly change the Act. Basically the section requires that such transfers be authorized in writing, verifying that the consumer is aware that they have been made.[96] The consumer may stop payment of any preauthorized debit by notifying the financial institution orally or in writing at least three days before the scheduled date of transfer. The financial institution can subsequently require written notification, which must be received within fourteen days of oral notification.[97] If a given preauthorized debit will vary from the authorized amount, either the financial institution or the authorized payee must notify the consumer in writing of the change at least ten days before the transfer is to be made.[98] This requirement allows the consumer to cover or stop the transfer if there are insufficient funds in the account. Such variances in the amount of transfer are common in such cases as payments for utility bills, which can vary substantially from one season to another.[99] In lieu of a notification each time the actual payment varies from the specified amount, consumers may arrange to be notified only if the transfer falls outside a specified range, high or low.[100] The Federal Reserve Board has interpreted the stop payment right to continue indefinitely once ordered, meaning that no payments for the stopped check occurs until the consumer reauthorizes in writing. This is only an interpretation, however, and is not clearly stated in the Act or regulations, nor has it been settled judicially. A consumer should check to ensure whether the financial institution has interpreted the stop payment order as indefinite, or whether it means only the next payment. Financial institution interpretation is likely to be found in the initial disclosures required by Section 205.7 (a) of Regulation E. Neither the EFTA nor Regulation E specify to whom a stop payment order must be delivered. The consumer must be careful to follow disclosure instructions in this regard. Notice to the wrong person at the bank, or via the wrong telephone number may be ineffective to stop payment of a preauthorized debit.[101]

There is good reason for allowing the consumer a stop payment right for preauthorized debits and not for instant transactions such as direct payment or ATM withdrawals and deposits. Originally the House and Senate EFT bills contained a reversibility provision. Consumer advocates argued that because EFT replaces mainly the check-based system, legislation should include reversal and "float" clauses since consumers had those benefits under the paper-based system. Opponents

argued that EFT transactions were more like cash payments; once made, the money is gone and the transaction
completed. They contended that allowing a reversal
period would negate any certainty of payment, one of
the major advantages of EFT to merchants and other payees.[102] Ultimately, those opposed to allowing reversibility and stop payment, except for preauthorized
debits, won the day. The decision not to allow reversal
and stop payment for instantaneous transactions makes
sense when one considers the compliance costs for a
payee to retransfer funds from a previously credited
account back to the consumer's debited account. In addition, bookkeeping would be difficult. Had the reversal
and stop payment provision remained, the high cost of compliance would probably have forced merchants and other
EFT payees to limit EFT payments to only high priced items.
Allowing consumers to stop payment of preauthorized transfers does not involve any of these risks or costs because
payment is stopped before transaction is completed. Under
the present Act and regulations, the consumer, knowing
the EFT payments are final, can plan accordingly. In most
cases, when there is a question of availability of funds
or the possibility of a need to reverse or stop payment,
the consumer will still be free to use a check instead
of EFT payment.[103]

SECTION 1693 f ERROR RESOLUTION

This section is of great importance to any consumer participating in the EFT services because an error in debiting or crediting a consumer's account could cause severe problems for any consumer who relied upon the EFT transaction for the payment of such obligations as rental or mortgage payments.[104] The issue is one of control and knowledge since the consumer must assume correct transfer, but is not always directly involved with the transfer, as would be the case in a paper-based system in which the consumer writes the deposit, withdrawal, and transfer documents in the form of a check.

A mistake by the financial institution could cost the consumer the amount of the transfer mistake if there were no error resolution procedures. More importantly, nonpayment or improper payment of other obligtions, such as a mortgage payment, could jeopardize the consumer's standing with creditors.

Because alleged mistakes often take the financial institution a long time to resolve, the National Commission on Electronic Funds Transfer recommended error resolution procedures to protect the consumer during the investigation period. There was, however, much debate in Senate and House hearings over what was a reasonable time in which to have errors resolved. [105] Bankers insisted error resolution procedures were unnecessary because financial institutions would resolve errors as quickly as possible as part of good customer service. They pointed out that other areas of the law, such as the UCC, had no error correction deadlines. Congress, however, recognized the nature of EFT made it imperative that some form of formal error resolution procedures be adopted. The early versions of error resolution bills specified periods ranging from three to forty-five days.[106] Neither consumer advocates nor the financial industry could accept the extremes. A financial institution often could not even gather the necessary information to determine whether the crediting was necessary in three days, while a consumer's financial standing may be devastated by a 45-day wait for recrediting.[107]

Finally a compromise was struck. The measure gives consumers adequate protection while giving financial institutions adequate time to complete a thorough investigation of any complaint of improper transfer. The consumer must give oral or written notice of an alleged error within 60 days of receipt of the information (i.e. periodic statement) in which the error was discovered. The consumer notification need not be precise but must contain enough information to allow the financial institution to investigate, including, to the extent possible, the type, date and amount of the error. The financial institution may require notification in writing within 10 days of oral notice, but the investigation period still begins at the time of the original notification.[108] Once notificaiton of an error is received by the financial institution, it has ten days to complete its investigation and either recredit the consumer's account or notify the consumer that the account will not be credited and state why there was no error.[109] If the financial institution cannot make an adequate determination within the ten-day period, it may extend the investigation period to forty-five days as long as the consumer's account is provisionally recredited by the amount of the alleged mistake. The financial institution may, however, withhold $50 from the recrediting.[110] If the financial institution concludes there was no error and refuses to permanently recredit the consumer's account, treble damages, including interest, shall be awarded if it is found the financial institution did not make a good faith effort investigation, or if there was no reasonable basis to conclude that no error had occurred. Treble damages may also be awarded if the financial institution does not act within the 10 or 45-day time period, whichever is applicable, or if it does not notify the consumer of its intention not to recredit the consumer's account.[111]

From the time of final determination that an error occurred, the financial institution has one business day to recredit the consumer's account, and three days to provide written notice and explanation if it finds that no error has occurred. [112]

The financial institution is required to investigate reported errors only to the extent of its own records, even if the alleged error concerns a transfer to or from a third party, so long as there is no agreement (i.e. contract) between the financial institution and the third party. [113] If there is such an agreement, such as where a third party merchant has agreed to honor the financial institution's access device, the financial institution must contact the merchant in order to see if the error can be found through a comparison of bank records with the merchant's records. [114]

For purposes of the EFTA and Regulation E, an error includes the following: [115]

1) an unauthorized electronic fund transfer;
2) an incorrect electronic fund transfer to or from a consumer's account;
3) the omission from a periodic statement of an electronic fund transfer to or from the consumer's account that should have been included;

4)   a computation or bookkeeping error made by the financial institution relating to an electronic funds transfer;

5)   the consumer's receipt of an incorrect amount of money from an electronic terminal;

6)   an electronic fund transfer not identified in accordance with the requirement of Regulation E, Section 205.9 or SEction 205.10 (a); or

7)   a consumer's request for any documentation required by Regulation E, Section 205.9, 205.10 (a), or for additional information concerning an electronic fund transfer. This includes any request for information in order to assert an error within the meaning of paragraphs (a) (1) through (6) of this section. It does not include a routine inquiry about the balance in the consumer's account or a request for duplicate copies of documentation or other information that is made only for tax or other record-keeping purposes.

Under number 7 above, a consumer's request for documentation or additional information is considered an error. The reason for its inclusion is that it permits consumers to use the error resolution procedures and time constraints if they discover an error after their initial inquiry is answered. The financial institution must respond to their request within ten days, just as if it were an original error report. If an error is found after the additionally requested information is reviewed, the consumer will still have plenty of time to report the error before the expiration of sixty days from the time of receipt of the information in which the error first appeared.

This provision allows the consumer adequate time

to investigate a suspected error. For instance, a consumer may check the account balance and believe it is
incorrect but will not be able to verify this until the
periodic statement arrives, which could be up to thirty
days later. By that point one half of the sixty day
period will have expired. [116]

Error resolution procedures do pose a number of
problems. First a consumer may not know what the financial institution requires in reporting an error.
Regulation E provides that a financial institution use
reasonable measures to refer consumers to the appropriate location for reporing errors. [117] For example,
if the consumer notifies the financial institution, but
at the wrong telephone number, the resolution procedure
may not be invoked. If the consumer then waits until
after sixty days to check the status of the investigation, the bank may not have to investigate at all since
the consumer did not properly notify the bank of
alleged error within the required 60 days. While the
regulations do specify that the financial institution
must use reasonable measures to refer the consumer to
the correct location, such as a phone number or address,
a better rule would be to either require that the consumer be made aware of the correct error reporting
location and telephone number both verbally and in the
initial disclosures, or to allow the consumer to notify
the financial institution by any reasonable means, such
as the general telephone number, or by notifying any
bank employee. It is much easier for the bank to refer

the consumer to the proper location than it is for the consumer to be certain to notify the right individual.

Second, financial institutions need only respond to "errors contained in preliminary disclosures, transfer receipts, periodic statements, or notifications concerning preauthorized transfers."[118] But a consumer may learn of an error before it is identified in some form of statement. The financial institution need not comply with the 10-day recredit limit until the error is formally recorded. This could create a severe hardship on a consumer if the next statement is not due for 30 days. A solution would be to require error resolution procedures to include investigation of errors not yet in documented receipt form.

A third problem faced by consumers is what to do if the financial institution concludes that no error was committed and either will not re-credit the consumer's account or debit the provisional re-credit. If the consumer still feels wronged he or she must initiate legal action. Despite the protection of the treble damages clause and other possible penalties for the bank,[119] the consumer may be unwilling to risk legal expenses if the amount of the alleged error is relatively slight, as it probably will be for the average consumer. A twenty-, fifty-, or even one hundred-dollar error may not be worth the time and expense of legal action. Further, for a poor consumer, if the re-

credit is not done immediately, even a successful lawsuit sometime in the distant future will not prevent
eviction, foreclosure or repossession due to failure
to make timely payments.[120]

SECTION 1693g CONSUMER LIABILITY

Unauthorized transfers are a major concern of both
financial institutions and consumers. In order to complete an EFT transaction, the account owner must usually
enter an access device, such as a debit card, into an
EFT machine. The individual must also punch in a code,
such as a PIN, in order to initiate a transfer. This
two-step process is designed to protect the consumer.
An unauthorized user will need both the card and the
secret number in order to gain access to a consumer's
account. The problem is that many consumers keep a copy
of their PIN either on their debit card or somewhere
near it. Gaining access to the card usually means gaining access to the code as well. Unauthorized use does
not always mean an unknown thief has stolen the access
device and code. The unauthorized user could be a member of the owner's family or someone who was previously
authorized to use the card and code but who no longer
has such authorization. A financial institution has no
way of knowing whether a user with an access device and
code is unauthorized. This particular problem is one
drawback of an EFT system as compared to a traditional
paper-based system in which the account holder must sign
checks, and the signature can be traced or verified.

A consumer is liable for unauthorized electronic fund transfers up to varying limits, depending upon circumstances. An unauthorized transfer is defined as one

> . . . from a consumer's account initiated by person other than the consumer without actual authority to initiate such transfer and from which a consumer receives no benefit, but the term does not include any electronic fund transfer (a) initiated by a person other than the consumer who was furnished with the card code, or other means to access to such consumer's account by such consumer, unless the consumer has notified the financial institution involved the transfers by such other person are no longer authorized, (b) initiated with fraudulent intent by the consumer or any person acting in concert with the consumer, or (c) which constitutes an error committed by a financial institution. . . .121

The Consumer is held liable for an unauthorized transfer if the access device used in the transfer was *accepted*, 122 meaning that the consumer has caused the device to be activated upon his request. In addition, the financial institution must have provided a means of identifying the consumer to whom the access device was issued, 123 and the financial institution must have provided the consumer with a summary of the consumer's liability and information as to how and where to notify the financial institution in the event of discovery of unauthorized use. 124

A consumer's liability for unauthorized transfer is fifty dollars or the amount of the transfer, whichever is less, so long as the consumer notified the financial institution of the loss or transfer within two days of learning of the loss or theft. 125 Consumer liability increases to $500 or the amount of transfer if the consumer

notifies the financial institution of the loss of transfers after more than two days. The five hundred-dollar
liability includes transfers made after the two-day
notice period that would not have occurred if notice
had been given in two days.[126] Liability of the consumer is unlimited if he fails to notify the financial
institution of any unauthorized transaction which
appears on a periodic statement within sixty days of
receipt of the statement.[127] The designated notification period can be extended if failure to notify the
financial institution was due to extenuating circumstances such as travel or hospitalization.[128]

The liability clauses and limitations are necessary
to protect the positions of both financial institutions
and consumers in the event of unauthorized use of EFT
access devices. If consumers were not liable or were
held liable for only a flat fifty-dollar limit, as with
unauthorized credit card transactions, financial institutions would face extreme costs in recrediting consumer accounts; consumers would be unmotivated to
report unauthorized use. Worse yet, because there is
no way to verify who makes an EFT transaction, fraudulent use by the consumer or an accomplice, with a subsequent report that the transfer was unauthorized, could
become widespread. Notice to the financial institution
of unauthorized use is complete when a consumer "takes
such actions as are necessary to provide the financial
institution with pertinent information" relative to
such unauthorized use.[129] Notice does not have to be

given to any particular person at the financial institution. Written notice is considered effective when
mailed, not when received by the financial institution.[130]

There are numerous problems in applying this section
of the EFTA and Regulation E. It may be unclear exactly
when a consumer discovered an unauthorized transfer.
Though the consumer is given two days from the time of
the unauthorized transfer in which to report it, the
financial institution may not be able to determine when
the discovery actually happened. For instance, if an
unauthorized transfer occurs two days before the consumer's next periodic statement is issued, the consumer
probably would not learn of the loss until receipt of
the statement. To adequately protect financial institutions, the requirement should be that consumers must
report the unauthorized transaction within two days of
the time when the consumer reasonably should have known
of such unauthorized use. In the above scenario, the
consumer could effectively claim that he learned of the
unauthorized transaction any time up to 60 days after
receipt of the statement on which the loss originally
appeared. The consumer is liable for a maximum of only
$50 unless the bank proves the consumer knew about the
unauthorized transfer.

Another problem under this section arises from
transfers initiated by a person whom an account owner
"furnished" with the access means to the account. Unless
the account owner tells the financial institution that

the person is no longer authorized to use the account, the account owner is liable for all transfers that person makes.[131]

Fortunately, consumer liability for unauthorized transfers is one area where some case law has been developed which helps in interpreting the section. In *Feldman v. CitiBank*,[132] the court addressed two cases which had been consolidated due to the similarity of the facts. In case number one, the plaintiff claimed that $770 had been stolen during six unauthorized withdrawals occurring on four different dates from February to May 1981. The plaitiff claimed to have no idea how the money was taken, saying that she had given her card and PIN to no one. Testimony showed that the plaintiff had noticed the original discrepancy in the amount of $150 on her February 1981 statement but she did not pursue the claims until the additional withdrawals occurred in May of that same year. She was apparently not sure whether or not she had actually made the February withdrawal herself. The court, following what was at the time the proposed version of the EFTA, allowed the plaintiff to collect only the original $150 unauthorized withdrawal. The court reasoned that the plaintiff could not have prevented the original withdrawal so held the bank liable for it. The remaining withdrawals, however, may have been prevented if the plaintiff had notified the bank after discovering the original unauthorized withdrawal.

Under the present version of the EFTA and Regulation E, the result would have been slightly different.
The consumer would have been liable for $50 of the first
$150 unauthorized withdrawal under Regulation E, 205.6
(b). The account holder's liability for the remaining
$620 would depend upon whether sixty days had passed
between the time she had received her February 1981
statement and the date of the remaining unauthorized
withdrawals. If the consmer reported the additional
withdrawals before the 60-day period had run, she would
have been laible for 1) the amount of withdrawals occur-
ring after the initial $150 plus $50, or 2) $500, which-
ever is less. In the *Feldman* case, number 1 above would
be $770 minus $150, or $620 plus the original $50, a
total of $670. Therefore, the maximum liability would
be $500 since it is less.[133] If, however, 60 days had
passed between receipt of the February statement, which
was probably received in early March, and the reporting
of the theft in May, the consumer would be liable for
the maximum $500 liability during the 60-day period plus
all transfers which occurred after the 60-day period.[134]

The second victim in *Feldman* claimed that $100 was
withdrawn without authorization only 37 seconds after
he had completed a withdrawal at the same bank but at
a different ATM terminal. The plaintiff noticed the
unauthorized transfer as soon as he received his next
statement, so the notice provisions limiting liability
were met. At trial, the plaintiff testified that he
gave his ATM card and PIN to no one, and that to his

knowledge he was alone in the ATM machine vestibule. The court, however, concluded that he must have unwittingly allowed some unauthorized person to learn his PIN and therefore gain access to his account. Since the infomation allowing unauthorized use was, though unintentionally, "furnished" to the unauthorized user, the transaction was deemed not to fit the definition of an unauthorized transaction. Therefore, the court would not grant the plaintiff relief. Under the present EFTA statute, the result would be the same. [135]

A second claim against Citibank, also decided in 1981, offers a scenario striking similar to that in the second *Feldman* claim above but with different results. In *Ognibene v. Citibank*[136] the plaintiff was the victim of a scam in which a thief pretended that one of two adjacent ATMs was broken and feigned calling the bank on the service phone located between the ATMs while the plaintiff-victim carried out his own transaction. Asking the customer for assistance, the thief stated that the bank wished the customer to insert his card into the allegedly broken machine in an effort to determine whether it had been repaired. The plaintiff, believing he was cooperating with the bank allowed his card to be so used. He did not believe he was in any danger of improper use because he had not given the thief his PIN code and since both the card and the code are required to effect a withdrawal. In this case, Citibank argued, as it successfully had in *Feldman*, that the consumer must have unwittingly allowed the thief to learn his PIN and that by giving the card to the thief, he had "furnished" access to his account. Therefore the transaction was not an unauthorized transfer as defined. If the transfer was not unauthorized, the plaintiff customer would be fully liable for the loss. The *Ognibene* court however, found that the consumer had not purposefully given his PIN code to the thief, and since Citibank produced no evidence proving that it was supplied to the thief unwittingly, the two necessary steps in furnishing access, that is, furnishing the card and the code, were not met. Therefore, the transaction was found to be unauthorized as defined in the EFTA and the consumer was due the protection of the consumer liability clause under the act.

Regulation E has finally solved the question of what constitutes furnishing access to the consumer's account. The Federal Reserve Board has interpreted "furnishing an account device" to mean that the consumer has knowingly granted actual authority to a third party to use the device. Access and use furnished via robbery or fraud upon the consumer, unbeknownst to the consumer, is regarded as an unauthorized transfer. The consumer is, under this interpretation, liable for transfers by those to whom authority was granted who exceed that authority until the consumer notifies the financial institution that such authority no longer exists for the third party.[137]

The final issue addressed under the consumer liability section of the EFTA and Regulation E is its relationship to the Truth in Lending Act (T.I.L.A.)[138] and Regulation Z,[139] which implements it. Basically, the Truth in Lending Act governs credit card issuance, use and liability. The TILA and EFTA conflict whenever a credit card is issued which also acts as an EFT access device (debit card). Regulation E provides that it controls whenever an unauthorized EFT transaction occurs through use or abuse of one of these "hybrid" cards.[140] Regulation E also determines liability if a hybrid card was used in a transfer that involved an extension of credit "under an agreement. . . to extend credit when a consumer's account is overdrawn or to maintain a specified minimum balance." . .[141] Unauthorized use of a hybrid card which does not involve an EFT transaction is governed by the provisions of the Truth in Lending Act.

Though there are issues under this section which must be resolved, the consumers are well protected so long as they act reasonably in the use of EFT access devices and in the reporting of unauthorized use as soon as it is discovered. This also presumes that the consumer properly reviews and balances his account upon receipt of periodic statements. The greater risk of loss, so long as the consumer acts reasonably as described above, is on the financial institution which provides the EFT service. Because financial institutions stand to suffer the loss once unauthorized use has been reported by the account holder, they will have a great incentive to provide adequate security and to update EFT systems as better security measures are developed. The use of the PIN, which presents the greatest security problem, will probably disappear over the next ten years or so.[142] More advanced identification methods, such as voices and fingerprint analysis, or signature verification are likely to be used as soon as they are developed to the point where they are cost-effective.[143]

Based on the similarities with the Truth in Lending Act and its apparent success since its inception in 1970,[144] the consumer liability structure under the EFTA and Regulation E should prove exceedingly effective.[145]

SECTION 1693 h LIABILITY OF FINANCIAL INSTITUTIONS

This section has not been implemented by Regulation E, so the EFTA is controlling. A financial institution is liable for damages proximately caused by its failure to make a properly instructed transaction, for failure to make a transfer due to insufficient funds if the financial institution failed to credit previously deposited money which would have provided sufficient funds, or if the financial institution makes a pre-authorized transfer after having been properly instructed by the consumer not to make the transfer.[146] The financial institution is not liable if its inaction or improper action was the result of circumstances beyond its control as long as it used reasonable care to prevent such an occurrence. Such occurrences could include a technical malfunction of which the consumer was aware,[147] insufficient funds in the account, funds that were subject to legal process, a transfer that exceeds the consumer's credit limit, or an ATM terminal that has insufficient cash to complete the transaction.[148] Unless the consumer plaintiff can prove that the financial institution intentionally failed to make a properly requested transaction, or to stop a transaction upon proper request, only actual damages are collectible.[149]

This section of the EFTA deals only with a financial institution's failure to *complete* a requested transaction. But the Act does not address the question of a financial institution's liability for withdrawals that are erroneously made (other than preauthorized transfers). For instance, what happens if a consumer instructs the financial institution to transfer $50 to a third party, and the financial institution actually transfers $500? Such withdrawals are not unauthorized transfers as defined in section 1693 a of the Act, so there is no redress under that section of the Act. If they were considered unauthorized transfers, the consumer might be liable for the first $50 even though the erroneous withdrawal was completely beyond his control, and in fact was solely the fault of the financial institution. It appears that the consumer's only alternative is to seek redress through the error resolution procedures, and if unscuccessful, bring a

civil action against the financial institution under
EFT Section 1693 m. If, however, the consumer is unaware that he can seek redress via the error resolution
procedures, and fails to notify the financial institution of the improper withdrawal within 60 days, there
is no other remedy under the EFTA. Although the consumer may have a right of action against the financial
institution at common law, once again the time and
expense of instituting legal action may outweigh the
amount of the erroneous withdrawal.[150]

In keeping with the stated purpose of the EFTA
to provide consumer protection, the Federal Reserve
Board should implement regulations updating this entire
section, specifically addressing the procedures for
solving claims of erroneous withdrawals. The intent
of Congress in enacting this section of the EFTA was
to set the same standards of liabilities for financial
institutions in EFT that apply to checking under the
Uniform Commercial Code.[151] Under the UCC, a financial
institution is liable for damages proximately caused
by wrongful dishonor of commerical paper.[152] A financial institution should similarly be liable for
wrongful (erroneous) withdrawals or transfers. The
EFTA, parallelling the practice under the UCC, would
provide proper consideration of financial institution
liability based upon the facts and circumstances,
rather than fitting the liability into narrowly defined
categories, as at present. Further, absent proven
intent by the financial institution, bona fide error

would be assumed. If the error is bona fide, the consumer will be limited to actual damages. The present law places a great burden of care upon the consumer to ensure that the financial institution makes the proper transfer, as an improper withdrawal or transfer by the financial institution can be costly to the consumer, particularly if he is unable to meet other financial obligations as a result of insufficient funds.

As a final protection for itself, a financial institution can add to the list of instances in which it is absolved from liability by specifying the altered terms and conditions in contractual agreements and initial disclosures with customers.[153]

SECTION 1693 i ISSUANCE OF CARDS OR OTHER MEANS OF ACCESS

This section, implemented by Regulation E Section 205.5, was included in response to two problems which were identified at the time credit cards first came into widespread use in the 1960's.

First, unlimited and unrestricted dissemination of the EFT access or debit cards may cause people who would not normally obtain such cards to use them irresponsibily, without realizing their rights and responsibilities as a user. Back when credit cards were widely distributed on an unsolicited basis, many consumers used them indiscriminantly, and subsequently found themselves deep in debt.

The second problem addressed under this section is that of EFT access devices being intercepted in the mail. Interception and use by an unauthorized person might go unnoticed by both the consumer and the financial institution for a period of time. If funds were diverted from the consumer's account, a consumer would be faced with the burden of proving that he never received or used the access device.[154]

As a result of these and related problems, the current regulations require that the access devices, whether they be debit cards or any other types, be issued only upon request of the consumer, or as a renewal of a previously issued accepted device.[155] Unsolicited access devices may be sent to consumers so long as the devices have not been validated. In addition, an unsolicited access device may be validated only upon consumer request, and upon verification of the consumer's identity. It is also required that the financial institution supply a full disclousre of the consumer's rights and liabilities upon validation of an unsolicited access device, as well as an explanation of how to dispose of the card should the consumer not wish to have it validated.[156]

The issuance and validation requirements are intended to protect both consumers and financial institutions. Those consumers who would not or should not use an EFT card due to spending haibts or temptations are protected. While they might not turn down a validated card if it were sent to them, they must now make a positive effort to have the card validated before it can be used.[157] If the access device is intercepted in the mail, the consumer is protected from unauthorized use since the card will be validated only following request and proper identification of the consumer. The financial institution is also protected by the request and identification requirement. Though some believe that unsolicited access devices should not be distributed at all, Congress recognized the mutual benefit of allowing financial institutions to do so. The distribution of unsolicited access devices will create competition between financial institutions for increased client bases and consumers will gain the benefit of banking options that they might otherwise not have had.

Access devices or debit cards which can be used for both EFT purposes (debit card) and charging purposes (credit card) are governed by both the Truth in Lending Act and Regulation Z, and the EFTA and Regulation E. The EFTA and Regulation E govern the issuance of pure debit devices, and the addition of access device capability to an existing credit card.[158] The Truth in Lending Act and Regulation Z govern the issuance of credit cards, the addition of credit card features to an accepted access device, and the initial issuance of dual-use (hybrid) cards.[159] Regulation E governs EFT access devices which involve credit characteristics only to the extent of providing overdraft protection.[160]

SECTION 1693 j SUSPENSION OF OBLIGATIONS

This section, unimplemented by Regulation E, provides:

If a system malfunction prevents the effectuation of an electronic fund transfer initiated by a consumer to another person, and such other person has agreed to accept by such means, the consumer's obligation to the other person shall be suspended until the malfunction is corrected and the electronic fund transfer may be completed, unless such other person has subsequently, by written request, demanded payment by means other than an Electronic Fund Transfer.

The key requirements under this section are that the transaction in question must be one initiated by the consumer, and that the third party must have previously agreed to accept payment by electronic funds transfer. If a preauthorized debit, therefore, does not occur because the system malfunctioned, the consumer is still liable for the preauthorized debit, since this type of electronic fund transfer is not a consumer-initiated transfer.[161]

This section acts to protect the consumer from pressure by those who agreed to do business with him under an EFT system when nonpayment of the consumer's obligation is completely out of the consumer's control. The creditor can rest assured in these cases that payment will be forthcoming as soon as the system is "on-line" again. Because of the intent of this section, it appears that a consumer's account can be automatically debited without further authorization if the consumer had authorized the transaction before the system mal-functioned.[162]

The Federal Reserve Board has opted not to address any issues which have arisen under this section, claiming that the section is "straight-forward, and requires no regulatory implementation. It remains for judicial determination to answer any questions raised under this section.[163]

SECTION 1693 k COMPULSORY USE OF ELECTRONIC FUND TRANSFERS

The Federal Reserve Board believed that this section too was straight-forward, so it has not been implemented by Regulation E.[164] It provides:

> No person may, 1) condition the extension of credit to a consumer on such consumer's repayment by means of preauthorized electronic fund transfers; or 2) require a consumer to establish an account for receipt of electronic fund transfers with a particular financial institution as a condition of employment or re=ceipt of a government benefit.

The EFTA does not prevent financial institutions from requiring that an individual accept EFT service capability. For example, a financial institution may require that an account include EFT capability though the consumer does not have to use it. Although an employer cannot force an employee to open an EFT account

at a particular financial institution as a condition
of employment, the language of the act implies that
the employer could require an employee to open such
an account at one of two or more fiancial institutions.
Similarly, the government can require receipt of benefits via direct deposits at one of a choice of financial
institutions.[165]

If an employer requires an employee to accept direct
payroll deposits at one of two banks, the employee
is faced with the possibility of being effectively
forced to establish an account at a bank which is far
away from the employee's home or which is differnt
from the financial institution with which the employee
has his account. Such an employee is faced with changing his account, and/or traveling a great distance
in order to conduct his banking business at an unfamiliar bank. This situation would seem to violate
the spirit, if not the letter of the Compulsory Use
section. This section in particular is ripe for inter-
pretive action by the Federal Reserve Board. Since
it does not appear that such action by the Board is
forthcoming, case law and enacted state regulations
can be implemented in order to adequately protect the
consumer.

Though a financial institution cannot, under this
section, require compulsory use of EFT, it is possible
for financial institutions to effectively require electronic payment from consumers with credit extension
obligations. A financial institution accomplishes

this by increasing the cost of other payment methods versus electronic payment.[166] In addition, the Compulsory Use section does not prohibit retailers and other service providers from establishing compulsory use of EFT. The New York Superior Court, for instance, upheld a lease requirement which said that if a tenant chose to pay rent by traditional means, such as by check, the tenant had to pay on time without being billed by the landlord, or the tenant could choose an electronic payment method via an authorized monthly debit.[167] Further, if the tenant closed the checking account from which the automatic rent payment was made without notice to the landlord, the tenant was considered in default, his lease terminable at will. The court upheld the automatic default provision under the "freedom of contract" theory, even if the tenant had made no late payments.

While this section of the EFTA does operate to protect the consumer from some forced use of EFT, the consumer may be placed in a position of virtual compulsory use in many situations. Since there is no indication that the Federal Reserve Board will address these issues in the near future, state law and judicial construction are left to determine the consumer's protection from compulsory EFT use.[168]

SECTION 1693 1 WAIVER OF RIGHTS

This section, primary under the EFTA since there is no implementing regulation under Regulation E, provides that:

No writing or other agreement between a consumer and any other person may contain any
provision which constitutes a waiver of any
right conferred or cause of action created
by this title. Nothing in this section prohibits, however, any writing or other agreement which grants to a consumer a more extensive right or remedy or greater protection
than contained in this title or a waiver given
in settlement of a dispute or action.

This section, which the Federal Reserve Board found to be self-explanatory, was included due to the concern of the drafters of the EFTA that financial institutions would condition the use of EFT services upon waiver of the protections provided by the remainder of the EFTA. This provision places the consumer on equal footing with the financial institution since both must observe the provisions of the EFTA and Regulation E if EFT services are to be provided.

SECTION 1693 m CIVIL LIABILITY

Under the provisions of this section, a financial institution is liable for failure to comply with any of the provisions of the EFTA. The Civil Liablity section is, however, subordinated to the Liability of Financial Institutions[169] and Error Resolution[170] pro- visions. A successful recovery under this section allows the consumer to recover actual damages plus a penalty ranging from $100 to $1000 dollars.[171] There is no minimum per-person recovery, and a class action is limited to a maximum of $500,000 or one percent of the net worth of the liable financial institution, whichever is less.[172] Attorney's fees and costs may also be awarded.[173]

In determining the liability of a financial institution under the Civil Liability section, courts are to consider the frequency and persistence of the compliance with the provisions of the EFTA, and whether such non-compliance was intentional.[174] In class actions, additional considerations by the court include the resources of the financial institution, and the number of persons affected by its non-compliance with the EFTA.[175] The financial institution has the burden of providing that any non-compliance was unintentional and a bona fide error. If this burden is met, no liability will attach.[176] So long as the financial institution complies in good faith with any rule, regulation or opinion of the Federal Reserve Board, it cannot be held liable, regardless of damages to the consumer.[177] The good faith provision also applies to the criminal liability provisions of the EFTA found at Section 1693 n.

A financial institution can protect itself from civil liability penalties by notifying affected consumers of discovered non-compliance with the EFTA, and by adjusting the consumer's account accordingly, including an appropriate damages payment.[178] If the consumer brings an action in bad faith, or to harrass the financial institution, attorney's fees shall be awarded.[179] Any action brought under this section may be brought in the United States District Court or any other court of competent jurisdiction, without regard to amount in controversy.[180] The statute of limitations under this section is one year. [181]

Relieving a financial institution of liability if it can show bona fide error is apt to be unfair to the consumer in some cases. If, for instance, all the funds in a consumer's account were withdrawn due to computer malfunction, yet the financial institution had taken reasonable precautions to avoid such malfunction, the consumer would be left to bear any losses which might result from his failure to meet other obligations, such as mortgage or rent payments.[182] This result obtains even though the damages resulted through no fault of the consumer. The consumer can collect for the money actually wrongfully withdrawn through a claim for unjust enrichment. Consequential damages, however, could be recovered only if the financial institution knew or should have known of the consumer's additional specific payment obligations. For the average consumer, who uses his bank account for the payment of many obligations, it is unlikely that the financial institution will know specifically of the obligations which must be met by the consumer. This is an area under the Civil Liability section which should be resolved by the Federal Reserve Board before costly litigation ensues. In the absence of such regulation, the individual states are left to implement additional consumer protection.

A final practical limitation to consumer-initiated suits under this section concerns the time and expense of litigation. It may be difficult for a consumer with a relatively minor loss to find an attorney who can handle the case for less money than the amount of the loss.[183]

SECTION 1693 n CRIMINAL LIABILITY

This self-explanatory section sets the penalty for giving false or inaccurate information, for purposeful failure to disclose required information, or for purposeful failure to comply with any provision of the EFTA, at up to $5000 and one year imprisonment.[184] The penalty for unauthorized, fraudulent or other illegal use of a debit instrument is up to $10,000 fine and 10 years in prison.[185]

SECTION 1693 o ADMINISTRATIVE ENFORCEMENT
SECTION 1693 p REPORTS TO CONGRESS

These particular sections, being procedural and self-explanatory, do not directly affect the consumer, so are not discussed here. Their full text is included in the EFTA at 15 U.S.C. §1693 et. seq.

SECTION 1693 q RELATION TO STATE LAWS
SECTION 1693 r EXEMPTION FOR STATE REGULATION

These final provisions of the EFTA are discussed together due to their relation to each other. They are extremely important in providing adequate protection to the consumer. Section 1693 q, *Relation to State Laws* provides at Federal law preempts State law only to the extent that the laws are inconsistent.[186] If a state law provides greater consumer protection than does the Federal law, state law is primary. It is through this clause of the EFTA that states will be able to enact provisions which fill the gaps found in the Federal EFTA. The final section of the EFTA, Section 1693 r, *Exemption for State Regulations,* allows the Federal Reserve Board to exempt a state from the requirements of Regulation E if the state has adequate regulations and penalties of its own.[187] A state may not, however, be exempted from the Civil Liability provisions of the EFTA,[188] even though provision is not implemented by Regulation E.

VI. CONCLUSION

The EFTA and Regulation E were enacted to provide legal standards for governing the relationship between consumers and financial institutions in EFT transactions. The passage of the EFTA and Regulation E was prompted by the rapid increase in the use of EFT combined with the lack of legislation to adequately regulate such transactions. The purpose of the EFTA is to provide a framework establishing the rights, liabilities and responsibilities of participants in EFT systems. The primary objective, however, has been the provision of individual consumer rights. Congress hoped that passage of the EFTA would promote financial industry and consumer confidence in EFT by defining each participant's part, thereby encouraging EFT development.

Basically the EFTA requires that:
1) financial institutions must make certain disclosures to the consumer at the time of contracting for EFT services, and that the disclosures state the respective rights, responsibilities and liabilities of each of the parties to the contract;

2) documentation of EFT activities must be provided at the time of each transaction, and at certain specified intervals;

3) alleged errors in debiting or crediting a consumer's account are to be resolved in a specified manner; and

The EFTA also specifies when and how the consumer or financial institution can be held liable for errors and mistakes.

Regulation E was promulgated to fill the gaps left in the EFTA. Congress granted liberal powers to the Federal Reserve Board to implement regulations under the EFTA, in order to more adequately protect the parties involved in an EFT system.

The EFTA has now been in effect for nearly four years. Though there are weaknesses, the lack of reported cases which interpret them is evidence of the overall effectiveness of the Act and Regulation E. The Act has assuaged the initial fears of consumer advocates, who did not think it would be protective enough of consumer rights. It has also stilled the early complaints of the financial industry that the legislation was unduly restrictive, placing upon financial institutions a too severe cost-compliance burden which would stifle the development of EFT services. For the most part, EFT has been well accepted by the American consumer as well as the business world. New ways to put the concept to use, such as interbank system sharing, are constantly being developed. The industry is also coming up with improvements which will all but guarantee proper authentication of EFT transfers and identification of EFT users.

The following are needs which the EFTA and Regulation E do not adequately address:

1) Requiring financial institutions to disclose the extent of consumer liability for delay in reporting loss or theft of EFT access devices under section 1693c.

2) Requiring *all* transfers to be properly documented whether initiated by consumer *or* the financial institution, under section 1693d.

3) Requiring more adequate regulations regarding financial institution's liability for consequential as well as direct damages resulting from erroneous transfers, under section 1693h.

4) Requiring more stringent compulsory use provisions under section 1693k.

Finally, an important aspect of the EFTA is that the states are free to institute their own legislation as long as it is as protective of the consumer, or more so than the federal law. Individual states may have to address the areas where adequate consumer protection is lacking.

VII. FOOTNOTES

1. 15 U.S.C. §1693 *et. seq.* (supp. 1983) [hereinafter cited as EFTA].

2. 12 C.F.R. §205 *et. seq.* (1982) 48 Fed. Reg. 14880 (1983),[hereinafter cited as Reg. E].

3. Connors, *The Implementation of the Electronic Fund Transfer Act: An Update on Regulation E,* 17 Wake Forest L. Rev. 329, 331 (1981).

4. Penney and Baker, *The Law of Electronic Fund Transfer Systems* par. 1.1 (1980).

5. *Id.* par. 1.01 (1).

6. *Id.* par. 1.01 (4).

7. In 1973 there were approximately 1700 Automatic Teller Machines in the U.S. In 1983 there were approximately 36,000. *Belsie, What's your password? Don't tell if it belongs to your automatic teller card,* Christian Science Monitor, Aug. 23, 1983 at 1.

8. Penney and Baker, *supra* note 4.

9. Brandel and Oliff, *The Electronic Fund Transfer Act: A Primer,* 40 Ohio St. L.J. 531, 534 (1979).

10. EFTS industry Report, June 6, 1979, at. 1.

11. Penney and Baker, *supra* note 4, par. 9.01-9.02.

12. *Id.* par. 9.03-9.04.

13. Lingl, *Risk Allocation In International Interbank Electronic Fund Transfers: CHIPS and S.W.I.F.T.,* 22 Harv. Int'l. L.J. 621, 626 (1981).

14. Penney and Baker, *supra* note 4, par. 9.04.

15. For a more detailed discussion of CHIPS, see. e.g. Lingl, *supra* note 13. For a case analysis of some of the legal issues of wire transfers such as CHIPS see: *Delbrueck and Co. v. Manufacturers Hanover Trust Co.,* 464 F. Supp. 989 (S.D.N.Y. 1979), *EVRA Corp. v. Swiss Bank Corp.* 673 F.2d 951 (7th Cir. 1982) and *EVRA Corp. v. Swiss Bank Corp.* 522 F. Supp. 820 (D.C.N.Ill. 1981).

16. Penney and Baker, *supra* note 4, par. 9.05.

17. For a more detailed discussion of S.W.I.F.T. see Penney and Baker, *supra* note 4.

18. Many financial institutions limit the amount of money that can be withdrawn such as $100 per transaction, or $200 per day.

19. Penny and Baker, *supra* note 4, par. 6.04(2).

20. *Id*. par. 6.04 (3) (a-d).

21. *Id*. par. 6.04(i).

22. *Belsie*, *supra* note 7, at 1.

23. Brandell and Oliff, *supra* note 9, at 534.

24. Penney and Baker, *supra* note 4, par. 4.02.

25. 15 U.S.C. §§1693 e (a), 1693d (b) (Supp. 1983).

26. *Id*. §1693 a (b) (e).

27. Brandell and Oliff, *supra* note 9, at 533.

28. Taffer, *The Making of the Electronic Fund Transfer Act: A Look at Consumer Liability and Error Resolution*, 13 U.S.F.C. Rev. 231, at 232 (1979).

29. *Id*. at 233.

30. Hearings on S. 2065 Before the Subcommittee on Consumer Affairs of the Senate Comm. on Banking, Housing and Urban Affairs, 95th Cong., 1st Sess. 39 (Oct. 3-5, 1977) testimony of Linda Hodak, Consumer Federation of America.

31. The Financial Institutions Regulatory and Interest Rate Control Act of 1978, Pub. L. No. 95-630, 2001, 92 Stat. 3641, Codified at 15 U.S.C. §1693 *et. seq.* [hereinafter cited as EFTA §1693 *et. seq.*].

32. EFTA §1693 g, governing consumer liability for un-authorized transfers, and EFTA §1693 i, governing issuance debit cards.

33. *Id.*

34. Connors, *The Implementation of the Electronic Fund Transfer Act: An Update on Regulation E* 17 Wake Forest L. Rev. 329, e.t. 331 (1981).

35. *Id.*

36. 12 C.F.R. §205 *et. seq.* (1982), 48 Fed. Reg. 14880 (1983) [hereinafter cited as Reg. E].

37. Connors, *supra* note 34, at 331.

38. Brandell and Oliff, *supra* note 9, at 541.

39. These are EFTA §1693 h, liability of financial in-stitutions.
    §1693 j, suspension of obligations
    §1693 k, compulsory use of electronic fund transfers
    §1693 l, waiver of rights
    §1693 m, civil liability
    §1693 n, criminal liability
    §1693 p, report to Congress.

40. Ellis and Greguras, *The Electronic Fund Transfer Act and Federal Reserve Board Regulation E. A Compliance Guide for Financial Institutions,* par. 1.1, (1983).

41. EFTA §1693 q (supp. 1983).

42. Ellis and Greguras, *supra* note 40, par. 1.2.

43. efta §1693 c (supp. 1983).

44. EFTA §1693 m (d) (1), (2) (supp. 1983).

45. *Id.*

46. 703 F.2d 936 (5th Cir. 1983).

47. EFTA §1693 a (6).

48. *Id.* § 1693 a (6)(E).

49. *Id.* § 1693 a (5).

50. EFTA § 1963 f.

51. Definitions added under Reg. E 205.2 include (a) (1) "access device", (a) (2) "accepted access device", (c) "act", (e) "credit".

52. Reg. E § 205.3.

53. EFTA § 1693.

54. *Id.* § 1693 a (6) (c).

55. Reg. E § 205.3 (c) (1982).

56. Connors, *supra* note 34, at 335.

57. Reg. E § 205 Supp. I (1983).

58. *Id.* § 205 Supp. II (1983).

59. Connors, *supra* note 34, at 336.

60. EFTA § 1693 (a) (2).

61. *Consumer Protection and Electronic Fund Transfer System; An Analysis of the Electronic Fund Transfer Act of 1978* 58 Ore. L. Rev. 363, at 370 (1979).

62. Reg. E § 205.8 (1982).

63. *Id.* § 205.7 (10).

64. EFTA § 1693 c (a) (7), Reg. E 205.8(b).

65. Reg. E §205 App. A (1982).

66. EFTA § 1693 g (a) (2).

67. 58 Ore. L. Rev., *supra* note 61, at 370.

68. EFTA § 1693 Congressional finding and declaration of purpose.

69. Connors, *supra* note 34, at 338.

70. 58 Ore. L. Rev. *supra* note 61, at 375.

71. EFTA § 1693 d (a) (1-5), Reg. E 205.9 (a).

72. Connors, *supra* note 34, at 340.

73. Reg. E §205.9 (a) (6).

74. EFTA § 1693 d (f).

75. Ellis and Greguras, *supra* note 40 at 95.

76. 58 Ore. L.Rev. *supra* note 61, at 376.

77. Budnitz, *The Impact of EFT Upon Consumers: Practical Problems Faced by Consumers*, 13 U.S.F.C. Rev. 311, at 377 (1979).

78. 96 Misc. 2d 142, 408 N.Y.S2d 870 (Civ. Ct. N.Y. 1978).

79. Ellis and Greguras, *supra* note 40 at 95.

80. S.C. No. 775-70 (D.C. super. Ct. unpublished order filed Jan. 19, 1980).

81. Exerpted from Ellis and Greguras, *supra* note 40, at 27.

82. Budnitz, *supra* note 77, at 377.

83. EFTA § 1693 d(b).

84. Reg. E §205.10 a (1) (iii).

85. EFTA § 1693 d (c), Reg. E §205.9(b).

86. EFTA § 1693 d(a).

87. Reg. E §205.9(b) (1) (iii).

88. Connors *supra* note 34, at 342.

89. Reg. E §205.9 (b) (1) (IV).

90. EFTA §1693 d (c) (2).

91. Reg. E §205.9 (b) (3).

92. Budnitz, *supra* note 77 at 378.

93. EFTA § 1693 d (c).

94. Budnitz, *supra* note 77 at 378.

95. *Id.* at 379.

96. EFTA §1693 e(a), Reg. E §205.10(b).

97. Reg. E §205.10(c).

98. Reg. E §205.10(d).

99. Connors, *supra* note 34, at 345.

100. Reg. E §205.20 (d).

101. Ellis and Greguras, *supra* note 40, at 109.

102. Brandell and Oliff, *supra* note 9, at 552.

103. For an argument in support of allowing reversibility and stop payment for all EFT transactions, see Budnitz, *supra* note 77, at 380.

104. Taffer, *supra* note 28, at 241.

105. *Id.* at 242.

106. Senate Hearings S.2065 Before the Subcomm. on Consumer Affairs of the Senate Comm. on Banking, Housing and Urban Affairs, 95th Cong., 1st Sess. 39 (Oct. 3-5, 1977).

107. EFTA § 1693 f (a), Reg. E 205.11(b).

108. *Id.* Reg. E §205.11(b)(iii).

109. Reg. E §205.11 c (2) (i).

110. EFTA § 1693 f (e), Reg. E §205.11 c (2) (i).

111. *Id.* § 1693 f (e).

112. EFTA § 1693 f (b).

113. Reg. E §205.11 (d) (2).

114. Connors, *supra* note 34, at 349.

115. Reg. E §205.11 (a).

116. Broadman, *Electronic Fund Transfer, Is the Consumer Protected?* 13 U.S.F.L. Rev. 245, at 262 (1979).

117. Reg. # §205.11 (b).

118. Broadman, *supra* note 116 at 264.

119. EFTA § 1693 n (a), for example provides for a $5000 fine.

120. Budnitz, *supra* note 77, at 392.

121. EFTA § 1693 2 (11) Reg. E §205.2 (1).

122. Reg. E §205.6 (a) (1).

123. *Id.* §205.6 (a) (2).

124. *Id.* §205.6(a)(3).

125. *Id.* §205.6(b).

126. *Id.* §205.6(b)(1).

127. *Id.* §205.6(b)(2).

128. *Id.* §205.6(b)(4).

129. *Id.* §205.6(c).

130. *Id.*

131.   Broadman, *supra* note 116, at 256.

132.   443 N.Y.S. 2d 43 (1981).

133.   Reg. E §205.6(b) (i), (ii).

134.   *Id.* §205.6 b(2).

135.   *Id.* §205.2 (1).

136.   112 Misc.2d 219, 446 N.Y.S. 2d 845 (1981).

137.   48 Fed. Reg. 14881 (1983), Supplement II, F.R.B. Official Staff Commentary - EFT-2, Q2-27.

138.   15 U.S.C. §1643.

139.   12 C.F.R. §226.

140.   Reg. E §205.6(d)(1).

141.   *Id.*

142.   Taffer, *supra* note 28 at 240.

143.   Greguras and Sykes, *Authentication in EFT: The Legal Standard and the Operational Reality*, 2 Comp. J. 67 (1980). This article provides a discussion of consumer liability for unauthorized transfers, and future developments in consumer identification in EFT.

144.   58 Ore. L. Rev. *supra* note 61, at 383.

145.   Taffer, *supra* note 28 at 241.

146.   EFTA § 1693 h (a)(1), (2), (3).

147.   *Id.* § 1693 h(b).

148.   *Id.* § 1693 h (a) (1).

149.   *Id.* § 1693 h (c).

150.   Broadman, *supra* note 116, at 262.

151. Senate Comm. on Banking, Finance and Urban Affairs, Fair Fund Transfer Act, S. Rep. No. 915, 95th Cong., 2d Sess. 2 (1978).

152. U.C.C. § 4-402.

153. Penney and Baker, *supra* note 4, par. 13.02 (3)(b).

154. Brandell and Oliff, *supra* note 9, at 559.

155. Reg. E §205.5 (a).

156. *Id.* §205.5 (b).

157. Brandell and Olliff, *supra* note 9, at 560.

158. Reg. E §205.5 (c) (1).

159. *Id.* §205.5 (c) (2).

160. *Id.* §205.5 (c) (1) (iii).

161. Penney and Baker, *supra* note 4, par. 13.02.

162. *Id.*

163. 44 Fed. Reg. 59464 (1979).

164. Penney and Baker, *supra* note 4, par. 13.03 (3).

165. Broadman, *supra* note 116, at 268.

166. Budnitz, *supra* note 77, at 362.

167. *Id.*, referring to *In re. Park Knoll Associates*, quoting from N.Y.C.J., Oct. 11, 1978, at 14, Col. 6 (N.Y. Sup. Ct., Westchester Cty., Oct. 1978).

168. For a more thorough discussion of the state laws relative to compulsory EFT use, see, e.g. Penney and Baker, *supra* note 4, par. 13.04(1).

169. EFTA § 1693 h.

170. *Id.* § 1693 (f).

171.   *Id.* § 1693 m (c) (2) (A).

172.   *Id.* § 1693 m (a) (2) (B).

173.   *Id.* § 1693 m (a) (3).

174.   *Id.* § 1693 m (b) (1).

175.   *Id.* § 1693 m (b) (2).

176.   *Id.* § 1693 m (c).

177.   *Id.* § 1693 m (d).

178.   *Id.* § 1693 m (e).

179.   *Id.* § 1693 m (f).

180.   *Id.* § 1693 m (g).

181.   *Id.*

182.   Broadman, *supra* note 116 at 269.

183.   Budnitz, *supra* note 77 at 396.

184.   EFTA § 1693 n (a).

185.   *Id.* § 1693 n (b).

186.   *Id.* § 1693 q, Reg. E 205.12 (a).

187.   *Id.* § 1693 r, Reg. E §205.12(d).

188.   Reg. E §205.12 (d) (2) (i).

Original research and preliminary writing by:

R. Timothy Phoenix, B.S. Community Development, University of New Hampshire, J.D. Franklin Pierce Law Center, former branch manager for international insurance service corporation, presently in private practice.